The Struggle for Meaning

This series of publications on Africa, Latin America, Southeast Asia, and Global and Comparative Studies is designed to present significant research, translation, and opinion to area specialists and to a wide community of persons interested in world affairs. The editor seeks manuscripts of quality on any subject and can usually make a decision regarding publication within three months of receipt of the original work. Production methods generally permit a work to appear within one year of acceptance. The editor works closely with authors to produce a high-quality book. The series appears in a paperback format and is distributed worldwide. For more information, contact the executive editor at Ohio University Press, Scott Quadrangle, University Terrace, Athens, Ohio 45701.

Executive editor: Gillian Berchowitz
AREA CONSULTANTS
Africa: Diane Ciekawy
Latin America: Thomas Walker
Southeast Asia: William H. Frederick

The Struggle for Meaning

REFLECTIONS ON PHILOSOPHY, CULTURE, AND DEMOCRACY IN AFRICA

Paulin J. Hountondji

Translated by John Conteh-Morgan

with a foreword by K. Anthony Appiah

Ohio University Center for International Studies
Research in International Studies
Africa Series No. 78
Athens

© 2002 by the
Center for International Studies
Ohio University
Printed in the United States of America
All rights reserved

09 08 07 06 05 04 03 02   5 4 3 2 1

The books in the Ohio University Research in International Studies series
are printed on acid-free paper ⊚

Published in the United States of America by Ohio University Press,
Athens, Ohio 45701

Library of Congress Cataloging-in-Publication Data

Hountondji, Paulin J., 1942–
   [Combats pour le sens. English]
   The struggle for meaning : reflections on philosophy, culture, and democracy
in Africa / Paulin J. Hountondji ; translated by John Conteh-Morgan ; with a
foreword by K. Anthony Appiah.
     p.   cm. — (Research in international studies. Africa series ; no. 78) Original
title: Combats pour le sens : Un itinéraire africain.
   Includes bibliographical references and index.
   ISBN 0-89680-225-6 (paper : alk. paper)
   1. Philosophy, African.   I. Title.   II. Series.

B5305 .H6713 2002
199'.66—dc21   2002075229

To my mother

To all my unfinished poems
To young Yabo Sèlomè Joana Mèhou-Loko

Contents

Part II. Critique of Ethnophilosophy

Part III. Positions

Foreword

Paulin Hountondji's *The Struggle for Meaning* is an extraordinary book. Its French subtitle, *Un itinéraire africain* (An African journey), suggests that it might be a memoir, which, in a certain sense, it could be said to be. But what it really is is an extraordinary—I think unprecedented—account of the development of an African intellectual, educated to the very highest level in the system of the French metropole, who has always taken very seriously the idea that his being-an-African is central to his vocation.

There is something of an irony in the fact that the author of this book, who has committed himself so totally to the development of philosophy in Africa in general, and in francophone Africa more particularly, is identified in many minds with a sort of eurocentrism. As is well known, some of Paulin Hountondji's critics have felt that his most famous thesis—that philosophy, in Africa as elsewhere, must be a set of texts written by individuals, not the shared and unanimous world-view of a people—makes Western philosophy the model for an African project, and thus reflects the mentality of a philosopher unable to tear himself away from the Europe of his education. What this memoir shows decisively is how, from his earliest days, he has always conceived of himself as fully situated in an African context with African obligations and a commitment to Africa's future. And it shows, too, that that commitment is fully consistent with his philosophical vocation.

The story begins with his teachers at the Lycée Victor Ballot in Porto-Novo in what was then Dahomey; but, after a few words of thanks to his first teachers there, Hountondji sketches his introduction to philosophy at the Lycée Henri IV in Paris, in the early '60s, and, by the second page, we are preparing for the entrance exams for the Ecole Normale Supérieure and moving from Sartre to Husserl. Hountondji manages, without immodesty, to indicate that the pedigree of his "formation" is, by French standards, impeccable: his teachers are Canguilhem, Ricoeur, Derrida, Althusser. If his earliest years in Porto-Novo had already led him to the philosophy of the *cogito* (Descartes being, of course, at the origin of any respectable French training in philosophy), the theme of the first part of the book is the centrality to his early thinking of his engagement with Husserl. But he shows, on the way, how he acquired, both from Canguilhem and from Althusser, a fundamental sense of the mission of philosophy and of his deep attachment to "la science" (which covers, of course, in French, a wider range of systematic knowledge than the natural or social sciences). For Hountondji, the project of "la science" is appealing not, as he says, because it is taken to be of value in itself, but because of its human meaning; philosophy is, for Hountondji, exactly the struggle for that human meaning.

This book provides an extraordinary sketch of Husserl's phenomenology of language and his "formal and transcendental logic," a review of the issues with which Professor Hountondji struggled, and an account of the texts he mastered in his years in Paris. In those same years, Hountondji discovered the work of Anton Wilhelm Amo, the Ghanaian philosopher of the German Enlightenment. In reflecting on Amo, he came to reflect upon his vocation: and to ask what the point of his work on Husserl was if it had no meaning within an African context.

"I concluded on the urgent need to put an end to the ex-traverted nature of all European-language African discourse; on the impossibility, henceforth, of being satisfied with partici-pating as individuals in the great scholarly and cultural debates of the industrialized world; and on the need to create pro-gressively, in our countries, 'these structures of dialogue and argument without which no science is possible'" (73).

If this was to be his project, publication on Husserl was ir-relevant, he thought.

> It was necessary both to come to terms with oneself and to main-tain one's roots, to express oneself unreservedly with no mental constraints, and at the same time remain intelligible to discuss everything one knew or sought to know, and at the same time share this knowledge and this quest. In any case, one thing re-mained certain for me, a political decision of sorts: the locus of this exchange should in no way exclude Africa. On the contrary, Africa must constitute its center, its point of departure, and, where applicable, be its primary beneficiary. (74)

His task was, as he puts it, to establish the legitimacy of an intellectual project that was both authentically African and au-thentically philosophical. It is this project, which takes up the second part of the book, that was to be his work in the late six-ties and the early seventies, and which led to the publication (in 1976) of *Sur la philosophie africaine* (*African Philosophy: Myth and Reality*, 1996) and its famous "critique of ethnophilosophy," which is now arguably the most influential work of African philosophy written in the French language.

This second part of the book begins by describing the con-text of debates in the late '60s and early '70s among the circle of *Présence Africaine*, at an important gathering in Copenhagen, where Hountondji was introduced to the figures and the sub-jects of African philosophy in the anglophone world, and in his early university career at Besançon, Kinshasa, Lubumbashi,

and, finally, back home in Cotonou. It thoughtfully locates
Tempels (author of *Bantu Philosophy*, which is a major focus of
his critique). But the discussion also makes clear how central
his own training in the (francophone tradition of) philosophy
of science and the history of ideas (with its great debts to German philosophy) was to his understanding of the prospects for
an African philosophy.

This section is an important addition to recent African intellectual history as it details the development of Hountondji's
ideas and the interactions that produced them. He details the
reception of his book, commenting wryly on various misunderstandings and recording the history that led to the publication of the English translation of *African Philosophy*, the result,
he says, of a collaboration between Henri Evans, the primary
translator, the philosopher Jonathan Rée, and himself. We can
be grateful that this translation, by John Conteh-Morgan, is
the result of a similarly fruitful collaboration with the author.

Part III is the most polemical part of the book (and it goes
beyond the material in the first parts, which was offered at his
defense for his *doctorat d'état* from the Université Cheikh Anta
Diop in Dakar). Here he seeks to locate himself in relation to
the critique of his work from many directions. He begins with
the response of an early generation, defined by the cultural
politics of negritude and beginning with the genial generosity
of Cheikh Anta Diop himself.

But he moves on to engage in a no-holds-barred debate with
critics for whom he has less affection or respect. Chapters 6
and 7, beginning with the death of his father and ending with
the death of his mother, cover a period of great international
activity, in the early '80s, and a period in the later '80s and early
'90s, when he turned his attention to the politics of his home-
land and played a key role in the re-emergence of democracy
there. (He calls this, rather too modestly, "my short foray" into
the corridors of power! [260])

The Struggle for Meaning offers a unique reflection by a philosopher of the very greatest importance on the intellectual substance of his life so far. It illuminates the debates about ethnophilosophy (offering, *en passant*, an extraordinary invitation into the world of Husserl) and demonstrates how deep the roots of Hountondji's analysis are in a profound philosophical reflection on "la science" (systematic knowledge) and "le langage" (systems of representation). It is not a memoir—personal details are offered just insofar as they relate to or illuminate the intellectual substance—and it is not a book that will have a popular audience, since it requires a willingness to engage with serious philosophy that is no more common in Africa than it is elsewhere. But for those who do read it I believe it will be one of the more rewarding experiences in the world of scholarly publication out of Africa in a very long time. Perhaps only the author of *African Philosophy* could have written a book that meets the standards of his most famous work while reflecting on its genesis and illuminating both its thesis and its reception.

K. Anthony Appiah

Preface

For many readers, my name, with that of a few others, remains linked to the critique of ethnophilosophy. Reading my brief "Remarks on Contemporary African Philosophy," and, later, my collection of articles, *African Philosophy: Myth and Reality*, some experienced a kind of intellectual liberation. The horizon seemed to clear, once the imaginary taboos that were placed on vast areas of philosophical research—judged too remote from African preoccupations—were lifted, as was the no less imaginary obligation placed on our young researchers to keep to Africa in their work, to survey in their own way, using their own conceptual tools, the narrow field that had been defined and mapped out by a long Africanist tradition.

Work on logic and epistemology became a possibility once again, where in the past one would have felt obliged, on pain of treason, to study *African* logic and epistemology. A study of values and of the foundation of ethics and politics, of aesthetics and of consciousness of beauty, of discourse and of the search for truth in general, all these became legitimate pursuits again, where in the past geographical confinement would have dictated that only *African* values, *African* conceptions of ethics, politics, and aesthetics, the *African* theory of knowledge, or in Tempels's term 'criteriology', be studied. The researcher could once again claim, without a bad conscience or false sense of shame, the duty to truth and the desire for apodictic certainty that are both integral to any true research. The philosopher, in particular, could once again assert a claim for universality that is the foundation of his discipline, by refusing to yield to the temptation of cultural relativism ("to each culture, its truth"), and by clearly acknowledging his vocation to enunciate propositions that are valid across frontiers, that are true to all, at all times and in all places.

If the critique of ethnophilosophy has had this liberating effect on some, it seems to have had on others a paralyzing effect, by preventing them, through excessive scruple or hesitation, from exercising on African culture and experience their talents as analysts and philosophers. It was as if any work on Africa was *a priori* suspect of ethnophilosophical contamination, and that to retain philosophical purity, one had to hover above concrete situations!

In referring to these two types of reaction, one fruitful, the other unproductive, all I wish to do is to draw attention to a problem that would be interesting to study in itself: that of the impact of the critique of ethnophilosophy. It would be interesting to assess this impact using the most rigorous methods, so as to judge the effects of this critique on intellectual productivity, and to determine its proper place in the history of African philosophical research, and in the broader field of Africanist research.[1]

However, the present work has another objective. On the one hand, it seeks to determine, through the various pieces of work that I have devoted to it, the unity and the evolution, the continuities and changes in accent of the critique of ethnophilosophy, and on the other, to place this critique in the context of the totality of concerns that inform it which I have also clearly expressed in other texts.

I will discuss first, from my earliest research, the work I did on Husserl, a *diplôme d'études supérieures* thesis on the notion of ύλη *(hylè)* and a doctoral dissertation on the idea of science in the *Logical Investigations*. Although they have remained unpublished, these pieces of student research express no less a fundamental demand which, in a way, sheds light on my future development: namely my valorization of science, my ideal of a philosophy conceived as a "strict science," to borrow the words of the German philosopher.

The critique of ethnophilosophy in a sense reflects this ideal. By recalling the principal arguments and the stakes involved in this critique, as well as the great debates to which it gave rise in African and Africanist intellectual circles, it will be possible to identify some of the problems and difficulties that will benefit from further study today.

But my critique of ethnophilosophy grew and developed, as did my earlier work on science undertaken under the influence of Husserl. My articles on scientific extraversion, the first of which goes back to 1978, bear witness to this development. In these articles, a marked interest emerges—outside, or at the very limits, of classical epistemology, and far from the preoccupations of Husserl's theory of science—for the scientific and technological relations of production on a world scale, as well as the outline of a sociology of science in the countries of the periphery. At the same time, the critique of ethnophilosophy led to a critique of ethnoscience in general, understood as a clever way of freezing traditional systems of knowledge by emptying them of their dynamism, of their power to transcend their limitations, their autonomous capacity for enrichment and improvement.

The seminar organized in Cotonou on traditional knowledges in 1987–88, which gave rise to the collective volume that was later published by CODESRIA in Dakar, is an important step in this development. The project of a critical reappropriation of endogenous knowledge—an indispensable complement to this vast and methodical appropriation of modern science and technology that is essential to giving Africa complete mastery of its destiny—resolutely took shape at this seminar with the contributions of colleagues from a variety of fields including history and archaeology, anthropology, hydrology, linguistics and ethnolinguistics, mathematics, botany, psychiatry and ethnopsychiatry, surgery, and philosophy.

It is, therefore, clear: from one end of the journey to the other hovers, against the background of the dominant problematic, a concern about the future of Africa that in the end becomes quite explicit: it is a *political* concern, political in the strictest sense of the term. Because I cannot specifically examine the articles and editorials where this commitment has been expressed, the present rereading will attempt to highlight, if need be, the political premises of the theoretical analyses themselves, and to place them in their general context.

Acknowledgments

This book is a revised and expanded version of the work I presented and defended for the *doctorat d'état ès lettres* degree by research and publication. The defense took place in Dakar on June 25, 1995. The document presented contained the first four chapters of the present volume. Chapters 5, 6, and 7 were written later.

Neither the initial work nor its subsequent expansion would have been possible without the support and encouragement of several people, and my sincere thanks go to them. I would like to mention in particular Souleymane Niang, rector of Cheikh Anta Diop University in Dakar, whom I had the pleasure of meeting again in Cotonou when I was Minister of Education in 1991 and of welcoming, together with other rectors, to a meeting of the African and Malagasy Council for Higher Education (CAMES); Marc Augé, whose friendship has always been a source of encouragement and who, during his tenure as director of the Ecole des hautes études en sciences sociales (EHESS), offered me all the facilities at his disposal during my research visits to Paris; and Aloyse-Raymond N'Diaye, Director of the International Fund for University Cooperation (FICU) in AUPELF, who was able to work a miracle—nothing less—by making it possible for the prodigal son, recently released from the grip of politics, to get back into academic work thanks to a research fellowship in Dakar. I would also like to mention my adoptive family in Dakar, Mamoussé and Marie Diagne and their children. I cannot forget the affectionate, very energetic Renée Senghor-N'Diaye, a great tease, whose death still defies the imagination.

Souleymane Bachir Diagne steered the defense process and, in spite of the academic "formalities," remained from the beginning to the end very friendly, as usual. Alassane N'Daw chaired the examination committee and Abdoulaye Bara Diop, Abdoulaye Kane, and Oumar Diagne were members of the committee. My thanks go to them.

On my return from Dakar, I found a particularly friendly reader in the person of Dominique Mondoloni of the French Cooperation Mission in Cotonou, a philosopher himself and my former adviser in the Ministry of Culture and Communications. I am indebted to him for having persuaded me, before his departure to Haiti where he has since been transferred, that this text could be of interest to a wider public, and for requesting a publication subvention for it from the mission. The patience of his successor, Michèle Nardi, was sorely tried by an author whose slowness was incompatible with administrative demands. I was determined to re-read the initial text and put finishing touches to it, but I had underestimated the necessary deadlines. My thanks to the French Mission, to Michel-Robert Gomez, Director of Flamboyant Publishers.

Let me express my gratitude to Rock Capo-Chichi, my former secretary, who has since become an expert in all types of computer work, for his invaluable assistance.

Finally, my long periods of study over the past thirty years, coupled with many other demands on my time, have often made me an absent husband and (later) father. I would like my spouse and four children—Hervé, Flore, Sophie (deceased young), Olivier—to know how much I have always appreciated their understanding and support.

Translator's Acknowledgments

This translation of *Combats pour le sens: Un itinéraire africain* (1997) has been in a real sense a collaborative effort between its author, Paulin Hountondji, and me. I wish to thank him for his encouragement and painstaking assistance. He read through every chapter carefully, and made many crucially important suggestions and comments on the translation. In trying to express his French style and his ideas as faithfully as possible, especially in the first two (technical and uncompromisingly philosophical) chapters on the philosopher who helped shape his thought, Edmund Husserl, I have relied on the English terminology developed for the German thinker by some of his eminent translators, who are cited in the bibliography. My thanks also go to the Ohio University Press reader for his helpful suggestions, to David Estrin for a meticulous copyediting job, to project editor Sharon Rose for her invaluable assistance and thoroughness throughout the preparation of the manuscript, especially the bibliography, and to my editor, Gillian Berchowitz, for her patience and understanding. Finally, I would like to thank my wife, Nyo, whose professional librarian skills helped me rapidly locate not just the English versions of the many books and articles referred to by Hountondji, but also the specific passages he quotes. All citations and page references in my translation refer to published English versions (where they exist) of the originals used by Hountondji. It goes without saying, of course, that the above assistance from others does not imply responsibility for the translation, which I alone bear. To my late brother, Ross, whose struggle was of another kind, I dedicate this translation.

JOHN CONTEH-MORGAN

Part I

DISCOVERING HUSSERL

1

Landmarks

1. From Porto-Novo to Rue d'Ulm

At Victor Ballot, the *lyceé* in Porto-Novo recognized at the time as the greatest nursery of Dahomey's future élite, there was a figure at once intriguing and fascinating. It was a young Senegalese philosophy teacher who, in the first half of the 1950s, was by his very presence proof that even philosophy, a subject reputed—rightly or wrongly—to be difficult, was within reach of Africans. His name was Alassane N'Daw.

I did not have the good fortune to be his student. He had already left by the time I reached my senior year of high school (1959–60). I had no cause for complaint, however, for there was Hélène Marmotin. She was French, as were most of our teachers then, with a methodical mind and a preference for dry, analytical rigor over intense flights of lyricism. In her very first lecture, she warned, "philosophy has to be learned." No question then of innate knowledge, of hereditary wisdom. One had to work.

What I retained from this introductory year, I believe, was a pronounced taste for conceptual analyses, and a certain fascination with doctrines of freedom. I had avidly read, from among the meager but precious twenty to thirty books in our library, Sartre's *L'existentialisme est un humanisme* (Existentialism is a humanism). That existence preceded essence strengthened my spontaneous resistance to all forms of fatalism, my rejection of any doctrine that tended to limit man, individually and collectively, or to deprive him of hope, of confidence in himself, of the certainty of being able to transcend himself, or of responding to the call from the unknown (Sartre 1946).

But it is to my teacher in *hypokhâgne*,[1] André Bloch, that I owe my interest in Husserl. This brilliant teacher—an artist, whose melodious voice held our attention all the more because it seemed to flow effortlessly, unmediated by writing—devoted part of his 1960–61 course at the Lycée Henri IV in Paris to introducing our young class of eighteen-year-olds to Husserl's phenomenology. He did this through a close analysis of Husserl's "Philosophy as a Strict Science" (1965). Other aspects of the course were devoted to Descartes (with special emphasis on the significance of the *'cogito'*), Kant and Hegel ("the history of philosophy is philosophy itself"), Kierkegaard, and other modern and contemporary philosophers.

The course by and large was designed to be practical, to demonstrate, as it were, motion in the act of walking, to answer one simple question: "What is philosophy?" or, in the absence of any confident answer that would not be another form of subtle dogmatism, to equip each student with the tools (a study of some of the great classics of philosophical thought, and an intimate familiarity with their authors) with which to formulate elements of an answer. Bloch taught us that there were no problems in philosophy, only themes; that one could not possibly expect from thought any guarantees that it would cease to develop, and that philosophy was permanent anxiety. Bloch never refuted a doctrine; he tried to understand it. Hegelian in his own way, he was more inclined to bring out the truth of a doctrine than to compare it with another. And, when he happened to compare doctrines, his interest was more in establishing their complementarity, in showing their dialectical unity, than in emphasizing their differences. It was, for him, a question of elegance, and decency to the authors. I can no longer remember which of my classmates once openly expressed surprise in class that Bloch was never in the least bit critical of an author. He replied by way of a quotation from Nietzsche whose reference I only recently located: "Where one can no longer love, there should one *pass by.*"[2]

In reality, then, our teacher had chosen to speak only of authors he liked; those whose works interpellated him, whose works he found convincing. There lay the secret of his enthusiasm and communicative fervor. On closer scrutiny, all the authors we studied had a family likeness. What Bloch introduced us to was the philosophy of the *cogito*, no more no less. And he did this brilliantly, even if subsequently—in a reading of authors including Hegel and Freud—he demonstrated its limitations.

I also had a passion for Latin, Greek, and French. I could easily declaim Cicero's *Catilinarian Orations*, the first of which I knew by heart. I was good in English, but reputedly hopeless in history. Among other teachers, I remember most vividly Raoul Audibert—who asked to be called "Prosper"—my French and Latin-to-French translation teacher at *hypokhâgne*. Impeccably dressed in his three-piece suit and bow tie, he embodied elegance. Then, in my second year of *khâgne*, there was Marcoux, my Greek and French-to-Latin translation teacher; Laurent Michard (the manual made flesh),[3] a tall man of Olympian calmness and vast learning who taught us French and French-to-Latin translation, and who had the decency never to refer us to *Lagarde et Michard*, for in spite of its pedagogical clarity and richness, we all preferred his lectures to this book. I have jealously guarded my signed copy of the volume on the twentieth century, the sixth and last in the series. It was published in 1962, the very year we became his students. "Prosper," I remember, never made a secret of his pride for his contribution in this last volume.

To return to philosophy, I was taught in my first year of *khâgne* by the affable and fatherly Dreyfus Le Foyer, a man already advanced in age, and whom, in our youthful insouciance and insensitivity, we heckled throughout class. In my second year we had Jacques Muglioni, who was determined to teach philosophy and not the history of philosophy, even if he could not conceal his own convictions during those wonderful lectures on perception that lasted an entire semester, and still less during his detailed explication of the supporting texts. A Kantian to the core, and a devoted reader and admirer of Auguste Comte, he gained public attention during and after a brilliant career as Inspector-General of Philosophy Education, as a result of his publications on Kant and Comte, and of his work championing the cause of secondary-school education (Muglioni 1987, 1988, 1993).

In short, be it at Porto-Novo or at the Lycée Henri IV, I was brought up during those years on a philosophical diet of the *cogito.* Louis Althusser brought this to my attention shortly after my entry into the Ecole Normale Supérieure. He made me write an essay to help me decide, after a long period of indecision, between a classics or philosophy major. He observed, in his remarks on this essay, that I tended "to shut myself up in the unthreatened space of a philosophy of consciousness."

My second stroke of good fortune, concerning Husserl, was Derrida. He was a breed apart. Among the authors whom he carefully and methodically analyzed—bringing out the cadences of their texts, the texts' inner breath, problems, and challenges, comparing them when necessary to the German or

English originals, and expressing himself with exemplary clarity and accuracy—were Hume and Husserl, authors whom the brilliant "cayman" of Rue d'Ulm made us read.[4] The author himself of a solid, but at the time unpublished, *diplôme d'études supérieures* thesis on Husserl, which he generously put at my disposal, as well as of the then recent and highly acclaimed translation, accompanied by a copious commentary, of *The Origin of Geometry*, Derrida familiarized us with such texts as Husserl's *Logical Investigations* and *The Phenomenology of Internal Time-Consciousness* (Derrida, 1989, 1994; Husserl, 1970, 1966).

During the same period, and this was my third stroke of luck, Paul Ricoeur's seminar at the Sorbonne gave us, in a different style, a clear picture of the great themes and the general problematic of Husserl's work. Ricoeur's particular focus was *Ideas: General Introduction to Pure Phenomenology*, whose translation of the voluminous Book I he had published with Gallimard (Husserl 1975; Ricoeur 1949, 1950, 1951).

It would be impossible for me to recount all that I owe to my teachers. Someday I may return to this topic and treat it more completely and methodically. Because I am tracing the genesis of some of the theoretical demands that underpin my critique of ethnophilosophy, however, I cannot leave out of my account the teachings of Georges Canguilhem, the austere director of the Institute of the History of Science and Technology—a man whose old reputation for strictness owes something, no doubt, to his past career as Inspector-General of Philosophy Education, and who apparently accepted me in his seminars on the basis of one of my oral performances at the *agrégation* examination, whose committee he chaired.

Canguilhem, it is well known, has no sympathy for nebulous metaphysics. All the elements that account for the beauty of his writings—rigorous analyses, an austere style, and conceptual rigor—were present in his seminars at Rue du Four. My participation in this seminar from 1966 to 1970 gave me the opportunity to share the concerns and preoccupations of a team of researchers from different geographical, ideological, and institutional backgrounds who shared the same high standards for clarity, accuracy, and rigor. These standards are valued and cultivated by all of Canguilhem's students.

It was in one of these seminars in 1969 that I first presented a paper discussing the results of my research on Amo, which was underwritten by a UNESCO fellowship. Claire Solomon-Bayet, also a student of Canguilhem and an editorial assistant at *Etudes philosophiques*, immediately agreed to ask the editorial committee to consider an article based on my paper for publication (Hountondji 1970b).

Last but not least how can the great but tragic figure of Louis Althusser be left out of this account?[5] The other "cayman" of Rue d'Ulm was, in a sense, Canguilhem's rigor and precision applied to a privileged object: Marx. This is not to say that Althusser was interested in nothing else. On the contrary, his genius lay in his ability to show, in the difficult ideological conjuncture of the period, that it was possible to have a nondogmatic and nonscriptural relationship with the work of Marx and the theoretical and political tradition deriving from it: an intelligent and open relationship with it that was not antithetical to the products of the mind, but, on the contrary, presupposed a real interest in them.

Althusser was particularly interested in Spinoza and Rousseau (to whom he devoted two unforgettable seminars) as well as Aristotle and Kant (both of whom he quoted often), Freud, Bachelard, and contemporary thinkers including Lacan, Lévi-Strauss, Canguilhem, and Foucault. It is to this vast learning that we owe his central contribution, which later made him famous: to inject a breath of fresh air into the ideological confines of Marxism (or rather to tear asunder its increasingly closed space and restructure it from top to bottom).

My class of 1963 witnessed a portion of the creation of *For*

Marx (Althusser [1965] 1990a), a book whose preface, "Today," is a real intellectual autobiography. It is the passionate story of an enduring resistance to doctrinal regimentation and policing of thought in the working-class movement from within this movement. Althusser's efforts to "think with Marx" was unheard of at a time when Marxism was perceived as a closed system with answers to everything, which left the individual with only two choices: blind submission to or outright rejection of it. In any case, this was a system that was incompatible with any form of thinking that is critical, personal, and responsible (Althusser [1965] 1990a).

My class also benefited from the seminar on *Capital*, and from the "Philosophy for Scientists" lectures that resulted, respectively, in *Reading* Capital (Althusser and Balibar [1966] 1990) and in the series of publications inaugurated by Althusser's *Philosophy and the Spontaneous Philosophy of the Scientists* ([1967, 1974] 1990b). *Lenin and Philosophy* ([1968] 1977) appeared shortly after, followed by *Positions* (1976, not available in English), *A Reply to John Lewis* ([1973] 1976a), and *Essays in Self-Criticism* ([1974] 1976a). My generation's luck was to have come in contact with Althusser at a time when he was most intellectually dynamic and intensely creative.

I drew some important lessons from Althusser's teachings. The first concerned the limits of our activism. *Our* activism: that of the African students belonging to various national associations and unions (for example, the Association of Dahomean Students in France [AED] and the General Union of the Students of Dahomey [UGEED]) and regional organizations, including the Paris-based Federation of Black African Students in France (FEANF) and the General Union of West African Students, based in Dakar.

My political activism was limited to these organizations. Although I was a student at Rue d'Ulm where, by the very nature of things, I was able to closely monitor the debates and factional strifes in the Union of Communist Students of France, I was never tempted to become a member of this organization, or to take sides in its debates, which I felt more directly concerned the French. My battlefield was elsewhere—in Africa. I became aware of this quite early on. Some of my French friends did not see it that way, and so misread the reserve and discretion of the attentive observer of French politics as political inactivism. For the same reasons, in May 1968, I was not on the barricades either in Besançon, where I was an assistant professor in the College of Humanities, or in Paris where I lived, although I followed events every day, and I was strongly interpellated, like so many others, by this extraordinary explosion of student revolt. I did not get involved. By temperament as well as by conviction, I kept my distance.

To return then to the struggles of African students: the objective was political independence; the *leitmotiv* was the denunciation of imperialism. We wanted real, not nominal, independence, and we denounced imperialism not only in its colonial form, which was disappearing, but also in its neocolonial guise, and we lambasted in passing the "local valets of imperialism," the *"comprador"* politico-bureaucratic bourgeoisie who served as the link or the transmission chain for foreign domination. FEANF's discourse never rose above this level. It was silent on many issues, notably on power relations within African countries, the place of liberties, the question of pluralism and monolithism as forms of political organization, the role of the army, and many other related questions.

The result of all this was that when, after a courageous "No" to General de Gaulle's 1958 referendum, Guinea became one of the most ferocious dictatorships in contemporary Africa, questions of human and democratic rights, the right to free speech and association, and the right of personal security remained taboo subjects, for such was our fascination with the narrative of independence, with the populist and nationalist discourse of Sekou Touré, which, in a sense, mirrored our own discourse.

I felt, therefore, that I was rediscovering in this type of activism the same theoretical indigence, the same conceptual limitations Althusser was fighting in the French Communist party. *Mutatis mutandis,* I concluded, we too were in urgent need of theoretical work, of a breath of intellectual oxygen, fresh air. We needed to be inventive. But how could we make this demand heard and understood in the context of our impassioned debates? This was the great question, one which in turn raised the fundamental issue of democratic debate (debate that *had* to be democratic), and the relationship between members and leadership in our student mass organizations. I remember raising these issues one Sunday in 1966 in a presentation titled "Culture and Politics" that I gave at a General Assembly Meeting of the AED at boulevard Poniatowski. The paper inspired lively discussions, but it obviously could not bring about radical changes to old habits.

The second lesson that I drew from Althusser's teachings was of a more general import. It concerned the nature, object, and true vocation of philosophy. He raised this question in his earliest essays, and constantly returned to it and reworked it. I appreciated the clarity of his answers as much as the reasons he advanced, when necessary, for modifying them. Althusser's revulsion for "ideology," his characteristically Bachelardian, uncompromising emphasis on 'rupture' as a precondition for the transition to science, his idea of philosophy as a theory of science—with none of philosophy's earlier and bizarre pretensions to "founding" science, but only to recognizing and identifying retrospectively its real procedures in order to give them conceptual clarity; in short, in spite of the enormous distance separating the author of *Formal and Transcendental Logic* (Husserl 1978) from that of *For Marx*, Althusser's courageous thesis could not find me indifferent, particularly as I was already familiar with Husserl's demands and concerns about science, philosophy, and the relationship between them.

Nor was I discouraged by the sharp clarifications in *Lenin and Philosophy* and *Essays in Self-Criticism*. On the contrary, these clarifications were a demonstration of the way in which concepts could be reformulated without being disowned. Philosophy, now understood by Althusser as the expression of the class struggle in the realm of theory, his critique of theoreticist deviation, recognized *a posteriori* as characteristic of his earliest writings, and the conceptual reformulation that, by the same token, affects his earlier theses, all this is proof that Althusser's thought—living, uncomplacent, and self-questioning—was the very opposite of the rigid dogmatism that some had curiously believed they could criticize in him.

2. Rationality as a Problem

Rationality is not self-evident. It must be perceived as a problem, a strange paradox. No one has better demonstrated this than Husserl. The most demanding form of rationalism is also the one that is most conscious of its limitations.

In a philosophical conjuncture still heavily influenced by the empiricist tradition in which the human mind, wrapped in itself and grappling only with its subjective "impressions," gave up on all claims to objectivity, universality, and truth, Husserl, early this century, suddenly unshackled the mind, brought it relief, as it were, by reaffirming a simple fact: that "all consciousness is consciousness of something."

The object is immediately presented to the mind. It does not have to be invented or laboriously constructed, but to be perceived in its flesh. *"Zurück zu den Sachen selbst!"* (Back to things themselves). Beyond all the florid writings and clever analyses that tend to dissolve the real in the flow of consciousness, beyond the learned speculations on the genesis of objectivity that is understood as an irrepressible but illusory form of belief, Husserl appealed to an immediate, pre-reflexive experience of the world that is always already there, and simply called for a description, prior to any explanation, or interpretation, of this primary experience. The object is always already given, and with each object is this horizon of all possible objects that we call the world. Consciousness is not a monad with neither doors nor windows; it always points to something other than itself, it is 'intentional'.

Now with this intentionality, this necessary object-directedness, or object-pointedness of consciousness, arises the outright possibility of objective knowledge or the rational. The refutation of psychologism that runs through the writings of Husserl is about nothing else but this possibility. Intentionality provides an escape from a retreat into the self; it removes the danger of solipsism and of being mired in the irrational.

Yet Husserl does not stop at this major assertion. Intentionality is hardly recognized when it is perceived as a problem. The relation to the object does not exhaust the real content of experience; it is borne by an entire stratum of non-intentional 'primary contents', the sensory data through which the appearing phases of things "manifest themselves perspectively." Husserl distinguishes, in every object perception, between the unitary 'sensile' experience, which in itself is not intentional, and the objectivizing apperception, which relates this experience to an objective correlate.

All this is very close to, and yet different from, Descartes. This is close to the Descartes of the second *Meditation* who, warning against the shortcuts of language, found it inappropriate to claim that men are 'seen' walking in the street, when in reality what is seen are hats and coats that could very well be concealing automata; or that the same wax is 'seen' now hard, cold, fragrant, resonant, now soft, hot, or odorless. This is also close to the Descartes who thus reduced sensation to its real content, separating it somewhat from itself, and disconnecting, for a while, its claims to objectivity. It is, however, different from the intellectualism of this same Descartes, for whom any object-thesis necessarily amounted to a piece of reasoning, an act of judgement, in the strongest sense of the word.

By positing the intentionality of consciousness, Husserl avoided having to superimpose such a reasoning on real sensitive contents: a syllogistic reasoning the truth of whose conclusion, deductively established, could at best only be probable, but never certain—not of that certainty that can only be generated by the presence of the thing itself.

Cartesian intellectualism resulted in keeping the self-evidence of the object somewhat out of reach, and breaking the immediate relationship to the world. It is this split that grounds the possibility of sensualism, psychologism and empiricism in general, and the possibility of all forms of relativism and skepticism. Thus, Husserl's opposition to all the figures of modern empiricism can be traced to this split. Intentionality makes it possible to avoid such a split; to ensure, at the level of immediate experience, the real presence of the object.

However, Husserl constantly returned to this very experience like an act of repentance to reflect at length on the genesis of intentionality. The relation to the object, though always already given, is neither instantaneous lightning nor sudden unannounced flash; it is not a pure relation, with neither consistency nor support. Rather, it points to the profound sensuality of an extremely rich and varied experience that, far from exhausting itself in this positioning of an objective opposite, encompasses the totality of experiences that Husserl negatively describes as nonintentional; that is, the 'sensory data', whether figurative or nonfigurative, includes sensations of pleasure and pain, and affective states and drives. It is the sum of these experiences, considered in their generic unity, that

Husserl calls the ὕλη *(hylè)* or 'matter', in opposition to μορφη *(morphè)* or 'form', thus borrowing the very Greek expressions used by Aristotle, but diverting them from their original context to apply them to a phenomenology of sensibility rather than an ontology of the sensible.

I worked on the notion of *hylè* in my 1964–65 thesis for the *diplôme d'études supérieures* at the suggestion of Jacques Derrida, to whom I had expressed my interest in Husserl. He recommended me to Maurice Patronnier de Gandillac, who kindly agreed to supervise my work. Re-reading this work—a touch schoolish—today, after a thirty-year interval, I still basically subscribe to the questions that it raises and its core arguments.

The thesis deliberately confined itself to a methodical reading of *Logical Investigations*, and to drawing, from a close examination of the incipient phenomenology, the full lessons and indications that were likely to shed light on the doctrine's future development. Now, three things are striking from this point of view. The first is the double movement of this major text which, from the *Prolegomena* through the *Fourth Investigation* included, attempts to defend the irreducible originality of logical concepts against psychologism, an attempt which leads to a powerful rehabilitation of ontology, but which does not prevent Husserl from effecting a sudden return to the ego, and to undertake, from the *Fifth* to the *Sixth Investigation*, a direct, systematic, and methodical thematization of experience.

What is also striking is that while attempting, all within the first movement, to establish objectivity, the ideal unity of the species, Husserl also makes parallel attempts to establish, whenever he discusses mental life, the primacy of intentional acts over nonintentional contents. The rehabilitation of ontology is thus grounded on the relativization of immanence in which, according to empiricists, lay the entire contents of consciousness; on the relegation to the background of these

"impressions," these "ideas" that constituted the real discovery
not just of Hume, but of all modern empiricists, and which are
seen in the history of thought as the latter's main contribution
(Locke 1975; Hume 1978).

It might as well be stated that Husserl did not invent the
notion of sensile content, but found it in his path as an em-
barrassing but unavoidable legacy. Putting an end to this
embarrassment meant, on his part, an interpretation that both
recognized and went beyond the heritage. The entire first part
of *Logical Investigations* is conscientiously devoted to this, as is
paragraph 85 of Book I of *Ideas*. By renaming nonintentional
contents in this paragraph with the generic term *'hylè'*, a term
that refers traditionally to its corollary, the *'morphè'*, Husserl is
clear that he is dealing with a 'functional' concept, and that in
reality nowhere in experience will a nonintentional stratum be
found as a real and separable component, but, all the same, it is
necessary to posit the idea of such a stratum in order to understand the possibility of intentional acts themselves.

What is also striking is that not once in the second part of
Logical Investigations, throughout the long phenomenological
study of experience begun in the *Fifth Investigation*, is this
privilege of intentional acts called into question. The return to
the ego does not entail a retreat into the ego. On the contrary
it reinforces the certainty of a necessary transcendence, of a
directedness of the subject toward the object. The analysis of
immanence, far from making immanence an absolute, is, on the
contrary, a long reflection on the meaning of transcendence,
and a description of the experiences that are constitutive of it.

One point, however, is worth noting. Whereas the first part
of *Logical Investigations* accepts the heritage of empiricism,
demonstrates its inadequacies, and posits the intentionality of
consciousness, the second part pays homage to Franz Brentano for having discovered the idea of intentionality in modern
times, while at the same time criticizing him for being igno-

rant of nonintentional contents. So after having implicitly played off Brentano against the empiricists, Husserl now plays off, in the *Fifth and Sixth Investigations*, the empiricists against Brentano.

It should be made clear, however, that Husserl received neither intentionality nor nonintentional contents as concepts merely handed down by history. He became forcefully aware of them through actual analysis. He makes historical references only later, in a retrospective commentary on insights grounded solely in phenomenological description. More precisely, the concept of intentionality and its corollary, the concept of nonintentional contents, were formulated in the *First Investigation* out of a phenomenology of language. To Husserl, words in themselves mean nothing. They only become meaningful through a speaking subject whose acts confer meaning to vocal matter that, without such acts, would remain mere sound, inarticulate noise, *flatus vocis*. It is this meaning-conferring act, this 'meaning-intention' that serves as a model for Husserl in his reflection on "objectifying apperception," this other act through which I spontaneously link my sensations to external objects. Thus, as Paul Ricoeur taught, Husserl first conceived intentionality on the model of the referential power of language and only later understood it as a structure of pure consciousness.

In a parallel manner, the sound phenomenon in a speech act—this perception of noise as noise, a perception that is prior to any meaning-generating interpretation, and that is always presupposed by it—serves as a model for the notion of primary sensile experiences which by themselves are devoid of meaning, therefore nonintentional, and are only later animated by apperception by being linked to an object.

I reflected long and hard not only on the status of the concept of nonintentional experience, but also on its acceptability. The truth is that I was unwilling to accept it, for it seemed so incompatible, in my view, with Husserl's fundamental discovery of intentionality. I was thus particularly attentive to the ambiguities and other difficulties of the text, as I was to whatever in Husserl's analysis could reveal signs of hesitation on his part, or indicate avenues for a possible reinterpretation of what to me remained a highly paradoxical notion.

The sensory datum was indeed for Husserl a boundary-concept, a μυθος *(muthos)*, rather like what the state of nature is for Rousseau; a state, according to the author of *The Social Contract*, that does not refer to any real historical moment, but which is nevertheless unavoidable as a critical concept if the course of real human history is to be properly understood.

Husserl himself does not tire of repeating that for him experience, in the broad sense, encompassing both intentional and nonintentional contents, is only an extension of the concept of experience *stricto sensu*, that is, of intentional experience. A being that had only sensory contents and was incapable of interpreting them objectively would not qualify as a mental being. He would almost be a body without a soul comparable to "phenomenal external things." Only the integration of sensory data with intentional acts, and by extension into the unity of consciousness, would confer experiential quality on these data. Intentionality is therefore the key concept. Intentionality is the "universal milieu which, in the final analysis, carries all experiences, including those that are not characterized as intentional."

A "functional" concept, a boundary-concept, just a manner of speaking, a *'muthos'* in the literal sense of the word, it is no coincidence that the *hylè* is at first characterized negatively, by the notion of nonintentionality. However, there exist two other determinations to this notion, and they are very positive.

The first consists in demonstrating that what is at work in empirical perception is a sort of dialectic of the one and the many. I cannot at one and the same time perceive all the sides of a tree. In order to have a full view of it, I will have to go round it. A physical thing is always perceived in successive phases through a manifold system of continuous percepts that all aim at it as the "same" object.

The empiricists who readily acknowledge this constraint only saw it, however, as proof of our finitude, of the ultimate limits of human understanding. Taking here the opposite position to Hume's, Husserl, on the contrary, sees in the necessary extension in time of empirical perception a universal constraint, one that is linked to the nature of physical objects in general. Even God, he affirmed, would perceive physical objects through patterns of appearances, because it is in the essence of such objects never to be apprehended through an adequate act of perception. In short, as Trân Duc Tao put it so well, where empiricists saw only the impossibility of a consciousness, Husserl, on the contrary, sees the consciousness of an impossibility (Trân 1951).

Now it is precisely this manifold system of continuous perspectives that Husserl calls *hylè*. Among the many other expressions variously used in *Logical Investigations* and in *Ideas* to describe this stratum of nonintentional experiences are: sensile matter, the phenomenological bed of 'primary', 'sensile', 'sensory and imaginative', 'experiential', 'figurative' or 'representative' 'contents'; the stratum of the 'sensory contents', of the 'sensory data', of 'presentative sensations', 'reproductive sensations', and 'intuitive representatives'.

The second positive determination of *hylè* is that which consists in including in the *hylè* the entire sphere of affective states such as feelings of pleasure, pain, itching, "as well as sensual phases in the realm of drives." Husserl acknowledges a generic relationship between such states and representative contents, but he carefully distinguishes them from affective acts and volitional acts proper, which alone are intentional. Warning against a serious ambiguity of language that leads to an indifferent use of the same word 'feeling' to designate both affective states as well as affective acts, Husserl separates feeling from itself by distinguishing two totally different uses of the word, uses which point to two realities that are not only distinct, but are in opposition to each other. Between affective sensations and affective acts, between 'desire sensations' (*sic*) and desires that are directed to and conscious of their object, there is only a relationship of ambiguity, but no relationship of generic community.

The fact is that Husserl's main objective, in this analysis, is to expand the notion of intentionality to the sphere of affective phenomena. Feelings in the strong sense of the word are not mere vibrations of the subject on itself, circular experiences with no relation to an object: they are intentional. There is no pleasure without an object of pleasure, neither is there displeasure without an object of displeasure. Pleasure and displeasure are acts of consciousness directed toward specific objects. The same is true of desires and drives.

Let it not be said either that feelings are mere states whose relation to objects only depends on the presentations to which they are associated. In such a case, intentionality would not be a real property of feelings themselves, but only of the presentations that are linked to them. On the contrary, in accordance with Brentano's teachings employed here by Husserl, not only does feeling, like any complex experience, have a presentation as its base, it is, in addition, a specific intentional act. In this way, one is dealing here with "*two* intentions built one on another: the founding intention gives the *presented* object, and the founded intention gives the *felt* object. The former is separable from the latter, the latter inseparable from the former." (Husserl 1970, 570).

However, if Husserl's strategy is to annex within the domain of intentionality the sphere of sentiments and drives, and if he partially succeeds in this, thanks to the notion of founded intention, it is the very same Husserl who attempts, in the second phase of his argument, to delimit the "very vast sphere" (*sic*) of nonintentional affective phenomena.

The method he adopts is simple. It consists in quite simply returning—beyond the thesis on the intentionality of feelings, which is after all quite laborious—to ordinary language usage. In ordinary language, feelings are first and foremost moods, like emotions—which is precisely what Brentano's opponents pointed out. Brentano himself preferred to place these so-called moods, like all the other sensory data, in the class of 'physical phenomena', and to reserve the quality of 'mental phenomena' for simple or complex, presentative or founded, intentional acts.

Husserl, on the other hand, although recognizing the intentionality of sentiments, emotions, and volitions seen as founded acts, agrees—on this specific point—with Brentano's adversaries in their adherence to ordinary language. For this reason, he felt the need to expand the field of 'mental phenomena' to include sensile affective states, feelings, emotions, desires, and drives—all apprehended in their inceptive state, before any conscious relation to an object.

Through this double characterization—as both a continuous flow of percepts, and as a sphere of sensile, affective states—the *hylè* ceases to be a residual concept, definable only negatively, in opposition to intentional acts, and instead becomes a positive concept with its own content.

I wondered, given these conditions, whether these two determinations were not better than the first. Defined as a continuous flow of percepts, the *hylè* is a clear concept, one that is unavoidable in its own way; but this is totally different from a nonintentional stratum of experience. Why can't these different percepts be seen as so many partial intentions merging spontaneously into one total intention, as is precisely suggested in a text in the *Sixth Investigation?* (Husserl 1970, 2:680–87).

I also continued to reflect on the generic relationship between 'sensory contents' and 'affective sensations' and on the way in which the latter 'fused' with the former, 'merged' with them. I was inclined to admit, and this was the thesis defended in the dissertation, that one was not dealing with two types of experiences that then came closer, but with one and the same class of phenomena. In short, there is always and everywhere a superimposition of affectivity on sensory data. 'Sensile affective states' do not merely overlay sensations as an additional extra, they are in themselves, from the outset, "sensations belonging to such and such a sensory field," and they are, additionally, invested with affective value. The affect is thus more than a mood; it always has a theoretical function—a knowledge function. The affect is not a pure, ineffable datum in its experiential singularity. It is the beginning of a statement, the foundation of a design, and the point of departure of some knowledge.

Conversely, 'sensory contents' have more than just a figurative function; they are emotion-laden and are, in their own way, affective phenomena. The emotional charge can vary in intensity, but it is always already there, and it comes first *over* the figurative function. The object affects me before I think about it. My contact with things is never serene. For as Koffka wrote, "an object looks attractive or repulsive, before it looks black, blue, circular or square" (Koffka in Merleau-Ponty 1962, 24).

Here then the initial perspective is reversed. The point of departure is no longer 'figurative contents', but the emotional and sensual depth of experience. By the same token, the description as nonintentional, which derived its meaning from the need to contrast representation with its intuitive base, loses most of its relevance. It is no longer necessary to affirm in any special way the nonintentionality of the affect. From a dynamic point of view, on the contrary, the real question is to account for the development of intentionality in different ways and in different degrees, from this initial shock: from this silent drive born of the mute contact with things.

Several indications by Husserl made it possible to attenuate—to relativize retrospectively—the basic distinction he establishes between affective sensations and intentional feelings: it is never purely a question of one or the other, but of "concrete complexions" where both are present and intimately linked. The ambiguity of current words is therefore not fortuitous. The ambiguity of the word 'feeling' is not a chance imperfection of language, but the expression of a dynamic relation between the intentional and the nonintentional in any real affective experience. Perhaps it must be admitted that affective sensations are already intentional, but in a rather confused, indeterminate manner, rather like these "intentions directed at no precise determination," conceptualized by Husserl in the *Fifth Investigation*, and that the transition to feeling *stricto sensu* is only an explicitation. Perhaps it must be admitted, above all, that both sensory contents on the one hand, and affective sensations, desire sensations, and drives on the other hand, are the same thing.

That was all I needed to cripple the idea of nonintentional experience. In my dissertation, I, in a way, played Brentano against Husserl without saying so, by refusing to admit that something inert that was not already carried along in movement could exist in experience. But I could not simply overlook the affects, desires and drives, or the sensual depth of experience where, in my view, lay the undeniable force of Husserl's demonstration. Brentano quite simply placed them on the side of "physical phenomena." But because he did not pay attention to the originality of one's own body, and to what makes it irreducible to pure exteriority, he remained unconvincing.

I therefore realized the need for a theory of the phenomenal body, a theory that attempts to go back to the most sensual sources of thought in general and explore in depth the most obscure meanders of the irrational, without entrapping myself there, but rather to observe the genesis of the rational at work.

The sensual *hylè* discussed by Husserl seemed in this regard an excellent clue, on condition that one did not stop at the abstract opposition between nonintentional content and intentional experience, but that the sensual component was integrated in a living temporality, in the flow of intentionality that sustains it, traverses it, animates it—a step that Husserl himself invites us to do in a good many texts.

The *hylè* thus interpreted seemed an unavoidable concept. It expresses our primordial interlacing with the world, and the initial complicity that conditions any later distance that might be observed; it expresses this place of silence where, before any enunciation and verbal expression, the configurations of our relation to the world and to others are sketched out. In this sense, the *hylè* was inseparable from what Freud, working in a different context, and from totally different theoretical preoccupations, called the "libido." A confrontation between phenomenology and psychoanalysis seemed to me both possible and desirable, in spite of the huge gap between their theoretical assumptions and preoccupations.

The debate was already sketched out in a number of precise indications given by Husserl. In this respect his successive treatment of the notion of the unconscious is significant: at first he dismisses the notion as a mere "makeshift hypothesis" irrelevant to a theory of knowledge, but he gradually rehabilitates the idea as he deepens his study of genetic phenomenology. Between the "universal depths . . . called the unconscious," which according to Husserl "is nothing less than a phenomenological nothingness but . . . a boundary-mode of consciousness," and this hidden force that, according to Freud, explains our *actes manqués*, I was convinced that a calm confrontation would be extremely fruitful.

More generally, I was attentive to the Husserlian project of a "hyletic science," understood as a theory of sensibility. This "transcendental aesthetic in a new sense" would be a considerable expansion of Kant's transcendental aesthetic, if only because it would no longer apply only to human subjectivity, but to whatever subject of any knowledge in general. It would function as the fundamental level of a *Weltlogik*, a logic of the world.

A question however remained: from this transcendental perspective, what becomes of the problematic of the real body? What becomes of this sensual depth of an experience that is so laden and dense? How, from the initial logical and gnoseological preoccupations, can an account be given of all experience without restrictions or arbitrary limits? Is phenomenology only transcendental logic—in other words, the exploration of the *a priori* subjective conditions of the constitution of logical and scientific idealities? If the answer is yes, then how can a transcendental logic account for the phenomenal body, the drives, the libido, and even more, for the daily struggle of men? How can it account for their misunderstandings, prejudices, wars, fanaticisms: for the scandalous fact of their suffering and death? But if not, if transcendental logic is only one application among many of phenomenology, how can one ensure that legitimate interest in the nonrational and *a fortiori* in the irrational does not lead to a neglect of the rational, and that along the labyrinth of experience's tortuous path, neither the demand for universality—the founding value of all authentic values—nor the Ariadne's thread of the logos, gets lost.

I was never able to devote the necessary time to these questions. Other urgent intellectual tasks awaited me. Any researcher necessarily faces such limitations. Only a good division of labor among members of a solid, coherent team can surmount them, by making it possible for others to carry out research that one cannot carry out oneself, to examine those questions that one has had to suspend temporarily.

2

The Idea of Science

1. An African Concern

When, after the *agrégation* examination in 1966, it occurred to me to register for the *doctorat d'état*, I immediately chose, after discussions with my supervisor Georges Canguilhem, a topic that, although not part of African studies, nonetheless seemed to provide some of the conceptual tools necessary for an effective intervention in this field: "The Theory of the Relationship between Social Structure and the Genesis of the Scientific Spirit from the Beginning of the Nineteenth Century."

Taking as a point of departure August Comte or, more precisely, the set of doctrines that led to the formulation of the law of the three stages by the author of the *Cours de philosophie positive*, I proposed to examine all that the history of ideas could teach us on the modes of existence of forms of knowledge and the conditions of the transition to science. My ambition was to identify and delimit, within the existing *corpus*, something like an archeology of science and technology, and apply it critically to Africa (Comte 1978, 1974, 1966).

This thesis never saw the light of day, in spite of the vast amount of material I accumulated, and that turned out to be extremely useful. Meanwhile, when Canguilhem "withdrew from cars," as he used to say jokingly, meaning that as he was retired he could no longer crush anyone, it was to another Georges, an Africanist this time, that I turned (incidentally on the recommendation of the former) to request supervision of my research. I took advantage of the change to modify my topic which, with Georges Balandier's consent, read: "A Critical Investigation of the Epistemological Status of Ethnology."

It was no longer a question of investigating the conditions of a possible transition to science, but of exploring the historical and ideological origins of the Western gaze on "other societies," including Africa's; of assessing the claims of this gaze to scientificity; and of examining the conditions for a reappropriation and reworking by the societies concerned of the knowledge accumulated about them.

This thesis was not completed either, but I made abundant use of the material I collected on it, like the previous material in my research on ethnophilosophy. Meanwhile, when I decided to write a *thèse de troisième cycle*, I decided to focus my attention on Husserl again, but this time on a topic that was close to my concerns as an African: the question of science. Paul Ricoeur agreed to supervise this work and to have me defend it in June 1970 in Nanterre before a committee that included Suzanne Bachelard and Emmanuel Levinas.

The doctoral dissertation could not possibly be, any more than my *diplôme d'études supérieures* thesis, a study of all of Husserl's work. It was, again, the incipient phenomenology that I chose to examine, specifically in the first volume of the *Logical Investigations* and the *First Investigation* of the second volume, even if this sometimes meant anticipating on later works. This restriction proved useful: among other things, it made it possible to re-establish, beyond the obvious thematic change, the continuity between the resolute objectivism of the first volume—the long refutation of psychologism which, in the *Prolegomena to Pure Logic* leads to a rehabilitation of Platonism—and the return to the subject begun, from the opening pages of the second volume, with the subtle phenomenology of language developed in *Expression and Meaning*.[1]

The aim of the critique of psychologism is none other than to ensure the objectivity of science, to guarantee under certain conditions, against any empiricist or relativist interpretation, the universal validity of human discourse. It thus leads to the notion of "truth in itself" and to the thesis of an objective articulation of the "domain of truth," of the "atemporal realm of ideas." The *First Investigation*, however, begins with an acknowledgment that every science is a language event. Based on this notion, it sets out to identify the acts of the speaking subject—the mental experiences that sustain or permeate language—proposing the first concrete example of phenomenological analysis in Husserl's work.

This return to the subject does not however imply a retreat into subjectivity—on the contrary! The investigation of experience seeks to confirm the objectivity of essences, by identifying in experience itself an internal element of transcendence that obliges it to recognize its objective correlate. It is not coincidental that this phenomenology of language leads, at the end of the *First Investigation*, to a concept that is on the face of it paradoxical: the concept of "meaning in itself," posited in opposition to "meaning expressed" that alone was examined up to that point. Through an unexpected reversal of perspective, the meanings of human discourse, whose ideality had been laboriously established, henceforth appear as contingent realizations of idealities of a higher level, truly universal, and existing prior to the given language and the human subject.

The lesson can be extended to Husserl's entire work. The interminable referral of the object to the subject and vice-versa, this constant balancing of the analysis between two poles, never leads to a method that is completely circular. Chronologically, the critique of psychologism—this critique inaugurated by the *Prolegomena to Pure Logic* but to which Husserl returned countless times as if to exorcise a specter that was never completely laid to rest, or to push aside a threat, a permanent temptation of the human mind—comes first. The result of this critique is the certainty of the objectivity of essences. This result authorizes the structural analyses based on the intuition of essences through the technique of imaginary variation. It is only subsequently, after having erected safeguards against skepticism, that phenomenological analysis proper, the in-depth exploration of subjective experiences in which the object "is constituted," develops. But never, not even in its most resolutely "subjective" approaches, does Husserlian phenomenology risk dissolving this already cleared terrain, of letting this hard and concrete ground of objectivity slip away. It will, rather, set itself the task of bringing out its meaning. The problematic of the *Weltkonstitution* itself—this powerful attempt to "constitute the world" from a transcendental subjectivity, an attempt developed from *Ideas* and especially in *Cartesian Meditations, Experience and Judgment*, and in all the later works (published or unpublished)—cannot make one forget the gains of the early, inaugural phenomenology: that of the intuition of essences.

The thesis of this thesis, or at least one of its lateral theses, is affirmed, in passing, in the analysis of the central theme (the idea of science). Specifically, it is that it is futile to contrast early Husserl with later Husserl: a Husserl dealing with structures with a Husserl metaphysician of the transcendental field; or a materialist Husserl—the one who proved so seductive to Marxists and, in the francophone world, inspired such well-known, powerful pages from a Trân-Duc-Thao or a Jean Desanti—with an idealist Husserl. Moreover, it is even more futile to present the shift to idealism as a turnaround, a fall, or a relapse: it is more fruitful to assume that the entire work has an internal consistency, a real unity. The thesis of this thesis is also that it is particularly enlightening to privilege, in the effort to find this unity, the first insights of early phenomenology (Trân 1951; Desanti 1963, 1975).

2. The Scientific Demand

"Science is but a value among other values of equal right." In writing these lines in *Philosophy as a Strict Science*, Husserl, far from expressing a personal conviction, is making, on the contrary, a big concession to his adversaries, one to which he clearly does not subscribe. It is obvious that in the hierarchy of cultural practices, science (for him) occupies the highest rung. To Husserl, no other form of thought, way of life, vocation, nor job (art for example, or religion) appears nobler.

This is not scientism, far from it: science is not valorized for itself, but for its human significance and its meaning for life. It is subordinated, like any other cultural production to ethics; its exceptional value—far from deriving retrospectively from the powerful technological accomplishments to which it gives rise—resides, on the contrary, in the fact that as a practice, it is intrinsically, in and of itself, bearer of norms and generative of values.

The idea is taken up insistently in the last texts, notably in *Formal and Transcendental Logic* and in *Crisis*. Science is the *telos* of human thought and of life in general—the infinite task that confers meaning as much on our individual existence as on humanity's collective history. But it is already clearly expressed in the *Logical Investigations*. It is there, in the texts of the incipient phenomenology, that I tried to delimit it more closely in order to appreciate its original meaning.

As a mathematician by training Husserl was predisposed to privilege, among all the approaches to philosophy, the logical or, more exactly, the epistemological approach. Thus philosophy appears to him first as a *Wissenschaftslehre*; a theory of science necessarily called upon by the very movement of science as realization, or at least the condition of realization of this need for integral intelligibility that permeates science.

Husserl is certainly aware of the fact that this is only one possible approach. Others exist that are equally valid.[2] It is remarkable, however, that whereas Husserl theoretically recognizes this plurality of paths to philosophy in general, and phenomenology in particular, he himself only practices two—the one logical, the other psychological.[3] And to demonstrate that this double approach is not the product of chance, he theorizes it on several occasions by expressly assigning a double function to phenomenology. The analysis of experience is both a theory of knowledge and a necessary prerequisite to any scientific psychology. On this account, it exercises, with regard to all the sciences, a universal foundational function, and with regard to psychology in particular, a specific foundational one.

Thus the plurality, at first acknowledged by way of a concession, of these "other possible paths for sense investigations with a radical aim" is in fact reduced to two. But there is more. The chronological succession of the two approaches in the development of Husserl's work is not coincidental either. If the need for philosophy first imposed itself on him as a means of elucidating the mathematical concept of numbers, it is because philosophy in general is first of all reflection on science. If, in addition, it must offer its ultimate foundations to a particular discipline—psychology—it is not because of an intrinsic privilege of this discipline, but rather because the reflection on science, by seeking in experience the origins of scientific concepts and the meaning of objectivity in general, sees itself obliged in its development to demarcate itself from another

kind of discourse with which one could be tempted to confuse
it. Psychology therefore has only a relative privilege. Its relationship to philosophy is both philosophically and logically
secondary, subordinate to the relationship of philosophy to the
sciences.

In this respect, Husserl's evolution on the question of the
relations between phenomenology and psychology is significant. In the first edition of the *Logical Investigations*, after having demonstrated the necessity of phenomenology as a means
of beating psychologism on its own ground by establishing the
intentional essence of the experiences of knowing, the author
nonetheless admits that phenomenology could be defined, if
one absolutely had to, as descriptive psychology in opposition
to ordinary psychology that likes to think of itself as explanatory. Twelve years later, the second edition, on the other hand,
categorically rejects this definition.[4] This is due to the fundamental reason that contrary to any psychology, even descriptive, pure phenomenology does not presuppose the real
existence of a nature. It also excludes by the same token any
presupposition of a real mental life belonging to real men or
animals existing in an equally real world. It presupposes, on
the contrary, what Husserl calls at the time in *Ideas* the transcendental *épochè*, the bracketing of the world, phenomenological reduction.

Now if such is the case, if the description of logical experiences must discard the thesis of the reality of the world, it is
solely because the truths whose subjective correlate it seeks
are truths in themselves, independent of the existence or non-
existence of a world. The proposition that $2 + 3 = 5$ would remain true even if the world did not exist, and even if no human
being existed to think it. And this holds true for any general
truth as truth. The universe of meaning does not presuppose
the real world. This is why phenomenology also has to discard
this assumption if it is not to fall into empiricism and into

making eternal essences dependent on the factual existence of a given world, containing men and animals that are also given.

I therefore admitted that the transcendental *épochè*, this bracketing of the world, so essential to the development of Husserlian thought, was, above all, a response to logical and epistemological motivations. For the objectivity of logical and scientific propositions in general not to depend, in the final analysis, on the real intentionalities of real psychological subjects, it was necessary that the experiences directed towards intemporal objects not have to exist empirically in a real nature, but that they be treated as ideal experiences, unreal temporalities removed from the empirical time of the history of the world. Husserl could not then take as a theme man as a real subject of knowledge, but the universal structures of any subject of knowledge in general: man or angel, god or demon. Real man could only serve, at best, as an example, a specific case, an empirical illustration of an essential possibility.

That said, if phenomenology, besides its universal logical function as a theory of knowledge, exercises another function: to give psychology a scientific foundation, "pure" phenomenological experience should not be conceived as a mysterious and elusive reality either, but as a universal essence of concretely given human experience. Phenomenological experience is thus not just another experience; transcendental experience is not just another experience, but the intelligible and intelligent kernel of real human experience. The break of the *épochè* only signifies that the real does not let itself be immediately understood, but that it requires a detour; a clear view of its essence presupposes that it be suppressed by thought and that it be divested of its initial attractiveness: in short, that it be de-realized. But essence thus liberated remains that of the real; the "fictive nature" is none other than the eidetic kernel of "real nature."

In this respect, "descriptive psychology" itself, to the extent that it does not aim at explaining the human mind but

at defining its essence, is already a transcendental phenomenology unaware of itself; transcendental phenomenology, in
turn, is a descriptive psychology that has become conscious of
its methods and of its deliberately exclusive interest in structures. In this sense also, the first definition of phenomenology
remains pedagogically fruitful and enlightening by its very
clumsiness. What it demonstrates is that it was possible to
practice phenomenology with the aim of founding scientific
discourse without necessarily being able *to interpret its content.*
What it makes clear is the gap between the *function* of phenomenology and its nature as a specific doctrine. Husserl's
error in the first edition of the *Logical Investigations* was on
this last point.

Beyond the *épochè*, I accepted that, in a general way, the
most fruitful approaches, the most decisive theoretical steps
among those that punctuate the development of Husserl's
thought from beginning to end—notably the refusal of psychologism, the imaginary variation, the rejection of the concept of pure self, and then the rehabilitation of this same
concept—derived above all from logical and epistemological
motivations aimed at enabling a better understanding of what
happens in the sciences. I admitted, in other words, that for
Husserl science was never just a problem among other problems, but the central preoccupation of his thought.

It is not surprising, therefore, that science, the object *par excellence* of philosophical thought, should also constitute its
model. Husserl is taking up a challenge as old as philosophy itself. Since Plato, philosophy has always claimed that it cannot
be reduced to mere *doxa*, a body of arbitrary opinions, but that
it is the search for the apodictic certainty of the *episteme* or, in
other words, as Kant put it, the commitment to "the royal path
of science."

It is true that philosophy's methods cannot simply reproduce those of the positive sciences. The rigor to which it as-

pires is something other than the exactness sought after by the positive sciences. *Philosophy as a Strict Science*, in fact, identifies some of the methods that will make this rigor *sui generis* possible. But even in these conditions, even after the bracketing of the existing sciences, philosophy remains guided, in this radical return to the subject, by the ideal of apodictic certainty promoted—but only achieved in part—by these sciences.

There is more. Being both object and model of philosophical thought, science is also the *telos* (the ultimate end) of thought and of human life in general, the infinite task that gives meaning to humanity's collective existence. In the *Logical Investigations*, European humanity or Europe is not yet mentioned as such. But mention is already made of crisis and of the role of pacification that, in this crisis, is thrust on philosophy.

What is shocking to Husserl—what appears scandalous to him in the intellectual landscape of the period—is the general disagreement in specialist circles on the essence of logic. He did not mince any words in describing this situation: one was dealing with a real *bellum omnium contra omnes* (a war of all against all). Husserl uses the very terms with which Hobbes described the state of nature. Logic, for Husserl, embodies all the symptoms of spiritual anarchy, from the moment there is no agreement on its object and method, in other words, on how it should be defined. Each person says what he wants about it and tries to impose his preferences, his personal theoretical choices, on everyone else. The state of logic is such that it is impossible to "make the distinction between a personal conviction and a truth that is valid for all." The surest sign of the non-scientificity of a discipline is this internal disorder: this absolute conflict among its practitioners. In contrast, science's effect will be to instill order in the realm of minds, to create agreement between them by making them submit to the same and only law: the scientific law recognized in its objectivity and universality.

I was thus struck from the outset by the ethical accents of Husserl's diagnosis of the logic of his period and, in consequence, by the ethical connotations of his understanding of science. Other authors before Husserl had deplored the endless quarrels between scientists and philosophers. Hume and Kant had used the same extended military metaphor—with the same touch of humor—to account for this situation. But with Husserl the metaphor is more than a metaphor. The intellectual disorder signifies, in his eyes, the absence of norms or the frontal clash of systems of norms that are supposed to regulate action and conduct. Intellectual disorder generates, as a result, a crisis that is not just intellectual, but also ethical—indeed, virtually social and political. If science has meaning for life, it is precisely because it is, in Husserl's eyes, a unique means of resolving such a crisis thanks to the consensus that it enables on values and norms, which consensus is itself founded on the universality of truth.

3. Truth and the Good

It is, therefore, necessary to examine the relation between truth and 'the good' to understand why, with the help of which arguments, and based on which analysis, Husserl re-affirms, in his own way, a hope that dates back, in the history of ideas, at least to Plato: the hope for a new order where virtue would derive from knowledge, where the vertical agreement of minds with the universal structures of being would lead to a horizontal agreement of minds between themselves, and to transparency, justice, and peace.

In truth I still wonder today whether I have not over-interpreted the *Logical Investigations*, whether I have not stretched the meaning of this relatively early text a little bit by bringing to bear on it ideas and themes that appeared explicitly only later, notably in *Formal and Transcendental Logic* and in *Crisis* (Husserl 1978, 1970b). However, I do not think I was wrong. An attentive reading of the *Prolegomena* and the *First Investigation* suffices to convince any non-specialist that the conceptual seeds of what will become later, in Husserl, a veritable philosophy of history are already in place and perfectly legibly in these short but powerful pages.

a) Method and Truth

In whatever manner it is defined, science is, first of all, a collective good, a cultural phenomenon, and a tradition: "Science exists objectively only in its literature, only in written work has it a rich relational being . . . in this form, it is propagated down the millennia and survives individuals, generations and nations" (Husserl 1970, 1:60).

Husserl will never retract this minimal sociological determination of science. On the contrary, he continues to affirm it right up to the texts of *Crisis*. Thus he recalls in *The Origin of Geometry* that without writing, the ideal formations of the sciences will be lacking the "enduring presence . . . the being-in-perpetuity": the possibility, that is, of surviving the inventor and his interlocutors of the moment, and that the decisive function of the written word is precisely to make communication possible in the absence of the addresser.

What becomes a theme in *Crisis* is, however, only mentioned in passing in the *Logical Investigations*, like primary evidence mentioned only to be immediately superseded. At this point in the analysis, it is more important to acknowledge that all the tradition—and all the world's scientific literature—is nothing if it does not become a lever for actual knowledge, if it does not offer the opportunity to a thinking subject to articulate the acts of knowing expressed through this corpus.

Thus, science only finds realization in actual knowledge. The German terms that follow play on words in a manner not easily translatable: "as is indicated by its name, science has knowledge in its sights"—the *Wissenschaft* (science) is a product of *wissen* (knowing) resulting from the knowledge acts of numerous individuals, and has no other aim than to enable the reproduction of these same acts by other individuals.

We are, therefore, thrown back to the subject and his intellectual life. This gives Husserl the opportunity to develop a subtle phenomenology of 'degrees of knowing' that cannot be examined in detail here, but which lead to an inevitable question: what determines degrees of evidence? Is it the subject or the object? For now, let us be content with taking note of this question.

But also, if science, as a body of texts, is nothing without its reactivation in actual knowledge, then an isolated piece of knowledge does not constitute a science, any more than a group of bits of knowledge that are simply juxtaposed one against the other constitutes a science. For there to be science, a body of knowledge coordinated in a systematic sequence is necessary. A second, inevitable, question immediately arises: what does the sequence consist of, and what determines it?

The answer to this double question not only gives Husserl the opportunity to demarcate himself from empiricism, it also provides us with elements for an ethics of true knowledge; or, more precisely, an ethic of effacement and self-denial as conditions for acceding to truth.

It is as if, in the *Prolegomena*, the transition from one level of proof to another was less a function of the disposition of the subject than of the intrinsic features of things or states of things. Thus, probability in a piece of knowledge that is simply probable does not only express a lack of clarity in the process of knowledge, but an intrinsic feature of the known state-of-affair itself. Probability is in the things. Between the existence and the non-existence of a situation or state-of-affair *(Sachverhalt)*, a middle term is possible—a positive indeterminacy that is inherent in the very things. In this regard, probable knowledge is still evident in its own way: it is the clear vision of the uncertainty inherent in the object. It does not simply depend on the subject that judges and his or her contingent limitations, but it is a result of the manner of being of the things themselves.

What is true of probable knowledge is all the more true of certain knowledge: the latter is never invention but discovery, the perception of an objective relation between a subject and its predicates, the reflection in human discourse of a relation between things.

This holds even truer for sequences of knowledge. The systematic character of a system cannot be reduced to a simple association of ideas founded on what Hume would have called human nature. It is not a psychological link: it is a logical one. The internal consistency of a discourse and the unity of propositions in a deductive theory are far from being gratuitous. They do not point to "a kind of aesthetic trait of our nature. . . . Science neither wishes nor dares to become a field for architectonic play. The system peculiar to science, i.e. to true and correct science is not our own invention but is present in the things where we simply find or discover it" (Husserl 1970, 1:13–14).

Therefore, there is an order of things, an objective articulation of being, a universal legality that regulates the sphere of truth. Scientific discourse must account for this preexisting order.

A question remains: how can this order be recognized and expressed? How can it be reconstituted while ensuring faithfulness to it? It is here that the need for a method arises. For if things are always already linked between themselves in a vast system, scientific discourse cannot reflect this structure outright, it can only do so in stages. If it were otherwise, there would be neither a history of nor progress in science. But the fact is that the order of things implies and grounds the order

of truths, and that the systematic links between truths, understood as truths in themselves, serve the person of science as
accessories, stages, springboards, "helpful ladders," as Husserl
puts it, to progress in his efforts to reconstitute the complex
system of truths in discourse.

But then, all sorts of "artificial devices" and "complications"
become inevitable. The individual subject and his arbitrary
choices then arise. For want of being the immediate and outright reflection of total truth in a mirror-consciousness, real
science only exists, in human history, in the form of a construct, a complex scaffolding erected with the help of a method.
Direct evidence is better: evidence proper is only possible for
"primitive states of affairs," that is, for some elementary truisms,
a few axioms, and postulates from which the researcher can
only proceed through constructs. It might as well be stated that
far from being co-extensive with evidence, science begins where
evidence ends. Method is what enables such a construction. But
because it is also known that "for the same proposition there can
be several validating methods," nobody can deny that methods
contain an undeniable component of arbitrariness and artifice, in
other words, of subjectivity.

What is remarkable is Husserl's effort to reduce this element of artifice to a minimum and the way in which he does
this. First, he substitutes the concept of method with that of
validation *(Begründung)* and demonstrates that "validations"
(Begründungen) in general, understood as modes of demonstration or reasoning, are not totally artificial and arbitrary,
but that they obey general norms that are binding on any
researcher. Validations are fixed, universal, and necessary
structures whose generality runs across the frontiers of the
different sciences and which enable, from one piece of knowledge to another, "systematically regulated progress": "A blind
caprice has not bundled any set of truths P_1, P_2 . . . S together
and then so instituted the human mind that it must necessar-

ily . . . connect the knowledge of S with the knowledge of P_1, P_2. . . . In no single case is this so. Connections of validation are not governed by caprice or chance, but by reason and order" (Husserl 1970, 1:64).

Husserl is expressing the same concern: to exorcise the myth of a human nature, posited as an ultimate reason for the associations of ideas. In contrast, Husserl discovers the formal and its *a priori* necessity, and posits at the origins of our intellectual procedures, as is the case with any truly validating association, the action of forms themselves.

Only retrospectively, after demonstrating what he wished to prove, would Husserl justify the substitution of 'validation' for method by showing that the first notion fits into the second. In point of fact, scientific methods are always either validations proper or abbreviations used to economize thought and, in this regard, substitutes for validations or auxiliary procedures that serve to prepare, facilitate, or consolidate validations.

In this series of interlocking concepts, I believed I detected a typical figure of Husserl's rhetoric. It could be described as a "sliding demonstration." It consists in bringing reasoning to bear on a term that is easier than that announced in the beginning, and then demonstrating retroactively the equivalence of both terms. This device reproduces at the rhetorical level a recurrent move in Husserl's intellectual method: the reduction to the theoretical. It is only a tactic in the general strategy of a discourse that loudly and clearly proclaims the primacy of the theoretical. Other examples will be seen later.

Meanwhile, it will be useful to see how Husserl overturns the traditional explanation of the empiricists. Instead of invoking the association of ideas as the ultimate source of theoretical interconnection, he considers it, on the contrary, as the effect in the subject of an *a priori* formal legality. Thus, the form of certain premises easily brings out the conclusion deriving from it, because syllogisms of the same form had earlier been successfully effected. Inversely, the form of a proposition to be proved can remind us of certain types of validations that had earlier produced conclusions with an analogous form. Form itself is what therefore acts upon, and determines an 'association', in the empirical subject, and in a more permanent way, the habits or dispositions of mind that guide him in his intellectual effort. There is no other explanation for the exploits of "the mathematical instinct" or "the philological sense"—the reflexes created in the specialist through a long practice of his discipline, and whose effect is to speed up progress in his research. They are the effect on the individual mind of the action of forms themselves, of the action of the structures, and therefore of a pre-personal legality which, to be valid, does not need the individual, but through which, on the contrary, the individual constitutes himself as a thinking subject.

b) The Theoretical and the Normative

The examination of the relations between theoretical disciplines and normative and practical ones will lead to the same conclusions. Husserl will demonstrate, on the one hand, that every practical or normative science contains a theoretical kernel. But he will also demonstrate the remarkable property of any theoretical proposition and discipline to transmit norms implicitly, such that, again, the rule *par excellence* is the effacement of the empirical subject and his personal preferences, the subordination of any contingent system of values to the universal legality of truth.

It is known that Husserl's problem, in the first volume of the *Logical Investigations*, concerns the status of logic. The question is whether logic is an art or a science, a simple technology of knowledge or, on the contrary, a genuine theoretical discipline with a specific object, distinct from that of the other sciences and, in particular, from psychology. Husserl's answer is known: logic is a specific science, purely formal, *a priori* and demonstrative; a science that, up to now in history, has had only a partial realization, and which still must be systematically developed in new directions that the author of the *Logical Investigations* aims to identify in precise terms. The force of this demonstration comes from the fact that it does not merely content itself with pitting, arbitrarily, one response against another, but starts by first bringing out the truth of the false answer. Logic is indeed a technology of science, but it is not only that; much more, it functions as such only because it has a genuine theoretical content. This is what is brought out in chapter 2 of the *Prolegomena* in the form of a necessary and universal relation: not only logic as a technology of thought, but any technology or practical discipline is based on at least one theoretical discipline.

In so doing, however, Husserl is far from underestimating logic's practical function. On the contrary, it is from this practical function that logic derives all its importance, and all its human value. And even when this function has been "reduced" (in the sense of bracketed) to let a specific discipline appear behind it—a discipline conceived as a formal theory of discourse—this theory in turn will derive all its value from the fact that it discovers, within discourse itself, an *innere Gesetzlichkeit*—an irreducible, unsuppressible intrinsic legality: the final rationale for the methodological rules prescribed for the scientist by practical and normative logic.

Once again, Husserl's rhetoric calls for close attention. In order to prove that logic as a practical discipline presupposes pure logic as a theoretical foundation, he brings his demonstration to bear on normative logic. It is only retrospectively that he indicates, in a few bold strokes, that what is true of normative logic is all the more true for practical logic (or the technology of science) that, in his view, is only an extension of the former: its application to man and to the empirical conditions of knowledge. It is another example of a sliding proof.

But if the functions assigned by Husserl to normative logic as a methodology of science, a comparative examination of "the foundations" and the "patterns of foundations," are examined and compared to those of pure logic established in the last chapter of the *Prolegomena*, it must be acknowledged that in the final analysis normative logic has no real content other than that of pure logic; that it is not really a different logic, but, to the extent that it is an *a priori* prescription to science of its rules and methods, theoretical logic itself applied to a regulative function of knowledge.

The distinction between pure logic and normative epistemology is therefore only clear as a phenomenological distinction. The first is characterized by the absence, the second by the presence, of the subject that is bearer of norms and charged with a scientific responsibility. "The purification" of logic, this reduction to the theoretical, undertaken by the *Prolegomena*, will mean an exclusion of the subject, an exclusion which, incidentally, is profoundly ambiguous, because its only consequence is to bring out the true meaning: the universal dimension of norms which, up to then, have been only naïvely interpreted as empirical rules that are only valid for us.

Practical logic, on the other hand, is more complex. As a technology of science, it does not have logic as its unique foundation, but must additionally take into consideration the real conditions of human knowledge, whose study derives from various empirical sciences, notably psychology.

It follows that if the transition from a normative to a practical logic, and more generally, from a normative discipline to a technology results, as Husserl states, from an "extension" of the functions of the former; and if a technology can, in this regard, be viewed as a "particular instance" of the normative discipline, it is Husserl himself who provides us with the means to distinguish radically one from the other by opposing the universally valid *a priori* norms to the "technical prescriptions specifically adapted to human nature." For my part I concluded from this that the break established by Husserl between a theoretical discipline on the one hand and a normative and practical discipline on the other could easily be shifted and reconceived as one between a *theoretical and a normative discipline* on the one hand, and a *practical and technological discipline* on the other. The first distinction is phenomenological; that is, it takes the subjective attitude into account, the presence or absence of a normative interest. The second is purely epistemological, and takes into account the origin (the *a priori*, or, on the contrary, the empirical character) of the concepts deployed.

Although the case of logic is an important theoretical detour, he does not stop there, but attempts to construct the concepts of normative science and theoretical science in general.

His treatment of normative science is highly significant. By formalizing value judgments, demonstrating the possibility of substituting a normative proposition (e.g., "a soldier should be brave") with its interpretive equivalent ("only a brave soldier is a good soldier"), Husserl tries to rescue these types of judgment from the pure subjectivity of their enunciator, and to demonstrate that they too stake a claim to objectivity. Formalization, however, encounters a limit: like a residue, it brings out a couple of value predicates ("good" versus "bad"), which are introduced into the class of objects considered by an act that Husserl calls 'valuation'. The valuations of a system all refer to an underlying valuation whose linguistic expression is the basic norm: the ultimate justification of all the norms of the system under consideration, the founding principle of this system itself as a normative discipline. Significantly, Husserl cites as examples of a basic norm the 'categorical imperative' in the group of normative propositions that make up Kant's ethics, or the principle of the "greatest possible happiness of the greatest possible number" in the ethics of the Utilitarians, or the 'pleasure imperative' in the ethics of the Hedonists.

Thus, there are as many examples that derive from ethics and establish it, by the same token, as the normative discipline *par excellence.*

The unavoidable role of basic valuation does not however deter Husserl in his efforts at formalization. For if valuation as an act is set aside, and exclusive focus is placed on its expression in the norm, it is easy to obtain a purely theoretical proposition. From the interpretive statement "Only an A which is B is a good A" one moves to a purely neutral statement "Only an A which is B has the properties C," in which "C" serves to indicate the constitutive content of the standard-setting predicate "good" (e.g., pleasure, knowledge, etc.). The "sidelining" of the normative interest thus frees the theoretical proper.

The move to the theoretical—this conversion of normative interest to pure theoretical interest—was of the greatest importance to me. I saw in it something like a self-effacement of the subject before the objective relations; a way for the former to neutralize itself, to be nothing more than a pure spectatorial gaze. This gaze is, however, still a subtle mode of presence: a deleted presence certainly, but not a simple absence; the presence of an almost non-existent subject that had to be elucidated at some point or the other.

A remarkable fact, however, remained: if a move from the normative to the purely theoretical was possible, a reverse move was also a possibility, and any theoretical proposition could be converted into a normative one.

Thus, in a proposition of the form: "Only an A which is B has properties C," where "C" happens to be valorized as such, the proposition will take the following form: "Only an A which is B is a good A," that is "A must be B."

This is what accounts for the fact that a mathematical truth can always become a rule of construction. It also explains the widespread illusion that logic is a normative science. For if

the laws of logic are purely theoretical, and are of the same nature as mathematics, then they can always become normative
propositions in the sense of prescriptions, on the condition
that the normative idea is interpolated in them. In a general
way, any theoretical law, whether it belongs to logic, mathematics, or to any other science, can be converted to the normative and applied to a practical, specific function: regulating
human knowledge.

Thus, for the author of the *Logical Investigations*, it is in this
regulative function that the human value of science resides.
Husserl's intellectualism, this extraordinary valorization of
the theoretical for which he was taken to task by his contem-
poraries in the name of the seriousness of existence (Chestov
1926), is in reality only a powerful attempt to found an ethics
of true thought—the central kernel of ethics *tout court*.

4. The Interconnection of Truths

We can now proceed more quickly and, after having sketched
out the significance of the scientific demand, define science itself more precisely. To do this, there are two possible approaches. Science can be approached *a parte subjecti* (from the
point of view of the subject elaborating it), in which case it appears like a construct, a body of methodical practices. But it
can also be viewed *a parte objecti* (from the angle of the object).
In this case, it is a result: an ideal system of truths, the identical content of a theoretical discourse that can be enunciated by
the most diverse subjects using methodical practices that are
no less diverse.

However, if Husserl's text is read more carefully, things become a touch more complex. First of all, the subjective approach can be understood in two different ways, depending on
whether by "methods" is meant the intellectual procedures and

the linkages of acts of cognition in which "foundations" proper reside, or whether what is meant is the material practices accompanying or sustaining them, such as the instruments used in these practices and described by Husserl, as we observed, as 'foundation surrogates'.

Depending on the case, therefore, science will have either a pragmatic definition, where it will be seen as an experimental montage, a body of regulated material practices, or a psychological definition, where it will appear as an intellectual construct—a psychological linkage of acts of cognition. Husserl mentions the first definition only to annex it immediately to the second: instruments and apparatuses will never be anything but 'extrinsic tools' linked to a unity of acts of thought. This annexation leads anew to a sliding demonstration. No special analysis is needed to demonstrate the weakness of the pragmatic definition. It is enough to show how the psychological definition of which it is an extension prepares and implies its own reversal in an objective definition, and how the linkage of acts in an immanent temporality, far from being the cause, is, on the contrary, the effect on individual psychology, of the chain of truths in an intemporal order.

On the other hand, the objective approach subdivides into two. The content of a science will no longer simply be reduced to its theoretical content, to this chain of propositions linked by relationships of premises to consequences. Behind the interconnection of truths, Husserl projects an "interconnection of things" that constitutes its ontological base.

There is no doubt about the significance of this reduplication. It results in a more complete effacement of the role of the subject, and a stronger emphasis on the reversal of perspective by which Husserl stands in opposition to the empiricists. The psychological interconnection of knowledges thus points, in the first instance, to the interconnection of things themselves, in the broadest sense in which all consciousness is consciousness of *something*. It is only in the second instance that we can, through a new kind of abstraction, reduce the interconnection of things to a pure system of truths.

The detour through things thus has the advantage of avoiding the psychologistic temptation, that of dissolving the system of truths in the flow of individual consciousness. It becomes necessary to think of the system of truths in relation to that of things and to acknowledge, by the same token, in the system of truths the same independence, the same objectivity. In short, the ontological reduplication of the logical definition of science has a pedagogical role. It helps to show that truth is not only a function of the subject, but also of a state of things that is strictly contemporaneous with the thing itself and anterior to subjective knowledge.

Thus, does one move towards the idea of a truth-in-itself, the necessary correlate of being-in-itself. The idea of a science without a subject then almost becomes conceivable; a science that connects all truths within itself, an absolute science which, far from being mistaken for the uncertain beginnings of concrete research would, on the contrary, precede any actual research; a science-in-itself that would express the interconnection of all things, and as such would be anterior to man and independent of any thinking subject.

The idea seemed seductive to me. It brought to the fore the ethics of effacement in which, to my mind, Husserl locates the human significance of science. But then I still had to be careful not to interpret the "interconnection of things" in a naïvely realist manner. Everything points to the fact that for Husserl, the field of objects of a science is absolutely contemporaneous with this science, and that being in itself, in its widest sense, is absolutely connected to science in itself, that is to the total system of truths. Thus, in Husserl's language, the 'thing' does not necessarily designate the material thing, but the object in general—be it a real thing, an ideal one, a species, a mathematical relation, a being, or a value. The thing can, on occasion, even be a truth. Thus, for logic, understood as a science of science, it is knowledge itself that becomes the object of knowledge.

It was necessary in these conditions, to reinterpret the Husserlian thesis of an interconnection of things, and all those texts where the author of the *Logical Investigations*, warning against any μεταβασις εις αλλο γενος *(metabasis eis allo genos)*, explicitly adopts the Aristotelian doctrine of classes of being. All things considered, I accepted that the articulation of being is, as a matter of fact, nothing other than the different scientific disciplines themselves. All Husserl sought to do was to recall the fact that the division of epistemological fields should neither be artificial nor gratuitous, that the effective sciences must be guided by an idea of science that owes nothing to experience, but that functions as an idea, a regulative idea in the Kantian sense. The decisive break is thus not situated between the articulation of things and the articulation of knowledge. Knowledge itself is shot through and through with this break, insofar as the mumblings of the human-constructed sciences are opposed to knowledge itself that is ideal, intemporal, and called upon to serve as a model.

All things considered, science, strictly speaking, resides neither in the linkage of acts of cognition, nor in the interconnections of things, but in the interconnection of truths. The question then was one of identifying the link that binds the truths in a science. That gave Husserl the opportunity to affirm a demanding, uncompromising, deductive ideal.

The most accomplished form of science is deductive theory: a closed sum total of laws resting on one "basic legality," or on a conjunction of homogenous "basic laws" arising out of it through systematic deduction. The real sciences are therefore the "abstract" or "explanatory"; 'nomological' sciences, to use terminology that Husserl borrowed from von Kries. The unity of propositions is derived from a common axiom from which the rest of the propositions are generated. In the descriptive sciences, on the other hand, the propositions do not exhibit an internal interconnection of this nature; their unity results from the fact that they all relate to the same field of objects. Geography, history, astronomy, natural science, and anatomy—to mention just these few examples—illustrate this type of external, extra-essential *(ausserwesentliche)* unity, and also show how the so-called descriptive sciences, far from being satisfied with describing their object, in fact always try to integrate the nomological model in their methodology.

The same can be said for the normative sciences. Propositions in this instance are not derived one from the other; they owe their unity to a common grounding in a basic norm. Here too, however, the nomological model is at play. Better still, unlike the so-called descriptive sciences, any normative discipline is founded, as we observed, on one or several theoretical disciplines.

Given this axiomatic vision and the fundamental and rich significance of the mathematical model of science in Husserl's work, how then does he conceive the experimental sciences? By their methods, these are clearly explanatory and not descriptive sciences: the theoretical physicist views the earth and the skies from a perspective different from that of the geographer or astronomer insofar as they only matter to him as "examples of gravitating masses in general" (Husserl 1970, 1:231). By their object though, these sciences necessarily have a solid content of real facts and, to that extent, can only enunciate probable laws which are "accordingly genuine laws, but epistemologically considered, no more than idealizing fictions with a *fundamento in re*" (Husserl 1970, 1:106).

With regard to the experimental sciences, therefore, Husserl professes a kind of probabilism. The Law of Gravitation is only one possible language among many. Mechanics, acoustics, theoretical optics, and astronomy are only theoretical models among other equally plausible models. An authentic legality is never, in the fields of the knowledge of facts, anything other than an asymptotic ideal. "Purely conceptual" knowledge on the other hand fulfills this ideal.

That is why if one wishes to know what science is in general, one must interrogate not the descriptive, normative, or experimental sciences, but the theoretical sciences in the strict sense of the word: the nomological sciences. This is also why the theory of science *(Wissenschaftslehre)* will neither be methodology nor history of the sciences, still less psychology of knowledge. It will be first and foremost logic in the literal sense of the word: a theory of logos, a science of the formations of discourse and of their conditions of validity.

It can clearly be seen in the last chapter of the *Prolegomena* where Husserl seeks to define the ambitious program of what he calls "pure logic": the determination of the pure categories of meaning (and its correlative, the pure categories of objects), the pure theory of meaning (and its correlative, plurality), a theory of possible forms of theory (and its correlative, multiplicities)—three tasks which by all evidence constitute as many stages in the research on language. However, to understand this relationship between logic and language, it was necessary to work out, by following the movement of the *First Logical Investigation*, the concept of "meaning itself." I devoted a lot of time to this in my thesis.

5. The Language of Things

The phenomenology of language comes into play in the *Logical Investigations* as an instrument of conceptual clarification. Its aim is to establish the meaning of terms commonly used in logic like concept, representation, judgment, reasoning, truth, etc., by dissipating once and for all the ambiguity that attaches to these terms, which are also used to designate mental acts. It is thus an attempt to overturn psychologism on its own terrain, by demonstrating that the acts of knowing that attract the exclusive attention of the psychologist-logician necessarily refer to ideal objects.

If such is the case, however, we must hesitate before speaking of a phenomenology of *language*. For language is not the focus of the analysis, but the difficulty that motivates it; it is not the object but the pretext. What is being dealt with here is a phenomenology of logical experiences, an analysis of the mental acts that sustain language, rather than a phenomenology of language.

However, under closer scrutiny, it appears that "language," in the deepest sense of the word, consists, in fact, of such mental acts. Speech is not merely a physical articulation but the expression and extension, as it were, of thought. Verbal articulation is only the accidental manifestation of an inner speech, which is a silent speech which, in turn, equates to the very act of thinking. The phenomenology of mental experiences is therefore a phenomenology of *language*.

For Husserl the linguistic signifier does not signify by itself, but its relationship to the signified is conferred to it by the subject. Behind the reference of the signifier to the signified, which a superficial linguist might see as inherent to the signifier itself, the phenomenologist discovers a signifying act which, by investing the given phonic or graphic matter, transforms it into a sign. No object is a sign by itself. An object only becomes a sign through delegation.

Now, even when this object ceases to be given—even when the silence of inner monologue replaces the rustle of real communication—consciousness continues to produce meaning: that is, thought. I concluded therefrom that thought is, in reality, the silent form of language: language amputated of its communicative dimension. Consequently, if the so-called phenomenology of language is always, as mentioned earlier, the identification of acts of thought behind language, inversely, if by language is no longer meant empirical communication, but this fundamental language that continues to be heard even in what Husserl describes as "the solitary mental life," then all phenomenology is, in the final analysis, a phenomenology of language. The *First Investigation* only indicated the path, by highlighting on the basis of a privileged example the essential function of all experience in general—which is to prepare and occasionally sustain language.

I paid the greatest attention to Husserl's effort to "purify the sign." First, he excluded from his concerns the indicative sign—a material and empirical sign that is neither discourse nor part of discourse—in order to concentrate solely on expression. Next, he excluded from discourse itself those body movements and various gestures that involuntarily accompany speech and still derive from empirical indication, in order to focus on expression proper—on the linguistic sign which alone is the true bearer of meaning. Finally, he amputated the communicative dimension from language in which expressions function simultaneously as indices, to concentrate solely on the expression in "solitary mental life;" in a context, that is, where the physical production of the word, and correlatively, its real perception, gives way to an imaginary representation of the same word by both speaker and interlocutor merged into one and the same person.

This progressive de-realization of the sign frees the essence of meaning in general, that is, of the meaning-conferring act *(Sinngebung)* that boils down to the act of thinking itself.

I noted in passing the voluntarist touch of the Husserlian concept of meaning, and more generally, of intentionality. Jacques Derrida had drawn our attention to this point in a seminar that resulted in his book *La voix et le phénomène* (1967): namely that through the successive stages of the purification of the sign, Husserl meant to stick to what the speaker really wishes to say, and to exclude from his field of concern all the meanings that might have escaped from him— the involuntary confessions, or what the interlocutor can rightly or wrongly interpret as such. The reduction to the solitary mental life boils down to a precise exclusion of the possibility of misinterpretation and misunderstanding, the possibility of imputing motives by uniquely taking into consideration conscious, deliberate, and "intentional" meanings in the most common sense of the word: meanings borne by a *Bedeutungsintention* (a signifying intention).

I, however, noted how Husserl sees himself forced, in spite of this voluntarism, to privilege, in his analysis of the acts of verbal expression, *the viewpoint of the listener.* The de-realization of the sign, the substitution of real words with words that are simply imagined, does not equate to—far from it—straightforward elimination. Even in inner monologue, words remain: *solitary thought is, in the final analysis, only an imaginary form of listening.*

Without that, it would be impossible to understand the first series of "essential phenomenological distinctions" established by Husserl. Among the partial experiences superimposed in the total acts of expression, the *First Investigation* distinguishes the "mental phenomenon" where the expression gives itself its materiality, meaning-conferring acts where reference to the object expressed is constituted, and finally, in the best cases, the meaning-fulfilling acts that give experience its intuitive fullness. What is remarkable is that these distinctions bearing on solitary acts of verbal expression, recognize, at the foundation of this experience, a moment of irrepressible passivity: "the phenomenon of expression" is not only necessary, in a real conversation, to enable the real interlocutor to understand what the speaker means, it remains indispensable in the inner soliloquy, to enable the lonely speaker to understand what he wants to say to himself, what is given to thought.

The three strata of the acts of expression will become a little more complicated as well. I knew, from the research for my *diplôme d'études supérieures*, that the notions of intentional act and of non-intentional content proceeded, in Husserl, from an extension to all experience of equivalent concepts elaborated in the analysis of expressive experience. I now saw how these general concepts, obtained by analogy, could in turn be applied to the act of expression itself.

Thus, in the end Husserl splits the physical nature of the word, distinguishing, as a result, four moments in the total act of speech: the "sensation-content," which gives the expression; the intentional grasp (perceptive or imaginative) of the expression as a sensible sign; the sense-giving act, where the specificity of the linguistic act resides—and by extension the specificity of thought as solitary discourse—and finally the intuitive act, which illustrates and, in the best instances, fulfills meaning.

Through all these subtle phenomenological distinctions lay an essential, unavoidable fact: namely the anteriority, in relation to any other step, of the sense datum passively received by consciousness. Even in the inner soliloquy, the supposed producer of discourse is already a listener and an interpreter. It can, therefore, no longer just be said that the significance of discourse points to the subject. The origin of meaning can no longer be merely located in the sense-giving act. For this act itself has a genesis: it is built on an initial non-act that can no longer be said to belong to a subject. The most solitary thinker cannot possibly coincide with himself. Listener of words from elsewhere, he is at best only a fissured subject.

To the "phenomenological distinctions" correspond, however, "ideal distinctions"; to the superimposed layers of acts of expression correspond the objects—material or immaterial (in a word the object-entities, as Husserl describes them)—that are posited or targeted through these acts. Here again, are distinguishable three steps that can be further complicated by a fourth.

To the physical phenomenon of the word corresponds the expression *in specie*, always identical to itself whoever the person enunciating it or whatever the variable circumstances of the enunciation. The sign, in this respect, is an ideal species, irreducible, that is, to its real production through the fleeting moments of its phonic realization and the multiplicity of its written instances.

This description is of crucial importance. The ideality of the sign implies the ideality of its meaning, its permanence through the multiple acts directed at it. Husserl asserts the ideality of meaning as a *consequence* of the ideality of expression. Intentional meaning is thus first and foremost only a "founded reality," a "non-independent" reality *(unselbständig)*, to use the terms in the *Third Investigation*. It is nothing without the expression; it is carried by it, transmitted by it like color by a surface.

Meaning thus understood points, however, to an object. Husserl makes a careful distinction between what an expression means and what it is about: its *Was* and its *Vorüber*. Several expressions may have the same meaning but different objects, and inversely again, they may have different meanings but the same object. "The victor at Jena" and "The vanquished at Waterloo" are examples of two expressions necessarily having as such two different meanings, but each referring to one and the same individual: Napoleon. That said, it is not the object, but the meaning-intention that is central to discourse as such. The relationship to the object is only achieved in privileged cases where the meaning-intention sees itself gratified with the actual presence of the object. How then does the encounter take place? It is here that Husserl makes his "ideal distinctions" a notch complicated by refusing to merge the object itself with its ideal correlate in the intuitive act, that is, in the act of perceiving or imagining. This ideal correlate is the fulfilling meaning as opposed to the empty meanings of mere discourse.

Because of this, truth arises by the retrieval of intentional meaning, and by fulfilling meaning. I did not, any more than Husserl in the *First Investigation*, expand on this important concept of retrieval *(Deckung)*. What fascinated me, though, was the concept of fulfilling meaning. This new concept was, to me, of the utmost importance. The object is no longer a mere thing in itself, independent of the subject and locked in itself. Every object became a sign. Everything has an intelligible nucleus, a 'form', in the Aristotelian sense of the term, an essence, a 'quiddity', something like a grain of meaning in a sort of immanent discourse that inheres in things themselves. Things, henceforth, speak by themselves. By so doing, they establish a universe of meaning that is anterior to man, that human discourse aspires to find.

By thus layering the signified object with a fulfilling meaning conceived as the ideal correlate of intuition, Husserl repeats, in reverse order, a method that I had already observed in the *Prolegomena:* the ontological reduplication of the logical definition of science, the gesture through which he projected, behind the theoretical content of a discipline defined as an interconnection of truths, a solid and permanent support: an interconnection of things. The result is however the same. The detour through things was, in the *Prolegomena*, only a pedagogical tool meant to warn against the temptation of dissolving the chain of truths in the linkage of the acts of knowing. This interconnection, it can be speculated, remained inaccessible: it was a mere regulating idea in the Kantian sense. With the opposite gesture accomplished, this time in the *First Investigation*—after the "ideal distinctions" that conclude the phenomenology of language—this semantic reduplication (as it were) of the targeted object results in throwing the latter out of the field of the accessible and the controllable, and in making it a regulating idea in the Kantian sense, rather than a constitutive idea. All in all, the human universe is from end to end a universe of meaning where things announce themselves without ever becoming truly present. Even in an ideal case, where human language coincides fully with the language of things, one would still be *in* language, at maximum proximity to things, undoubtedly, but still outside of them.

Ordinary language does not have this good fortune. It is woven, through and through, with empty meanings that fill up only occasionally and then incompletely. The essence of human discourse is this universe of "intentional meanings" that correlates to the total system of expressions and links directly to this system. The ideality of meaning, we observed, is nothing other than that of the expression as a sensible sign. It follows that, hypothetically, one and only one meaning corresponds to each expression. Such is Husserl's exact postulate.

This postulate is shaken by a simple fact: the existence, in ordinary language, of an incalculable number of ambiguous expressions. It is not merely a question of accidental ambiguities that can be easily eliminated by forging more complete and precise expressions. It is a question of the insurmountable ambiguity of certain verbal categories such as personal pronouns, demonstratives, adverbs of place and time, the definite article in some of its uses, and such other "essentially subjective and occasional" expressions whose meaning depends on the person speaking or his situation, in contrast to "objective" expressions whose meaning depends—or can depend—simply on their reality as phonetic phenomena. Thus, if the function of the pronoun "I" is always to refer to the person speaking (what Husserl calls the 'indicative meaning'), the representation of this function outside of any context cannot replace the unique representation of the person speaking in the specific, given context (which is the indicated meaning). "I am happy" does not mean, "any one who, by speaking, is designating himself, is happy."

Ordinary language is replete with such "fluctuating expressions." They represent a real challenge to the Husserlian ideal of univocity that is inseparable from a certain vision of science.

The way in which Husserl meets this challenge merits some attention. It boils down, in effect, to attributing to the poverty of human languages and, more generally to the limits of human knowledge, the need to have recourse to fluctuating expressions, for lack of an infinite number of stable expressions necessary to describe the different situations, the different particular cases imaginable that are themselves infinite. Normally, it should be possible to substitute a stable expression for each use of the fluctuating expression. The limited vocabulary of natural languages, the impossibility of foreseeing *a priori* all the possible situations of the speaking subject render such a substitution inapplicable in reality. The important thing, however, is that it remains possible in principle, and that we can always remedy the deficiencies of vocabulary by making words fluctuate, depending on what we wish to say. "Rightly seen," writes Husserl, "such change in meanings is really change in the act of meaning": in short, the movement of the eyes leads to an imperceptible shift from one meaning to another and engenders, like a kaleidoscope, the illusion of a movement of meanings themselves. Why is it so important to dissipate this illusion? Because these fixed, unchanging, and discrete unities that the ideal meanings are understood to be would be dissolved in the flow of signifying consciousness. This is also, and more simply, because, as Husserl says, the affirmation of the "unbounding range of objective reason" cannot be abandoned.

This way of resolving the problem clearly indicates that the ideality of meaning is no longer simply perceived as a consequence of the ideality of expression. To say that the universe of meaning is richer than the richest of our vocabularies is to abandon the idea of meaning considered as a "founded" reality and to acknowledge for it the same independence or autonomy *(Selbständigkeit)* as for any ideal species.

It is not at all surprising, in these conditions, that Husserl should suddenly reverse positions by positing abruptly, beyond the "meanings in expression," a universe of "meanings in themselves," the first of which would be a partial and contingent realization in the language of humans. It is, however, necessary to understand the significance of these "meanings in themselves." They do not coincide with the objects themselves, individual or general, but constitute perspectives on the objects, or multiple representations pertaining to them. Thus, the mathematical object "4" is targeted through several meanings, including: "the number 4," "the second even number in the series of numbers." Richer than human languages, the universe of meanings is also richer and considered wider than the world of objects.

It appears to me that this notion of "meaning in itself" concludes a constant attempt, throughout *Investigations*, to exclude the subject, after its initial consecration as the condition and the primary source of meaning. If the proper object of a phenomenology of language, as of any phenomenology in general, is to show the subject at work behind the production which, at first sight, hides it, the clearest result of Husserl's analyses in the *First Investigation* is, paradoxically, to reveal the subject at the end of the journey and to subordinate it to a necessary and intemporal order that precisely establishes it as subject by giving it the task of carrying this pre-existent order to the expression.

In this manner, experience is taken seriously only long enough to be transcended, relativized, and subordinated to a presubjective *a priori* that grounds it.

In these conditions, the categorical rejection in the *Fifth Investigation* of the neo-Kantian notion of a "pure self" becomes easily understandable. To me it was the logical outcome of the entire movement of the *Logical Investigations*: the theoretical acknowledgment of a gesture of exclusion that had been at work from the beginning of the book.

I attached the greatest importance to this criticism of the absolute subject, to this approach that sees in the real self an "empirical object," like the self of the other or of any other object in the world. By reducing this empirical self to its purely phenomenological nucleus, one is faced with a complex of experiences blending one into the other in the same temporality; but nowhere above this lived temporality can an 'egological principle' *(Ichprinzip)*, sustaining all the contents and unifying them all a second time, be found. The "I think," of which Kant said, "it should accompany all our representations," is thus a theoretically superfluous notion. The unity of experience takes care of itself through a progressive and horizontal articulation, in an open, unfinishable process. Husserl's long controversy with the neo-Kantian Natorp clearly shows the extent to which he was averse at the time of the *Logical Investigations* to bringing this process to a premature conclusion (Husserl 1970, 2:548–51).

These initial positions of Husserl's were later to become historically influential. Sartre relied on them to affirm the "transcendence of the ego." The self thus became an object of the empirical world, constituted by an originary consciousness that could itself be a "transcendental field without a subject" (Sartre 1965). Sartre also pushed Husserl's analyses to their most radical limits by emphasizing the uncontrollable spontaneity of prereflexive consciousness. And it is easy to see how such an approach led to the existentialist position and all the issues relating to the analytics of the *Dasein*, of 'being-there'.

What I found missing, however, in this interpretation was a clear understanding of the logical motivations of Husserl's method. The idea of "truth in itself" advanced in the *Prolegomena*, the correlative idea established in the *First Investigation* of an *a priori* universe of "meanings in themselves," this repeated insistence on the objectivity and intemporality of meaning, all this necessarily made it impossible, even before the opening of the *Fifth Investigation*, to posit the idea of a pure self that could be the source and producer of thought experiences. On the contrary, these experiences had to be determined in the final instance by the ideal forms themselves, and the logical experiences in particular had to be the contingent realizations of an impersonal, presubjective, and universal meaning.

From then on, the later rehabilitation of the concept of self undertaken from *Ideas* and the second edition of *Logical Investigations*[5] could no longer merely be seen, as does Sartre, as an arbitrary change of opinion, something like a gratuitous and fortuitous turnabout. I proposed, for my part, another working hypothesis: Husserl's sudden change of position on this question was also in its way a response to logical demands. The transcendental Ego is rehabilitated only insofar as it is the bearer of a scientific responsibility, the subject of an incomplete discourse that he feels duty-bound to pursue, the site of a concern or, as Husserl frequently puts it, of a "theoretical interest" without which the "truths in themselves" could never be brought to the point of expression.

We find ourselves, however, on a level different from that of pure description: the transcendental Ego will be a normative idea and not a descriptive concept.

6. The Impossible Closure

Once the concept of "meaning in itself" had been produced, the tasks of logic remained to be examined. If science, as was observed, is only a particular form of language, a sub-system of true meanings in the universe of "meanings in themselves," then the theory of science must demonstrate the transition from genus to species, from general system to sub-system—in other words how truth arises within language.

A science of the conditions of possibility of science, logic could not, as a matter of fact, be reduced to the study of the noetic, or subjective, conditions of scientific knowledge. It is first and foremost the study of the objective conditions of possibility of the *result* of this knowledge, namely the theory, the linkage of propositions expressive of this knowledge. Better still: the noetic conditions of knowledge are nothing themselves without these ideal conditions. On the contrary they derive from the latter through a simple inflection *(Wendung)*, a simple transposition *(Uebertragung)* that precisely announces "these conversions to the normative" *(normative Wendung)*, which enable, as we observed, the transition from pure logic to normative epistemology.

I paid particular attention to a question raised by Husserl on the meaning of the word "possibility" in the expression "conditions of possibility of a theory." This term is normally reserved for objects. It can only be applied to concepts and theories by an obvious transposition, by metonymy, as it were. A "possible" concept is not one that could exist because it is understood that it does exist; but it is a concept whose object *could* exist, a *valid concept*. Similarly, a "possible" theory is a theory that expresses possible states of things, a theory that is valid, coherent, and non-contradictory. The task of formal logic will precisely be to determine *a priori* the foundations of such validity.

By defining at the end of the *Prolegomena* pure logic's triple tasks, Husserl was keenly aware of his project's novelty. It was impossible for me not to be struck by the programmatic nature of his vocabulary. For the author it was not merely a question of bringing out the structures of an existing discipline, but of founding a new one. It is only later, and retrospectively, that entire areas of what passed for a logic were to be annexed to the new discipline.

It was equally impossible not to notice the nuance between this hierarchy of tasks and the hierarchy of levels established in *Formal and Transcendental Logic*. According to Suzanne Bachelard, this difference in perspective explains the absence, in chapter 1 ([1929] 1989), of any allusion to the theory of theories, and its separate treatment in chapter 3 (S. Bachelard 1989, 38–42).

What the three tasks consist of is known. The first consists in establishing a pure morphology of meanings, and correlatively, a pure morphology of objects. The second, consists in defining the conditions of formal truth or, more simply, of the theoretical validity of the signifying structures thus formed—a move that will lead to the establishment of theories of reasoning and, correlatively, of theories including theories of plurality and of number. The third, finally, consists in constructing the different types of possible theories and, correlatively, a doctrine of multiplicities, that is, of possible fields of knowledge.

The difficulty in understanding these tasks is linked to that of the very concept of form. I pitted myself against it as best I could. I first had to understand the notion of pure category of meaning in its distinctiveness from primary meanings, and to avoid being led into error by the very ambiguities of a text where Husserl is still feeling his way. What seemed important to me, however, was first to understand the function of this pure morphology of meanings, which is to establish the "laws of meaning" in general, in contrast to senselessness *(Unsinn)*, to enunciate the laws of complication of the first elements of discourse: the rules that govern the combination of meanings.

The *Fourth Investigation* achieves, at least in part, this first task of the *Prolegomena* under the name of a pure "logical grammar" by establishing in passing some concepts of concepts and strategic distinctions such as the distinction between 'categorem' and 'syncategorem', or between independent and non-independent meaning. I could not help noticing the relative paucity of the results of this investigation, the disconcerting banality of these laws of meaning established after long and complex analyses. However, Husserl himself anticipated this objection, proposing humorously to define philosophy as "a science of banalities." I acknowledged, like him, that depth is never obscure and that, in any case, the *Fourth Investigation* could not exhaust the entire field of pure grammar, but could only bring out its project and establish its foundations.

The most important point, however, was how Husserl moved from a pure morphology of meanings to a pure morphology of objects—from a pure logical grammar to what I would call the grammar of things. Thus the idea of a "formal ontology" appears for the first time in philosophical literature: the expression, absent from the first edition, was used in the second edition of *Logical Investigations;* Husserl explains, in *Formal and Transcendental Logic*, the scruples that held him back from using it at the time of the first edition (Husserl 1969, 27:86).

I could not help but notice that the pure morphology of objects—the first level of formal ontology—was later concretely illustrated in a study on the *Theory of Wholes and Parts* (the object of the entire *Third Investigation*), with the same breadth as the correlative idea of pure grammar exemplified in the *Fourth Investigation.* Noting, further, that this *Fourth Investigation* presents itself explicitly as an "application" of the results of the preceding *Investigation,* I concluded that in the horizontal duality of superimposed levels of logic, the two correlative theories could not be on the same level, but that on each occasion, formal ontology founded the analytic and preceded it theoretically—even if in the real movement of the *Investigation*—the project of a formal ontology only appears as a corollary of the analytic.

The second task of logic was easier to understand because it was more familiar, given that it had received celebrated treatment in traditional syllogistics. Husserl later clarified the point in the *Fourth Investigation* that the laws of pure grammar do not belong to formal logic proper, but that their only function is to delimit the field of meaning that constitutes the proper field of logic by excluding, among the innumerable language formations, the immense field of senselessness. Formal logic, *stricto sensu*, is indeed the theory of 'reasonings', the formal analytic that, once senselessness *(Unsinn)* is excluded, seeks to also exclude nonsense *(Widersinn)* by providing the means to distinguish concordant from non-concordant meaning.

I could not help but be struck by the subdivision in *Formal and Transcendental Logic* of this second group of *Investigations* where Husserl was finally to distinguish a "logic of consequence" or pure analytics, from a "logic of truth" or analytics in the wider sense. The *Fourth Investigation* was already suggesting that formal or analytic absurdity (e.g., "All As are Bs among which some are not B") not be confused with the absurdity referring to things, the material absurdity of a proposition that is formally correct but untrue (of the type "A square is round," for example) or of any false proposition in pure geometry. If the function of the logic of consequence is to exclude formal absurdity, I acknowledged for my part that a logic of truth necessarily had to aim at eliminating material absurdity. My argument was, therefore, that the difference between the two disciplines was not only phenomenological—linked, that is, to a "change of attitude" as Husserl put it, in the logician who, in the first instance would consider the judgments as mere judgments, and in the second would, on the contrary, see them as means of knowing. This change in attitude entailed a difference in content.

The logic of truth could not be content with translating the pure analytic in a different vocabulary, as if it were enough each time to replace in the same discourse the word "noncontradiction" with the word "truth" and the word "contradiction" with the word "falsehood" to produce another discipline; as if all that was needed, in short, was a mere difference in terminology to demarcate objectively two theories. The logic of truth, as I understood it, could not be satisfied with enunciating the laws of the formal concordance of judgments, but must, additionally, establish the conditions of their material concordance: that is, the compatibility of their ultimate concrete kernels as substrata of the same judgment.

I felt it necessary at this point to part company with Suzanne Bachelard's interpretation that observed the letter of Husserl's text. I saw a problem in what seemed obvious to her, namely the inclusion of this logic of truth in formal logic. Seeking to resolve this paradox, I observed that, strictly speaking, the logic of truth was not Husserl's focus in the texts under consideration, but that it was mentioned in them only to be immediately excluded in favor of the logic of consequence alone. Because Husserl's aim was to "purify" traditional logic, he referred to the logic of truth in chapter 1 of *Formal and Transcendental Logic* only to highlight, *a contrario*, the originality of the pure analytic, and thus to give to logic its true meaning. He could, nonetheless, consider the logic of truth as a formal logic in the broad sense of the term where 'formal' would practically be synonymous with '*a priori*'.

I also caught a subtle distinction of Husserl's that could enhance an understanding of how a logic of truth could still be formal: the distinction mentioned in passing in *Formal and Transcendental Logic* between the clarity of anticipation and the clarity of possession of things themselves, a distinction that occurs in the context of what could be termed a differential phenomenology of degrees of proof (Husserl 1969, 16:56–62).

According to Husserl, pure morphology indeed demarcates the sphere of confused proof, whereas pure analytic delineates the more restricted sphere of the proof of distinction, that is, of concordant meanings; the logic of truth demarcates the sphere of the proof of clarity. The first thing I could not help but observe was the inversion in relation to Descartes. Whereas for the author of the *Principles of Philosophy* the progress of thought proceeds from clarity—defined as the presence of the ideas to the attentive mind—to distinction—understood as specification and precision with regard to related ideas—for Husserl the move is from a sort of zero degree of proof to distinction and finally to clarity (Descartes 1984, 20).

The reason is that the author of *Logical Investigations* does not start, like Descartes, from a sense perception that must then be "reduced," but from language. It is in language, the site of production of meaning in general, that a confused meaning offers itself to be thought out, that is, a meaning that is merely possible, in contrast to senselessness, mere cacophonous *flatus vocis* with no echo. It is again in language that the work on meaning takes place before any real perception, work whose effect is to exclude formal nonsense, that is, contradictory meanings, in favor of only concordant meanings that are likely to be thought out as a whole, articulated in one and the same intellectual move. It is in this way that the proof of distinction is produced.

The next stage will be that of the intuitive fulfilling of these still empty meanings. From this fulfillment and the compatibility to which it attests between thought and reality will arise truth. But it is there precisely that the nuance that is of interest to us occurs. Truth proper almost presupposes that one moves out of language and that the "clarity of the possession of things themselves" succeeds the evidence of distinction. It is not necessary, however, to await this parousia; it is always possible to anticipate it. One is thus satisfied with the "clarity of anticipation." Thus, by the same stroke, a logic of truth that remains formal becomes possible, a logic that establishes *a priori* (before any empirical verification, and without claiming to move outside of language, that is) the conditions of meaning that are not only compatible, but intuitively possible.

The prevailing idea here is that if clear lines of demarcation can be drawn between sense and senselessness, and then between contradictory and concordant meaning, no solution of continuity exists, on the other hand, between formal concordance and truth, only a continuous progression. From empty meanings to full meanings, one witnesses an uninterrupted process of fulfilling, where the signified/intuited things are never totally absent or totally present, but continuously approached up to this absolute proximity that is never anything other than a dream, an asymptotic limit.

The *Sixth Investigation*, the last and the longest, returns at length to this problem, and proposes, in passing, the following equation:

$$i+s=1$$

where s designates the signitive, merely symbolic content of a discourse, i its intuitive content, and 1 the discourse itself. Two extreme cases can then be imagined:

a) $i=0, s=1$

b) $i=1, s=0$.

Neither one nor the other of these cases normally occurs: a discourse is never purely symbolic and devoid of all intuitive content, nor entirely full and devoid of any signitive content. Human language is always situated, in different degrees, between these two extremes (Husserl 1970, 2:§23:732–33). This is what gives authority to our interpretation and shows how a logic of pure consequence is always a logic of truth, and a logic of truth also always a logic of pure consequence.

Logic's third task is presented in the *Prolegomena* as a "complementary task" and not as a new stage of logic *stricto sensu*. It is, therefore, not surprising to see it receive separate treatment in *Formal and Transcendental Logic*. Whereas the formal analytic, in a pure or general sense, constructs the idea of theory from its constitutive elements, the theory of possible forms of theory proceeds from the idea of theory as such to construct *a priori* the different types of theory. Correlatively, the task of the doctrine of multiplicities *(Mannigfaltigkeitslehre)*—the crowning achievement of formal ontology—will be to establish the different possible fields of knowledge.

Husserl believed he had found in the mathematics of his time, and in particular, in the theory of multiplicities, "this fine product of modern mathematics," a partial realization of this ideal. The theory of theories to him is thus far from being an idle dream. The progress of contemporary mathematics amply justified this ideal of an all-encompassing science that would make it possible to predict, and control in a virtual sense even before they historically appeared, the forms of all future theory. The theory of theories would be this exhaustive science of the pure logos, of its possible specifications and their connecting laws. Every scientific theory would have its space assigned in advance in a sort of Periodic Table of Logic. In imagining such a theory, Husserl clearly sought to limit the surprises of history, the uncontrollable plurality of future theories, and the unpredictable development of knowledge. He posited, as Jean Desanti observed, a principle of "phenomenological closure," which, it is feared, would lead him to fall quite simply into idealist metaphysics (Desanti 1963).

The rest of the story is known. Published in 1931, Gödel's theorem established the incompleteness of any theory richer than arithmetic, that is, the possibility of enunciating, in such a theory, undecidable propositions. Almost all mathematical theories are in fact in this situation. Because the Husserlian theory of possible forms of theory can only be applied to complete, or in Husserl's words, "definite," "closed," theories, it follows, as Cavaillès wrote, that Gödel's theorem definitively invalidates Husserl's project (Cavaillès 1938, 144–51; 1947, 68–78).

I, of course, followed this debate attentively. I was tempted to acknowledge, with Trân-Duc-Thao and Suzanne Bachelard, that the *de facto* impossibility of a theory of possible forms of theory was not enough to reduce Husserl's project to naught, but that the latter retained all its meaning and value (Trân 1951, 35; S. Bachelard 1989, 52, 53–55). I, however, remained uneasy, convinced that the objections of the specialists could not be brushed aside. For even if the mathematician, as Husserl readily wrote, is but "a higher level technician," that is, even if one is entitled for this reason to distinguish fields—by being careful not to use the same criteria of validity for products of philosophical thought and those of calculation—this separation of fields itself still had to be thought out, to be justified, and its limitations brought out.

With this feeling of unease, my research on Husserl temporarily came to an end, although I promised myself I would return for more in-depth study. I did not even think it necessary to conclude: any conclusion, provided at this precise stage of my thinking, would have seemed premature to me. I necessarily left the reader dissatisfied, and even I had the feeling that I had interrupted myself midway through a sentence, and that I had to return to it immediately, as soon as I had closed the parenthesis of my doctoral defense.

It has been twenty-five years since I defended my doctorate and there has not been a single publication from me on this topic. I have not even been able to follow up on the advice of my master, Paul Ricoeur. With his usual indulgence and generosity, his concern to see what new contributions have been, or could be, made by even the most modest of student-researcher, he had strongly urged me to complete this work with a view to publishing it. So what happened?

I think I very quickly asked myself a question: that of the public I would be addressing. As much by temperament as out of principle, I was against writing only for a foreign public, or over the heads of my compatriots. I had just published, early in 1970, some months before my defense, the article on Amo that was later included in 1976 in *African Philosophy*. In it I clearly raised *in fine* a question that I myself described as dreadful: that of the real destination of Amo's discourse: both its target audience and its historical fortunes. I considered it a failure that the work of this *African* philosopher could only be part, from beginning to end, of a *non-African theoretical tradition*, that it exclusively belonged to the history of Western scholarship. I concluded on the urgent need to put an end to the extraverted nature of all European-language African discourse; on the impossibility, henceforth, of being satisfied with participating as individuals in the great scholarly and cultural debates of the industrialized world; and on the need to create progressively, in our countries, "these structures of dialogue and argument without which no science is possible" (Hountondji 1970b, 46).

So for this reason, I observed a pause. To publish on Husserl was not the obvious thing for an African academic. But if such is the case, why research on Husserl as I had just done? Why lecture on Husserl endlessly, as I had just done for three years in Besançon, before my doctoral defense, and as I was probably going to continue doing, barring the unexpected, in Lovanium University in Kinshasa where I was expected after my defense?

Up to what point is such a hiatus between research and publication, teaching and publication tolerable, such a divorce between two modalities of scholarly activity—the one, private, could tackle any subject and encompass any field of research, the other, public, would be limited to topics judged appropriate or, at the very least, compatible with the identity and cultural origins of the author, or significant for his society of origin?

I could not accept this dichotomy either, this sort of double-speak, or these arbitrary limits imposed on my horizon. It was necessary both to come to terms with oneself and to maintain one's roots, to express oneself unreservedly with no mental constraints, and at the same time remain intelligible, to talk about everything one knew or sought to know, and at the same time share this knowledge and this quest. In any case, one thing remained certain for me, a political decision of sorts: the locus of this exchange should in no way exclude Africa. On the contrary, Africa must constitute its center, its point of departure, and, where applicable, be its primary beneficiary. The result of all this was that, reluctantly, I had to abandon, temporarily, for conjunctural reasons if not for reasons of principle, not only all publication, but even the in-depth pursuit of my research on Husserl. The time was not right. Too many conditions still had to be met for Africa to be able to listen, without a feeling of self-repudiation or distraction, to a discourse on Husserl, or on any other such author or doctrine anointed by the Western philosophical tradition; or even more, for her to be able to show active interest in such authors and doctrines, to ask them her own questions and expect answers, to take up their questions and appreciate their relevance, in short to develop authentic research on them.

To be more specific, some authors had, so to speak, clearly passed the adoption test. An African publication on Marx would have shocked no one: Marxism, it was believed, proposed a politics to us and therefore one could, by this means, develop a philosophy from him. But what is the relationship of authors such as Plato, Aristotle, Descartes, Malebranche, Spinoza, Locke, Leibnitz, Kant, Wittgenstein, and all the others to Africa? Why on earth Husserl, specifically? What is the relationship between phenomenology and African cultures, between *Logische Untersuchungen* and Bantu philosophy? Why Husserl, especially today, when not a few philosophers, even in Europe, consider him completely out of fashion (Desanti 1975)?

Here then are many prerequisites that must be examined, and if possible, met, before one could claim to proceed any further. I therefore had to work on the margins and, rather than plunge head-first as a narrow specialist on an author or a current of thought, to clear the field patiently, establish the legitimacy and the outlines of an intellectual project that was at once authentically African and authentically philosophical.

This is the task I set myself since then, through my critique of ethnophilosophy. In the process, I realized that this critique did not concern only ethnophilosophy, but scientific extraversion in general, and that it required, because of this, a theory of the scientific and technological relationships of production on a world scale, and suggestions for a new science policy. Only my work on those theoretical and political issues has been published to date.

However, if I judged it appropriate to mention my unpublished work in a book such as this one—which is supposed to present a synthesis of my research—and if I took the liberty to comment on it at length, it is first because it provides a measure of the theoretical work then in gestation—work that at a very minimum had to be postponed, if not definitively sacrificed. It indicates by the same token what could be called the theoretical (scholarly) cost of the critique of ethnophilosophy. It is also because this critique draws, as could be expected, from the long study of Husserl, and beyond him, of the entire tradition of Western philosophy, some of its weapons, bearings, and conceptual instruments.

Part II

CRITIQUE OF ETHNOPHILOSOPHY

3

Anger

[handwritten annotations: ethnophilosophy — subsumme philo. under a specific title (ie African) to Discredit its contribution to Discourse as a whole]

1. From Husserl to Tempels

It could not be otherwise: the critique of ethnophilosophy is still largely a Western affair, because the ethnophilosophy that it denounces is itself an invention of the West. One of the main results of this critique had to be the dispelling of a widespread illusion that saw ethnophilosophy as an invention of negritude, and by extension, as the way of philosophizing worthy of an African, the only one that could preserve the originality of the black man.

I was to show, on the contrary, that ethnophilosophy had a more ancient history that was linked to the history of anthropology in general—that is, to the history of the Western gaze on so-called primitive societies; that the invention of an African philosophy, such as happened in the 1940s, was only the application, to a particular field, of an older hypothesis; that moreover, this application was, in the beginning, the work of European theorists intervening in a European debate, and that the encounter with the negritude movement took place only later.

Thus the true history of ethnophilosophy made it possible, from the outset, to get rid of the imaginary obligation placed on the African philosopher to give an account of an African philosophy to the exclusion of any other theoretical preoccupation, as it made possible the lifting of the no less imaginary law forbidding any incursion into the arcane conceptual elaborations of Western philosophy.

On the contrary, to appreciate fully the ethnophilosophical project, it was necessary to confront it with the idea or the ideas of philosophy that undergird Western philosophical practice, to question the consistency of the founding procedures and presuppositions of this project, and the conditions of its emergence in the history of Western thought. For this necessary confrontation, I had been prepared by my reading of Husserl, among other landmark figures in the history of philosophy.

2. An Exceptional Crucible: *Présence Africaine*

I am indebted to Alioune Diop for having associated me at a very young age with the work of the African and Africanist intellectuals of *Présence Africaine*. I was hardly twenty-two when, at the launching ceremony in Paris of Nkrumah's *Consciencism*, I happened to laboriously stammer a presentation that made headlines by portraying the Ghanaian leader's project as more progressive than negritude. In that same year, I was included by Alioune Diop in a delegation that took part in a summer colloquium at the University of Perugia, organized by the Association of the Italian Friends of *Présence Africaine*, on "The Presence of Africa in Tomorrow's World."

In the presentation I gave at this occasion, which was carried in the local press, I insisted on the plural nature of African cul-

not just a 'common body of thought'

ture. Citing approvingly *L'Afrique ambiguë* by Georges Balandier—whose seminar at the Ecole Normale Supérieure I had
just taken, and who was himself participating in the colloquium—I warned against the temptation of a reductive, unilat-
eral, and overly simplifying reading of cultures, and especially, of
the worldviews of the African continent (Balandier 1966).

Three years after Perugia, Alioune Diop had me invited once
again, in August 1967, to an important colloquium. This time it
was in Copenhagen. Organized by a Danish academic, Erica
Simon, under the sponsorship of, and thanks to funding by, the
Danish International Development Agency (DANIDA), this
forum brought together a group of African and Danish intellectuals to reflect on the theme "African Humanism-Scandinavian
Culture: A Dialogue." The proceedings of the conference were
published three years later by DANIDA under the same title
(Lundbaek 1970).

It was an unforgettable colloquium. Besides the Scandinavian
intellectuals, I was privileged to meet people including Cheikh
Anta Diop, Joseph Ki-Zerbo, John Mbiti, Engelbert Mveng, and
the voluble Pathé Diagne regularly for almost a week, in a float-
ing hotel on the shores of the Danish capital, and in an atmosphere of the greatest conviviality—and all this under the
protective and enigmatic eye of Alioune Diop.

At *Présence Africaine*, I had the pleasure of speaking with the
philosopher Jacques Howlett, a French collaborator of Alioune
Diop's and, I believe, one of his oldest and most trusted
friends. Like his friend, Howlett cultivated an important quality—the ability to listen, a quality that did not prevent him, of
course, from having his own ideas and holding on to them, but
which certainly had the advantage of facilitating dialogue and
moderating, on occasion, the excessive passion of the most aggressive opponents.

I also had memorable encounters at *Présence Africaine*. I would
probably never have met Césaire were it not for my frequent

visits to this place. The first time I saw him was in 1962 or 1963 at the bookstore at 25 bis, rue des Ecoles, where he stood by the shelves absorbed in his reading. He was alone with the bookseller. I came to buy, for the umpteenth time, the *Discours sur le colonialisme*, which I kept losing to frequent borrowers. I called out the title and the author to the bookseller. Her amused smile, and the movement of the man—who at this point turned completely towards the shelves, looking discrete as if intimidated—puzzled me. I had seen one or two photos of him; I do not think, taking dates into account, that I had by this time read the humorous portrait of the character that Baldwin was to depict in *Nobody Knows My Name* (Baldwin 1963). I thought I recognized the glasses, but I was not sure of anything. I took my book and left.

Occasions for encounters were, however, not long in coming. One of them was a small colloquium organized by the African Society for Culture at UNESCO in Paris, during which I was openly rebuked by my former *hypokhâgne* classmate Yambo Ouologuem, who no one suspected would later win the Renaudot book prize for the novel that he was then preparing, *Bound to Violence*. The nationalistic verve of my opponent, provoked by a few criticisms I had dared stammer out against the idea of a collective philosophy, became frankly aggressive and turned abusive. Césaire who was chairing the meeting wanted, I think, to defend the weak party. He came to my rescue by putting an end to the discussion.

I did not meet Senghor in *Présence Africaine* although he was Chair of the African Society for Culture. However, on Alioune Diop's recommendation in 1967, a year after my philosophy *agrégation* examination, I took the liberty of writing to him while he was passing through Paris. Pathé Diagne and Bakary Traoré jokingly made me understand later how rather casual it was to write to a head of state by pneumatic mail (something that still existed at the time).

[handwritten marginal note: Criticizes Senghor for claiming need to reclaim a "black identity" instead of an individual identity]

The Senegalese president replied me as soon as he got back to Dakar. My "cheek" had not been too badly received. I was impressed by the extreme courtesy of the statesman. For all that, Senghor remained no less Senghor, that is, in my view, the ideologue of a negritude that I did not accept, and one of the bridgeheads of French neocolonialism in Africa. Of course, I sent him a signed copy of *African Philosophy: Myth and Reality* as soon as it appeared early in 1977, and received *feedback* from him.[1] But it was not until I saw him, and listened closely to him, at the end of May 1980 in Germany that I requested an interview with him. The poet-president was the guest of honor at an international symposium organized by the Federal Ministry of Foreign Affairs on "International Cultural Relations: Bridges Across Frontiers." Childishness on my part? I don't know, but I was charmed by the man, and secretly proud of him. I had chosen my seat on the second or third row just behind the officials, in a huge reception hall where the few black heads present could be counted. After Senghor's speech, I walked up to his entourage. I wrote him a letter. A few weeks later, I was received in his Paris apartment. I left with a signed copy of *La poésie de l'action* that had just appeared. I think Senghor's official functions and political choices counted heavily for the negative reception of his work by Africa's progressive youth. From the moment he demonstrated, by resigning, the extent to which he put these functions themselves in perspective, he is being read with new eyes, being rediscovered.

3. The Copenhagen Presentation

Every thought, however original it may be, is to some extent shaped by the questions that it is asked. By asking me to present a paper on the subject "African Wisdom and Modern Philosophy," the organizers of the Copenhagen colloquium had hit right on my preoccupations at the time, thus setting me off, quite unintentionally, on a path that I was to tread for a long time, namely that of the critique of ethnophilosophy.

Other requests had the same effect. That, for example, of Professor Raymond Klibansky of McGill University in Montreal who, on the recommendation of Georges Canguilhem, asked me in 1969 to contribute to volume VI of his vast reference book on contemporary philosophy (Klibansky 1971), or that of Jacques Havet, then Assistant Director-General of UNESCO for the social sciences, who was directing a study on "Current Research Trends in the Social and Human Sciences" and asked me to contribute a piece on "Man in African Philosophy" (UNESCO 1970; Havet 1978).

My approach in all three cases was the same. It consisted first of all in taking note of the question asked by recognizing its spontaneity and apparent legitimacy, then in becoming suspicious of it by bringing out its paradoxes, and then finally in formulating, behind this badly framed question, the real problem (Hountondji 1970c, 1970d, 1971).

The first question, incidentally, differed significantly from the last two. In a sense it was better, because it was more informed. Its authors had clearly seen a difficulty that went unrecognized in the other two: that of identifying, in the cultural heritage of Africa, a philosophy in the strict sense of the word. They wisely referred to wisdom. Their problem, therefore, was one of comparing a wisdom and a philosophy, of determining their respective value, of examining the possibility of a transition from one to the other.

In this colloquium, where the rule was to have each topic treated concurrently by at least two participants, the question was also independently handled by M. A. Kissi of the University of Ghana at Legon.[2]

Using as an epigraph the famous eleventh "Thesis on Feuerbach," I started by reflecting on the role of philosophy in

Grounds philosophy
a nation through
rigorously & systema
philosophizing

Africa. I was of the view that it had to be something other
than Hegel's owl, Minerva's bird, which flies only at dusk: an
instance of an ideological justification of the real leading, in
practice, to the most absurd type of conformism. Philosophy
must, on the contrary, bring about the transformation of the
world (Marx 1947).

How could it achieve that objective? My answer to this
question was Althusserian, or more exactly, was inspired by *a
certain* Althusser, the careful reader of Bachelard and Marx,
the man fascinated by the notion of rupture through which
The German Ideology sought to found, that is to ground science
(Althusser 1990a, 1990b; Althusser et al. 1990).

For my part, I acknowledged that in Africa as everywhere
else, theory has meaning only if it is organized and subordinated to practice, that it derives its legitimacy—insofar as it is
itself a form of practice—from its foundational role in relation
to other practices. Among these other practices, I spontaneously privileged "political practice" and more precisely, "liberating action." My question then became the following: how
can philosophy serve as a foundation to politics, and notably to
the anti-imperialist struggle? It could do that perhaps, I
thought, through the mediation of "another type of theoretical
practice, one that is more rational and more certainly generative of the indispensable efficacy": science which I saw, following a fashionable trend at the time, as both the ultimate
achievement and the death of philosophy—even if this view
meant leaving unresolved large problems connected with science itself.

The appeal to science was, however, only an hypothesis. It
shifted, without resolving it, the problem of the relations between philosophy and politics, by forcing a reflection on the
relation between science and politics, between positive knowledge of the real in general and of society in particular, and the
practical transformation of this society. The question was not

posed, but it was at most adumbrated: it could not be otherwise within the limits of this text.

Linked, however, to this idea of the role of philosophy was a conviction that expressed itself forcefully, and not without a certain candor: the idea that the inferiorization of black cultures should not be considered as the cause, but rather as the result of colonization seen as an economic, political, and military phenomenon. Undoubtedly I would today expand my view by linking colonization to a more ancient phenomenon—the slave trade—and by broadly taking into account the total process of integration of Africa in the world capitalist market and its context of violence. That, however, would not change anything to my conclusions at the time: the myth of white superiority cannot be effectively combated by holding up against it a countermyth: a sound critique of imperial ethnology and of its mythology has, on the contrary, to start by linking the latter to its foundation, namely, the real and material relationship of force between so-called primitive societies and European societies.

Inversely the awakening of so-called primitive peoples today creates the conditions for a critique of ethnocentrism. "The cultural follows the political," I wrote as a comment on Frantz Fanon's assertion that: "The responsibility of the native man of culture is not a responsibility *vis-à-vis* his national culture, but a global responsibility with regard to the totality of the nation whose culture merely, after all, represents one aspect of the nation" (Fanon 1968, 232–33).

This acute sense of the omnipresence of the political has never left me. Césaire and Fanon at the time intellectually nourished me, and I think they have never ceased to live in me since then. The reading of *Black Skins, White Masks* had already inspired me to write the first article that I ever published: "Charabia et mauvaise conscience: psychologie du langage chez les intellectuels colonisés" (Double Dutch and guilty conscience: The psychology of language among colonized intellectuals) (Fanon 1961; Hountondji 1967). I had

[margin note:] influenced by Fanon? Césaire to think about political dynamics

written this article to exorcise my fear of language and, somewhat linked to this fear, the tendency that I shared with the immense majority of the people of colonies and ex-colonies to overestimate the language of the colonizer:

> Le français de France
> le français du Français
> le français français
> ⌈The French of France
> The French of the French
> French French⌉,

as Léon-Gontran Damas jokingly wrote (Damas 1966).

Reading Fanon had helped me track down the political right into our very relation to language. And beyond Fanon, I encountered Césaire anew, this unrivaled awakener of consciences, portions of whose work were quoted to us in my last year of high school by an enthusiastic history teacher, Albert Tévoèdjrè, and whose *Discourse on Colonialism*—a text which became bedside reading for me as much as did his short but powerful *Letter to Maurice Thorez*—displayed, in my view, exemplary clarity and rigor (Césaire 1972, 1956).

To return to our problem, Tempels's approach in *La philosophie bantoue* seemed to me to be an attempt to debunk Lévy-Bruhl, but in the worst way possible.[3] I saw it as "the art of combating a myth by another myth," by playing at length on a "dangerous ambiguity: the meaning of the word *philosophy*." For Africa does not have a monopoly of wisdom; every people has one that springs from the depth of the ages, that is anonymous, implicit in various degrees, that belongs to no one in particular, but is lived and practiced by all. And if African wisdom has to be compared to something, it should not be to Western philosophy, but to Western wisdom. At a stroke, the initial problem disappeared, but then it gave rise to this other one: why then such a misunderstanding? Why the desire at all cost to compare a wisdom and a philosophy?

Once I had settled down on this new terrain—the critical terrain—all I had to do was to present the content of *La philosophie bantoue* and to assess it. I readily granted Tempels the merit of holding up to the theorists of primitive mentality, who believed in an irreducible difference between savage and civilized man, "a wager in favor of the identity of the human mind beyond the diversity of cultures." I, however, recalled Césaire's sarcasm: in light of the agitation that was taking place at that very period in a Belgian Congo in ferment, of the social and political demands of the colonized masses, Tempels's approach was strangely surrealistic. The respect for Bantu spiritual values, which to him was the fundamental demand of the Blacks, could not in any case suffice to really calm spirits down.

On this political criticism that, on Césaire's own admission, only attacked a certain use to which Bantu philosophy was put, I articulated a theoretical critique that called into question the very project of a synthesis of collective representations that could, *a priori*, hold itself up as a philosophy, indeed as *the* philosophy of the Bantu in the singular. I found unacceptable, on principle, the claim of such a project to erect as a norm for every African—past, present, and future—a form of thought, a system of beliefs that could at best only correspond to a specific phase in the intellectual itinerary of black peoples, and which carried the risk of denying the status of African to present-day Africans, in particular those who have been to school and are considered, rightly or wrongly, as Europeanized and, therefore, unnatural.

I pointed out, besides, that on Tempels's own admission, not just any black man could be expected to make a coherent exposé of his so-called philosophy, and that this task rested solely with the European intellectual, a kind of public writer, secretary, or interpreter who was comforted *a posteriori* in his analyses by the expression of gratitude of Blacks who naively exclaim: "You have understood us, you now know us completely, you 'know' in the same way that we 'know'."[4]

I saw in this noisy expression of gratitude, assuming that it was sincere, a "sign, among many, of the falseness of human relations in a colonized society." I added that the fact that Bantus found in Tempels's construct elements of their culture in no way signified that they recognized themselves in this construct itself, and that it was possible to propose, from the same elements, other forms of systematization. What was presented as a "Bantu philosophy" was therefore not really the philosophy of the Bantu but of Tempels, the Belgian missionary, who had become the occasional analyst of Bantu mores and customs, and whose sole responsibility was at play here.

[margin note: key problem w/ book Bantu Philo.]

The comparison with Alexis Kagame's *La philosophie bantu-rwandaise de l'Etre* reassured me in this assumption. My attitude towards the Rwandan abbot was ambivalent. On the one hand, his work on the universals identifiable from the syntactic structures of Bantu languages seemed to me a more substantial and a sharper theoretical project than Tempels's. Using as his model Aristotle—whose ontology, according to him, consisted in nothing more than constructing, from his reflections on Greek syntax, the table of categories in use in his mother tongue—Kagame set out to establish in turn the table of categories of the *koinè* in use in Rwanda, Kinyarwanda, and to construct, in so doing, an original ontology that would represent an alternative to the Aristotelian philosophy of being. I found the project daring and attractive (Kagame 1956).

On the other hand, I could not accept any more with Kagame than I could with Tempels the claim to be the spokesman of a culture, and to reveal once and for all the system of founding concepts of this culture by locking up in advance all future thought in a vise. I also noticed, throughout the book, a surreptitious slippage that led the author to move imperceptibly from a formal determination of the grammatical

[handwritten note: one person can't delegate themselves as spokesperson for a culture]

structures of the language, to the material determination of
the content of belief. This content necessarily pointed, I thought,
to the author's own options, to his philosophical and ideological choices.

That is not all. Even if one set aside this content, and only
interrogated the formal procedure, one could catch Kagame
"red-handedly partial, as it were, in his choice of operative concepts." In short, why Aristotle and not another? Why brush
aside the entire critical tradition, in particular the notion of
category as it appears in Stuart Mill as reworked by Kant?
Without necessarily wishing to challenge Kagame's choice, I
nonetheless wanted it to be recognized that it was his choice
and not that of the Bantu people. I put my cards on the table: I
announced my preference for the critical approach, but quickly
added that the real problem was not there:

> The immense revolution created by Kant, the outdated naiveté of a
> realist metaphysics that claimed to know things-in-themselves, and
> thought it possible to ignore the very act of this knowing—all this
> critique of dogmatism through which Kant saw himself as the
> Copernicus of philosophy did not suffice to catch the attention of
> the Rwandan philosopher, or to inspire caution in him in his han-
> dling of the notion of "category." In itself that was his right, for
> here we are within the limits of philosophical choice. But then let us
> be spared talk of a Bantu philosophy that exists in itself and for it-
> self for all time, unchanging, always identical to itself, whereas in
> reality it gets its problematic and its status from without, namely
> from a specific doctrine, at a specific moment in the Western ratio
> that has been erected by the philosopher-ethnologist into a privi-
> leged point of comparison, indeed into a universal norm. (Houn-
> tondji 1970c, 195–96)

It was clear: I was a Kantian. I did not, however, require
everybody to become one. My conclusion was different: with
Kagame began the era of African philosophy *stricto sensu*, that
is, of the acceptance of responsibility for philosophical dis-

each person must be a unique thinkers criticizer

course by the Africans themselves; however, rather than pursue the movement of his thought to the end by positing outright the intellectual responsibility of the thinker in the production of his discourse, this assumption of responsibility stops half-way. The African philosopher "is frightened by his own freedom and responsibility as a thinker." That is why "he massively projects . . . his own thought onto a mythical philosophy that he attributes to his people, hiding behind the latter's authority."

I did not accept the idea of a collective thought at this time:

> A collectivity does not think, at least not in the literal sense. What is known as "public opinion" is nothing more than the statistically determined result of contradictions between innumerable "private" opinions. The collective consciousness has never been anything but a "myth." Even more so a collective philosophy, provided it is accepted that philosophy is not narrative, but creation; that it consists not in telling stories or in repeating things that were heard, but in challenging, explaining, interpreting with a view to transforming.

Does this mean that precolonial Africa was a *tabula rasa?* Not at all. I was pleading for a less reductive approach, which sought to restore the richness, complexity, and internal diversity of our intellectual heritage instead, and in place, of this smaller common philosophical denominator that is proposed by ethnologists. Beyond the hasty generalizations on *the* thought of Africans taken as a whole, it was necessary to find out both in our common past and our present, those that were, or are, considered as spiritual guides, in order to reconstitute the great discussions, the debates of ideas between these master thinkers, between them and their disciples, between them and their opponents, all in a fruitful confrontation whence a history can be articulated.

At a stroke, the question of writing became unavoidable: to what extent could one conceive a history of African thought in the absence of a writing that would have enabled the different doctrines to situate themselves in relation to others? I was only posing the problem and expressing my doubts in this regard, without claiming to provide the solution. I concluded, however, on the necessity of taking full advantage today of our access to writing, with a view to developing an expanded intellectual debate and to promoting, from one generation to the other, what could become, in the active sense of the word, a true *tradition*.

4. A "Set of Texts"

Already in place in the Copenhagen exposé, with no rhetorical niceties, no circumlocutions, are the main elements of a critique of what I called, shortly after, ethnophilosophy.

On my return to Paris from Copenhagen, Alioune Diop entrusted me with the task of creating a philosophical rubric for the periodical *Présence Africaine*. I wanted to display great openness in the choice of articles, but also to be absolutely clear about the principles involved. I immediately issued a warning: any article that was merely satisfied with philosophizing in the third person, and which, in place of responsible and clearly articulated theoretical positions, proposed instead a hypothetical reconstruction of some collective thought, would be rejected. From this view, the article by Eboussi-Boulaga "The Bantu Problematic" fulfilled my wishes. After a number of heated but always friendly discussions with the editorial board, I had the pleasure of opening the "Philosophical pages" of *Présence Africaine* with this intelligently iconoclastic text (Eboussi-Boulaga 1968).

Alioune Diop also asked me to run the "Inter-African Commission on Philosophy" of the "Société Africaine de Culture" (SAC). I did that with love. The commission was made up, for the most part, of students who were preparing doctoral dissertations or master's degree theses in philosophy, history, anthropology, or in some other subject in the social sciences or the humanities. Each person discussed his or her own work and tried to interest the others in it. Some of the most solid and lasting friendships I made go back to this period. Also, we were constantly on the lookout for black intellectuals passing through Paris, and readily invited them. Marcien Towa led, within this framework, a particularly lively discussion on the work of Senghor as a prelude to the rather fierce critique of him that he later published (Towa 1971a). We published a *Bulletin de liaison* that, with only pedagogical ambitions in mind, was distributed mostly to the senior classes of high schools in francophone Africa.

As this practice of a plural discussion developed, we progressively felt the need to agree on a short text that would spell out the main points of our common concerns and preoccupations, something like a charter or a manifesto. This text, finally published in 1969 with the title "The Theoretical Bases of the Work of the Inter-African Commission on Philosophy" was to lead, unfortunately, to an open conflict between the commission and the administration of the African Society for Culture and, from one misunderstanding to the other, to the collective resignation of the commission (SAC 1969).

By asking me to contribute to his *Chroniques de philosophie*, Raymond Klibansky, without realizing it, enabled me to sharpen my thoughts on the meaning that had to be given, from the perspective of a world history of philosophy, to the expression "African Philosophy." After Copenhagen, my mind was made up: only that which was comparable should be compared—not a wisdom with a philosophy, but a wisdom and a wisdom, and, if necessary, philosophies between themselves. I refused, as a matter of principle, all confusion of genres, all conceptual slippage. African philosophy, if the expression was to mean

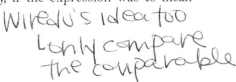

Wiredu's idea too
L only compare
the comparable

anything at all, had to exist historically on the same mode as all the philosophies in the world: as a literature.

Now it so happens that such a literature does exist: Kagame's work is proof of it, and it is not the only one. This literature therefore had to be taken into account, its weaknesses and strengths recognized, like its main orientations, its dominant, and if need be, marginal and counter-currents; in short the same treatment had to be applied to it like to any other philosophical literature in the world.

It is such a treatment that is outlined in "Le problème actuel de la philosophie africaine" (The current problem of African philosophy) (Hountondji 1971). This philosophy's problem, the difficulty in reading it resided, in my view—beyond its explicit themes—in its unawareness of itself, in its self-denial, its effort to efface itself as completely as possible to make room for an object that would never have existed, however, without it: the worldview of Africans. The problem was the "absence, throughout the long analyses devoted to this 'African philosophy' of any questioning of the status of these analyses themselves; the absence, in a discourse that wanted to be purely descriptive, of any question about its own function."

For my part, I made the opposite hypothesis: African philosophy, strictly speaking, was not so much the worldview of Africans as the discourse that sought to restore that view; less an implicit collective thought that was almost mute and unconscious, as the intellectual work that claimed to give an account of it.

To me, it was no coincidence that *La philosophie bantoue* had been written by a European and was, on the admission of its author, meant for a European public: the book was meaningful only within a debate that was internal to the West itself, where the Belgian missionary, in disagreement with the thesis of the prelogical mind, felt it necessary to challenge a certain ethno-

Philosophy — written by Africans for an african audience

logical discourse with another type of discourse. I noticed, by the same token, that by making this preoccupation theirs, African intellectuals, in turn, were taking position in a debate that was of no concern to their people and were necessarily developing in these conditions an extraverted discourse.

It was no coincidence either that *La philosophie bantoue* had been written by a priest, or that Tempels's African successors came, for the most part, from the ranks of ecclesiastics. The reconstitution of the Bantu worldview was only a step towards the conversion of the pagan, a way of recognizing his deepest convictions the better to change them.

The success of this book with well-known European philosophers and the praises they heaped on it came as a surprise to me. It was my view, however, that these philosophers were seduced by a sense of play, and by a fascination with the unknown—which is not to minimize the pressure exerted on them by the book's African publisher. That Bachelard, Lavelle, Gabriel Marcel, Jean Wahl, Camus, and some others were able to accept the thesis of a collective philosophy without batting an eyelid, regardless of their own philosophical practice, which would never have been possible without personal, methodical, responsible thought, and without a constant preoccupation with theoretical justification was, on the face of it, something worrying but, in the end, perfectly understandable in light of the ideological and political context of the period.

I took note of the persistence of this myth among quite a number of African authors including A. Kagame, A. Adesanya, A. Makarakiza, F. M. Lufuluabo, V. Mulago from Congo-Kinshasa (who I incorrectly thought was Cameroonian), B. Fouda, and J. C. Bahoken. African philosophy was first of all that: the set of texts devoted to the definition of an African worldview, a touch theoretically inconsistent, but which had, first of all, to be acknowledged. Also, to be noted, were African texts that went counter to this myth: those by Césaire, a diasporan

African that I had no difficulty in including, by Nkrumah, by Eboussi-Boulaga, and by the Inter-African Commission on Philosophy. We held then to what I called, using an Althusserian expression, a "theoretical break" born of new demands whose political nature had to be recognized, and which—in place of this laborious attempt to rehabilitate African culture by presenting the world with a constituted philosophy—prescribed instead a new task for our discipline: "to contribute, directly or indirectly . . . to the awareness of African realities and their revolutionary reappraisal" (SAC 1969).

It is clear: my friends and I were activists to the core, but with no dogmatism. I think I was expressing a general feeling within the commission faithfully when, denouncing the extraverted nature of the traditional philosophical discourse, I acknowledged a political origin to this phenomenon, and declared the wish to see "established in Africa an autonomous, theoretical debate, which would be master of its problems and its themes rather than simply . . . being a distant appendage to Western theoretical debates." "To the usual discourse *on* Africa must be substituted the discourse *of* Africa itself, with its uncertainties, its hesitations and its internal disagreements." Now, to the extent that this cultural autonomy presupposes real economic and political independence, the philosophical demand, while becoming deeper, intersected with a series of extra-philosophical preoccupations. Again, Césaire and Fanon showed the way.

I no longer remember the circumstances in which I came to submit to Jean d'Ormesson, then Secretary-General of the International Council on Philosophy and the Human Sciences (CIPSH), and to the editors of *Diogène*, a journal published under the auspices of the Council, a revised version of the text that I had just written on the invitation of Jacques Havet. The article was well received, and was published in number 71 of the third quarter of 1970, shortly before the Copenhagen exposé, which appeared that same year, and my contribution to Klibansky's work, which appeared the following year.[5]

I knew, by the way, that these last two texts would not be known to the wider public even after they appeared. I could therefore use their main themes without too many scruples for the *Diogène* readership. In terms of content, "Remarques sur la philosophie africaine contemporaine" (Remarks on contemporary African philosophy) did not add anything new to the Copenhagen exposé (Hountondji 1970d). It, in fact, omitted the entire preliminary reflections on the role of philosophy and the responsibility of the philosopher in Africa. But besides the fact that the remarks were illustrated with a "minimal bibliography" which was proof, and there can be no possible argument about this, of the existence of an African philosophical literature, the statements were perhaps more cutting, the concepts better honed, and the presentation clearer. The readers were first of all surprised by the abrupt definition with which the article opened: "By *African Philosophy,* I mean a set of *texts:* specifically the set of texts written by Africans and described as 'philosophical' by their authors themselves" (Hountondji 1970d, 102).

Begging the question? It was certainly not the case, of course. I wanted only to stick to the declared intention of authors who meant to intervene, through their writings, in a field that is conventionally acknowledged as that of philosophy. I wanted to take note of the *fact* of their writings, outside of any assessment or value judgment.

I did not claim, either, to reduce this literature only to written texts, although I spontaneously let out, as it were, a reference to writing. Written texts no doubt had the merit of existing, of an undeniable, material existence, of an existence that is blindingly obvious. That was, however, their only privilege. The proposed definition had to be understood as a minimum delimitation. It did not exclude later expansions that would take oral texts into account—expansions that were clearly suggested, by the way, in this article itself, in note 19, which refers to Ogotommêli, Griaule's old interlocutor. Oral texts, however, are still explicit discourses—what Kagame called "institutionalized documents." The minimal definition, as a result, excluded the idea of an implicit, unarticulated philosophy. It pointed to the only possible site of emergence of philosophy, its most general genre: human speech. The reader saw himself brought down to earth unceremoniously, with no warning, after the profusion of hypotheses and conjectures to which he had been accustomed on "African philosophy." He was literally aghast.

Besides, I used the word "ethnophilosophy" in this article for the first time to designate a specific genre to which *La philosophie bantoue* belonged. Anxious to dispel all ambiguity, and to distinguish, for reasons of clarity, words that were traditionally confused, I suggested writing *"philosophy"* in quotation marks to describe the collective worldview, and quite simply *philosophy* without quotation marks to designate the discipline, and *ethnophilosophy* to describe this form of philosophy (this branch of the discipline) concerned with reconstituting a "philosophy" (a worldview).

For the rest, the *Diogène* article restated exactly what was contained in the two previous articles, which had until then not been published: an analysis of *La philosophie bantoue*, a restatement of Césaire's critique, a comparison of Tempels and Kagame, and, finally, a conclusion on the necessity of a break with extraversion, and on the political prerequisites for a liberation of theoretical discourse.

The journal's editorship had, however, noticed my complete silence on a French author who could not be ignored: Griaule embarrassed me more than did Tempels. I nonetheless agreed to make up for the omission by pointing out in a note what to me was the merit of *Dieu d'eau: Entretiens avec Ogotemmêli* in relation to *La philosophie bantoue*. Voluntarily assigning to himself the humble task of secretary, custodian, transcriber of the worldview of *a* black sage, of *one* spiritual master among others, the French ethnologist gave the example of scientific patience and, in my eyes, did more useful work than the ethnophilosophers proper who were in a hurry to reach definitive conclusions on African philosophy in general (Griaule 1965).

This judgment was to become considerably nuanced later and, without questioning the project of solid research on oral literatures, to recognize, however, the unavoidable role of writing not only in the transmission, but in the very constitution of philosophical and, more generally, of scientific thought— thus confirming, at the end of a long and sinuous detour, this valorization of writing that was spontaneously effected in my first definition.

For the moment I had not yet got to that point. It was sufficient for me to have dealt with the weighty, burdensome myth of a philosophy that was at once collective and implicit.

5. Developments

The article in *Diogène* had a considerable response. Six years later, I was to make it the first chapter of *African Philosophy: Myth and Reality* with the title: "An Alienated Literature."

From the article to the book, there were, however, other texts, only a few of which were included in the collection. A substantial portion of these texts had only one aim: to give details on the contours of the new concept of African philosophy, by bringing out its polemical significance, its meaning and implications; to show on which refusals and inversely, on which hypotheses, certainties and hopes this concept is constructed, to make explicit what, in its early formulation, was only implicit.

The article, written in 1970 on the heels of the previous one and published only four years later with the title: "History of a Myth" before being used with some modifications in chapter 2 of the book, remained for a long time in my files, because in my estimation it added nothing really new (Hountondji 1974b; 1996, 47–54). I did, however, finally publish it as "'the passionate witness' of a refusal, the blunt and unadorned expression of a break whose fruitfulness did not take long in appearing, in the new (practical) tasks and the new (theoretical) research directions that since then had made themselves necessary" (Hountondji 1974b, 3).

In reality, if this article was only, indeed, a kind of epilogue to the *Diogène* text, this epilogue sheds light in a new way on the previous analyses, and comments on its results in clear and uncompromising language. It is no coincidence that Jacques Howlett, attentive to this discourse of rupture, to this will to "liberate the theoretical creativity" of African peoples, and comparing this orientation to the project of a cultural hermeneutics defended by the Nigerian Theophilus Okere, was able to write in the same *Présence Africaine* issue this sibylline sentence that delighted other commentators in Zaire—something that he himself could not obviously have foreseen: "The distance between P. Hountondji and Th. Okere is one between a *philosopher* who happens to be African and an *African* who happens to be a philosopher" (Howlett 1974, 24).

Another epilogue along the same lines is the "Myth of Spontaneous Philosophy" piece, which was initially meant to constitute the first chapter of a *Manuel de philosophie* that was never written but which, in the end, I turned into an article for the maiden issue of *Cahiers philosophiques africains* (Hountondji 1972).

Different in style and purpose, these articles both carefully distinguish a general from a narrow sense, a popular from a more rigorous usage, of the word "philosophy." They also shared the idea of a generic relationship between philosophy

Althusser
L philosophy as a
theory of
science

as a theoretical discipline and the sciences in general, and both emphasized the methodological rigor of conceptual proce- dures by which philosophy demarcated itself from sponta- neous thought, and resembled what is commonly known as science. Finally they had in common a declared Althusserian- ism, one that could be clearly seen on the one hand in the op- position between the ideological and the scientific—the first term tinged with a pejorative, and the second with a positive connotation—and on the other hand from their conception of philosophy itself viewed as a theory of science.

In more than one respect, I found the notion, then defended by Althusser, of a "privileged relationship" of philosophy to the sciences, one in which probably lay "the specific *modality* of philosophical propositions," enlightening. Althusser had for- mulated it in 1967 in his "Philosophy for Scientists Lectures," which were to appear only seven years later, but a first version of which was already doing the rounds in the form of lecture handouts (Althusser 1990b, 75). I set little value on the mas- ter's nuances, warning in the same lecture that philosophy had no object as do the sciences, but stakes. For me, as for any dis- ciple in a hurry, things were simpler: philosophy differed from mythical thought in both method and object.

Finally these texts had in common a forceful restatement of some of the refusals and anger[6] that are at the root of the critique of ethnophilosophy. They develop, following the *Dio- gène* article, a kind of "psychoanalysis of the ethnophilosophi- cal consciousness,"[7] by recognizing, behind this identitarian discourse of the African philosopher, a "desire to show off" which easily gets caught in its own trap and "grows increas- ingly hollow until it is completely alienated in a restless crav- ing for the most cursory glance from the Other" (Hountondji 1996, 44); a desire whose result is "to provisionally put on hold conceptual knowledge, covering for a while (with its) noise the language of science." It is a desire for rehabilitation, a drama of recognition that can lead "to the use of every and all means available" by having recourse to the most ambiguous of arguments, those that can be most easily turned into their opposite.

It is a disastrous inconsistency that "for the past twenty years at least" has made us waste precious time "trying to codify a thought that is believed to be given, constituted, instead of quite simply jumping into the water . . . to think new thoughts"; a movement of withdrawal that is totally unproductive and still makes us, in reality, "prisoners of Europe," whose respect we are still determined to extract, but that leads us to "petrify," to "mummify" our cultures "by making them topics of myths for external consumption." "And what do we find at the end of the road? The same subservience, the same wretchedness, the same tragic abandonment of thinking by ourselves and for ourselves: slavery" (Hountondji 1996, 50).

Freud was fashionable. Lacan's seminar, hosted at the Ecole Normale Supérieure by Althusser every Wednesday (if my memory serves me right) in room Dussane at coffee time, had made the theory of the unconscious a must for many students at the Ecole Normale at the time, and although I attended it as an amateur and only occasionally, it had led me to read or reread Freud—incidentally with pleasure. I, however, think that I was more influenced by Frantz Fanon's use of Freudian concepts—by the way he applies them, from the beginning to the end of his work, to a kind of "socio-pathology," to a diagnosis of abnormal, collective forms of behavior, to visible and invisible forms of cultural alienation[8]—than I was by my episodic presence in Lacanian circles.

Beyond this psychoanalysis, which, by the way, was pursued in later texts, both articles draw the conclusion from an "enormous fact": the fact that *La philosophie bantoue*, on its own admission, was addressed only to a European, or more generally,

How do we speak about Africans [?] [?] Don't eliminate them from the Discourse [?] (handwritten annotation)

a Western readership. Based on this observation, these articles articulate a critique of exclusion that, in its scientific guise, consists in excluding African peoples from theoretical debates concerning them. They demonstrate how scientific exclusion connects to political exclusion and how, in the case in question, the double problematic of Europe's "civilizing mission," and inversely of the "heightening of the soul" expected from Bantu cultures, is only meaningful as the "ideological problematic of triumphant imperialism" (Hountondji 1996, 49).

The exclusion practiced by the European scholar becomes, when it is taken over by the African intellectual, extraversion. There again, the two articles develop a critique begun in the *Diogène* article, and show how the non-African endpoint of African philosophical discourse explains, in part at least, this discourse's tendency to give credence to the most fantastic myths or, at the very least, to sharpen the angles, to deepen the differences between African and Western thought.

The struggle against intellectual extraversion presupposes the creation, in Africa, of an autonomous space for reflection and theoretical discussion that is indissolubly philosophical and scientific. Only such a space can enhance an effective participation of African peoples—and not just some individuals of African origin—in the debates about them. That will be the condition for intellectual freedom.

The critique of exclusion and of its corollary, extraversion, thus begins as an impassioned plea for a plural world, where the current peripheral countries would start, at last, to be self-sufficient and would progressively become, in turn, decision-centers alongside other decision-centers, in an egalitarian system of generalized interdependence.

At the same time as exclusion, the illusion of timelessness that is associated with any reductive reading of African civilizations, the tendency to mummify them, to empty them of their history, evolution, diversity, of their creative tensions, is questioned. What is demanded, instead, is that the internal dynamism of African cultures—and, in particular, the pluralism of beliefs and systems of belief transmitted by these cultures—be taken into account.

This impassioned criticism leads, however, to a most practical question: what is to be done? Beyond the fiery statements, which may be considered too general or too trenchant, a precise task is indicated: that of organizing in Africa "an autonomous debate that will no longer be a far-flung appendix to European debates, but which will directly pit African philosophers against one another." In reality this is a double task. Individual speech must at once be liberated, and the multiple speeches thus released confronted, related one to the other; thought must be brought out of its Africanist ghetto by acknowledging its right to be occasionally interested in something other than Africa—for instance in Plato, in Marx, "in the theoretical heritage of Western civilization to assimilate and transcend it"—and, at the same time, to act in such a way that each thinker finds in his own society his primary interlocutors and partners and gives priority to the horizontal, inter-African debate (over the vertical exchange with philosophers and intellectuals in the Western capitals) in a form of exchange that, in the language of international bureaucracy, is called south-south cooperation.

The Nairobi presentation "African Philosophy: Myth and Reality" reformulates and gives details on the distinction between a "vulgar concept" and a "new concept" of African philosophy (Hountondji 1974a). Besides, in its revised version, rewritten under the title "The Idea of Philosophy"—the third chapter of *African Philosophy*—it elaborates on the refusals and the "anger" *(colères)* expressed in previous texts.

By illustrating, through a copious list of publications, each of the two visions of African philosophy, the presentation advances, at the same time, a reading grid and a principle of classification for a rather special corpus, one to which no particular attention had been paid up to that point.

To be more precise, one is dealing with *two* corpuses: one whose unity is that of a current of thought (the ethnophilosophical current) and rests on an inspiration, a thematic, a common theoretical and methodological approach; the other whose unity is extrinsic, and rests neither on common presuppositions nor a common methodology, but rather on the fact of belonging to a common site of production, thus on a kind of accidental proximity that has nothing to do with the content of the corpus, in other words, on the common relation of the different components of a corpus to an identical geographical base.

The unity of ethnophilosophy, as a project of reconstitution of the worldviews of so-called primitive peoples, is obvious in itself. In truth, I was only interested for the moment in the application of this project to Africa, an application illustrated not only by Tempels, but also by numerous other European authors and a growing number of African authors. The examples that I quoted were necessarily debatable: there is always some injustice in categorizing an author or a work by privileging one of its facets at the expense of others. These authors were not all as simple as Tempels or as easy to classify. But beyond their contribution, which was sometimes enormous, beyond their richness and complexity, the sometimes vast distance and important nuances separating them,[9] the authors cited shared, in different degrees, the hypothesis of a "permanent, stable system of beliefs, unaffected by evolution, impervious to time and history, ever identical to itself." All of them made a passionate effort to locate "beneath the various manifestations of African civilization, beneath the flood of history which has swept this civilization along willy-nilly, a solid bedrock which might provide a foundation of certitudes . . . a specific, permanent metaphysical substratum." (Hountondji 1996, 59–61).

⌐ problem

In the unity of this current of thought, however, beyond the theoretical solidarity of authors of diverse origins exploring the same thematic field, I thought it necessary to focus specially on African authors. Why? Their work was not necessarily better or better informed. It dealt with the same object and was based on the same methodological presuppositions as those of Africanists of other origins. Nonetheless, a "demarcation line" remained possible and necessary "because, the subject being African philosophy, we cannot exclude a geographical variable, taken here as empirical, contingent, extrinsic to the content or significance of the discourse, and as quite apart from any question of theoretical *connections*" (Hountondji 1996, 64).

According to such a reading, Tempels's book belongs to European scholarly literature, in the same way as anthropology in general remains an avatar of Western scholarship, although it deals with non-Western societies. On the other hand, the work of African authors cited belongs to African scholarship. Is this division, within a theoretically homogenous corpus, an arbitrary decision? Such a division of ethnophilosophical literature has neither to be justified nor to be refuted. You see it if you look in that direction. Nobody has to do that. Nobody can be blamed for doing so either.

Once this division is carried out, however, once the African terrain has been cleared as a site of scholarly production, what is left is to circumscribe it, and to effect a finer characterization of its production. Then, and only then will it be noticed that in this area coexists, in the field of philosophy, alongside the ethnophilosophical current, a lot of other works with different interests. Some of them openly challenge the method and the presuppositions of ethnophilosophy; others, steering clear of these controversies, develop ideas on or based on authors and works of Western, or more generally, of non-African philosophy; still others strive to elucidate concepts, philosophical

questions of universal application, without any privileged relation to African or to any other civilization for that matter.[10]

The return to the real thus shatters into smithereens the
founding myths of ethnophilosophy: the myth of primitive
unanimity—the idea that in "primitive" societies, everyone is
in agreement with everyone else—from which it is concluded
that there could not possibly exist individual philosophies in
such societies, but only collective belief-systems. In reality an
unbiased reading of the existing intellectual production reveals something else. The African field is plural, like all fields,
a virgin forest open to all possibilities, to all potentialities, a
host to all contradictions and intellectual adventures like all
other sites of scientific production. The best and the worst can
be born there. Nothing can hold the continent's freedom in
chains—either in the area of thought or action. Hence our
hope. Hence also our responsibility.

Thus the unanimist prejudice cannot stand up to scrutiny.
It is enough to open one's ears and eyes: In Africa, no more
than elsewhere, it is impossible for everyone to be in agreement with everyone else. Pluralism is first of all a fact. It is not
invented, it is acknowledged. Diversity exists. Better still,
such diversity is not necessarily an evil; on the contrary, it is,
in the life of the mind, the condition for the greatest intellectual productivity, for the most intense creativity, on condition
it is accepted with an open mind by each and every one—what
is known as tolerance—and pressed into service in a true
spirit of research.

In this way, cultural plurality, at first simply acknowledged,
can be valorized or erected into an imperative. This praise of
pluralism, properly understood, had something subversive
about it.[11] What I was interested in first of all, however, was to
draw methodological conclusions from it: the unanimity pos-
tulated by ethnologists has never existed, neither in the past
nor today. From this point of view, it is necessary to undertake

a rereading of so-called traditional cultures to discover their dynamism, their imbalances, their internal tensions, beyond their unchanging aspects, which classical anthropology had, on the whole, unilaterally emphasized until then. Similarly, it is necessary to recognize the internal dialectic, the creative pluralism at work in contemporary African culture and in each of its components (for instance philosophy). Finally, once the unanimist illusion has been dispelled, it is necessary to try to organize, to construct pluralism in a manner that makes it possible to make maximum use of it, both from the theoretical as well as the practical point of view. A paper read in Louvain-la-Neuve some months before the Nairobi presentation, and revised as chapter 8 of *African Philosophy*, specifically examines this issue of cultural pluralism.

4

The Issues at Stake

African Philosophy took shape all on its own. I had not set out
to write a book, and when Yves Bénot asked me to work on
one, this was not the book that he had in mind. My friends
on the French Left were rather expecting a political work
that would develop—and give in-depth treatment for a
wider audience—the issues raised in the booklet that I had
written for the occasion following the October 26, 1972,
coup d'état in Dahomey. This collection of articles had en-
joyed considerable local success that could only be explained
by a deep thirst, on the part of activists, for theoretical
analyses and direction.

I could, indeed, have returned to and clarified these analyses, taken stock of the country's history from independence,
explained the cascade of coups d'état and the developments
that led to the events of October 26. I could have proposed a
synthesis, assessed the dangers, identified the tasks ahead. In
short, I could have sketched a promising path, albeit one
fraught with pitfalls, with the same critical concern, the same

sense of nuance and, indeed, the same internationalist outlook that had accounted for the success of *Libertés: Contribution à la révolution dahoméenne* (Hountondji 1973a).

I did not feel up to the task of such a book. Besides, I was aware that it would only have been meaningful as the product of teamwork that caps a common reflection on a common experience of struggle. The initiative for such a book could be launched, but its result could not be immediate. I realized, on the other hand, that with the articles on ethnophilosophy, the analyses inspired by the "anger" diagnosed by my master Canguilhem (anger that grew more intense with the turmoil in Dahomey), material for a book already existed. I decided to select some pieces from among these articles, arrange them in a manner that brought out their complementary qualities and, if need be, their progression, and work out a conclusion. I chose eight articles in all, one of which was written in 1969 (and published in 1970), two in 1970 (published, respectively, in 1970 and 1974), and five in 1973 (published in 1973 and 1974). I grouped them into two sections titled respectively "Arguments" and "Analyses." The first raised questions of method and conceptual clarification, developing the arguments of my critique; the second examined, by way of example, two authors, Amo and Nkrumah, and outlined the contours of a new vision of cultural pluralism, the only coherent alternative to ethnophilosopy's reductiveness. Finally, I added, by way of a conclusion, a postscript.

More than nine years had elapsed between the lecture in Copenhagen and the publication of *African Philosophy*. The young *agrégé* professor had meanwhile built a career and, more, had acquired a certain political experience, by teaching successively in Besançon, Kinshasa, Lubumbashi, and Cotonou. The book that appeared with Maspéro at the end of 1976 can only be fully understood in light of this experience.

1. Political Anchoring

a) *Learning to Keep Silent*

In Kinshasa-the-Beautiful, life then was beautiful. Each evening was a feast in clubs in the working-class districts, with orchestras, some of which had won well-deserved fame across Africa. The zest for life could, however, barely conceal the poverty. After the tumultuous history of the early independence years—the Katanga secession, Lumumba's murder, the national adventure of the ex-secessionist Tshombé—the country was living under the jackboots of a "pacifying" general, endowed, incidentally, with exceptional oratorical qualities.

It is sometimes wrongly imagined that no freedom of expression is possible under such a regime. I discovered quite early on, from my arrival in 1970, that the press could perfectly well attack every high ranking dignitary of the regime *but one*, and that the best way to proceed was precisely to attack all the others, in the name of the true thought of the generous Father of the nation.

The propaganda was intense. Huge billboards—in Lumumba Square around the Limete grade separation, as well as on the June 30 Boulevard, and more or less all over town—carried some of the slogans and official watchwords. I was surprised to read on one of them a quote attributed to Mobutu: "In the beginning was action." I could not help but think of Goethe: "Im Anfang war der Tat." But the sycophant on duty must have forgotten to consult his dictionary of quotations.

The party controlled the State. Everything flowed from the founding-president and everything led back to him: "One leader, one party, one nation!" Africa's good old tradition was opportunistically invoked, solicited, and interpreted in the service of this act of political control. Nowhere more than in Zaire had I felt this collusion between cultural nationalism and dictatorship. Nowhere had I seen power take such massive recourse, and so openly, to traditional "philosophy" to justify or hide its worst excesses, its most atrocious violations of human rights.

By appealing to Zairians to be themselves, and to reclaim a threatened cultural identity, the "philosophy of authenticity," the state's official doctrine, managed to reduce this identity to its most superficial and abjectly folkloristic level. The safari suit replaced the three-piece, or lounge suit and tie,[1] and loud indigenous first names, turned last names, replaced old European ones. There was nothing particularly profound in all this.

If the promotion of the main national languages, the mastery and excellent handling of Lingala (and the guide's interminable speeches are a particular instance of that) gave the Zaire of the period a head start in cultural policy over many countries in francophone Africa, the messages transmitted were hardly different, no more than the political, social, and economic practices that lay hidden behind this exaltation of the collective self. Worse, this self was not just collective. It was supposed to be embodied in a Person. The sanctification of the leader indicated for all the conditions of legitimate discourse that could not be questioned by any criticism. His moods carried the force of law. The political police stood permanently ready to refresh the memory of whoever was tempted to forget this simple fact.

On the campus, however, was a young, hard-working student body that was anxious to learn, intelligent, and consciously anti-authoritarian, poor on the whole, but full of dignity. A creation of the Catholic University of Louvain, Lovanium University was the largest in the country, next to the Free University of Congo (ULC) in Kisangani, and the state-controlled Official University of the Congo (UOC) in Lubumbashi.

But then in June 1970, on the anniversary of a student demonstration that had led to the death of one of their number, the students at Lovanium organized a remembrance march in Kinshasa. Tracts were distributed, some of which were judged disrespectful of the "national helmsman," and still worse, of the memory of his then-recently deceased mother. That was too much. The helmsman got angry, and all the students at Lovanium were drafted into the army. The three universities were, from then on, merged into only one—the National University of Zaire, with three campuses in Kinshasa, Kisangani, and Lubumbashi, respectively.[2] No sooner said than done. There were no protests, no counter proposals, not even from the university community. Only colleagues from the country could have initiated a collective response. In this atmosphere of feverish nationalism, anyone else, even African, would have been put on police files, savagely criticized for meddling in the country's internal affairs, and, most certainly, expelled even before a court hearing.

I learned to keep quiet. Being a new arrival at the university, and one of the youngest, I observed. This, then, was how the dictatorship operated. Once fear was internalized and the appropriate ideological environment was created, the tyrant could sleep peacefully. Now in this particular instance, the ideology was the doctrine of authenticity, whose relationship to ethnophilosophy seems crystal clear to me, which was one more reason, then, to pursue my efforts at deconstruction. In Lubumbashi where the three Faculties of the Humanities had been placed, intellectual work was still possible. I had to cling on to the job and not waste time.

b) The Desire for Revolution

However, as soon as the possibility of returning to the only country where I could freely exercise my rights as a citizen arose, I jumped on it. The Dahomey of the Presidential Council, run by a triumvirate of three political leaders controlling the south, center, and north of the country, was in a state of unstable equilibrium. Shortly after my return, a military coup d'état took place in October 26, 1972. At the end of a proclamation Commander Kérékou haltingly read over the national radio, the representative of the coup leaders shouted out: "Long Live the Revolution."

The population was jubilant, happy to be rid of a régime that to many was very corrupt. I took leave of my friends in the Universities of Ife and Ibadan, and of the late Lamine Diakhaté, then Senegalese Ambassador to Lagos, a poet and an old *Présence Africaine* friend many years my senior, whom I was visiting. I returned home.

The article in the daily *Daho-Express* that attracted a lot of attention and gave me national prominence had not been commissioned by anyone. Written between November 10 and 13, 1972, "What is a Revolution?" was a personal and spontaneous contribution to an important, ongoing national debate at a time when the soldiers, for once well meaning, had had the reflex, after the coup, to invite the country's citizens and its lifeblood to come together and recommend a vision and program to them. The student movements and other activist organizations that met at the presidency for that purpose were constantly settling old scores and, in the end, broke up into two separate working-groups. A loner by habit as well as by method, but always with ears to the ground, I took my pen first as a sniper.

What the public liked in "What is a Revolution?," I believe, is first of all the very approach itself. The article, an independent reflection, free from dogmatism, acknowledged the desire for revolution expressed by the soldiers. Observing that an identical national uprising had raised the same hopes nine years earlier only to see them dashed, it warned against the fascination with counter-models (Sekou Touré's Guinea was clearly aimed at without being mentioned) and reflected on what could, in the situation of the period, constitute radical change.

The analysis was based on a simple diagnosis: the Dahomey of 1972 was characterized politically by the loss of all meaningful sovereignty, by its international mendacity, servility in its relations with great or middle-level powers, its inability to keep to its internal and external financial commitments, and its "creepy-crawliness" and obsequiousness. Economically, it remained a private hunting ground for the former colonial power, and did not seem to have any strategy for development, or for harnessing its own resources. Culturally it had lost all confidence in itself, in its professionals and in the collective future. "The Dahomean State has crawled again and again. . . . In the eyes of the world . . . we look like a population of reptiles, of servants, of powerless talkers" (Hountondji 1973a).

It is in light of this situation that the "minimum" that a revolution could contribute stood out for itself—which is to bring an end to shame, to make the formal independence obtained twelve years earlier real, to take responsibility as a sovereign state, and to take the fatherland seriously. Economically, it meant widening our range of international partners, "taking money where it can be found, which is in our soil and sub-soil" while, at the same time, ensuring that our "undreamed of resources are rapidly and efficiently developed." It meant promoting regional and sub-regional integration, but before all that, it meant rebuilding our self-confidence and "the collective genius of our three million minds."

In sum, "independence is possible": a renewed faith in, and commitment to, it was necessary. I however immediately added: "Just like independence, democracy is possible." The least that a revolution could usher in was not only the restoration of freedoms, but their effective promotion through the creation, at all levels, of structures for dialogue and consultation, and the relentless struggle within those structures, against all forms of orthodoxy and conformity. I defended the right to free speech of the "ordinary, average citizen . . . living far from the mysterious workings of power, a stranger to all the inner circles where momentous events and actions that would only later break out in broad daylight were secretly planned." I could not accept what, to me, seemed like "the problem of almost every political and trade union organization that had existed up to now," namely the avoidance of discussion at the grassroots level, the monopolization of information by the leadership apparatus. This problem results in legitimating the myth of the expertise of the leaders, and inhibiting the slightest signs of opposition by the rank and file, thus ensuring the triumph of dogmatism.

The critique of centralism was and remains one of the important lessons of the May 1968 movement in France and Europe. I had read attentively the abundant literature (incidentally of very uneven quality) that was produced by the movement and in particular Cohn-Bendit's *Obsolete Communism: The Left-Wing Alternative* (1969). I do not think I was an anarchist, but I was in profound agreement with this form of iconoclasm indispensable, in Africa as elsewhere, for dealing with the permanent temptation to sanctify the State and even more, with some of the claims to revolutionary expertise and orthodoxy:

> The internal structure of an organization is always the image in miniature of the type of society envisaged; the relations between the grassroots and the leaders in a party or a union are a foretaste of the relations envisaged by the party or union within the future nation. It is finally time to learn to free individual talents, not to stifle them. It is time to accept the adventure of truth. (1973a)

Beyond this minimum which, as can be seen, is quite a program, the "ultimate" objective of the proclaimed revolution could not but tie in, directly or indirectly, with that of "the revolution in the singular—that unique process unfolding in different forms across the world, whose aim is to abolish the exploitation of man by man, and to usher in its place, a classless society." I defended the right to utopia, "the courage to dream . . . to imagine a possible world beyond the platitudes of the present, to have the horizon cleared wide open." Moreover, I found it difficult not to admit, as the classics of Marxism had taught (and, closer to home, as Nkrumah did), that imperialism was the last stage of capitalism, and neocolonialism the last stage of imperialism organized, in turn, in a vast international plot. The struggle against foreign domination, a minimum platform for the proclaimed revolution, necessarily had to lead to a class struggle on a world scale. It was the only way of resisting the temptation to chauvinism, of avoiding "racist or national-fascist acts," and of not replacing imperialism with imaginary enemies.

At the same time, however, I warned against the danger of an empty Marxist-Leninist verbiage that could serve as a smoke screen for all sorts of recuperation. I drew attention to the failure of the Prague Spring four years earlier and to the reality of social-imperialism.

I concluded on a paradox: the cascade of coups d'état in Dahomey since independence must be seen as both a sad record but also as a source of pride. For beyond the obvious inconvenience, the chronic instability was also a sign of good political health. We were on the right track. Of course a lot remained to be done. We had to remain vigilant, to fully appreciate the risks of excess, chief among which is "the internal threat of fascism" that hangs over any attempt at a revolution from the top. But the opportunities were wide open. Hope was possible. What attracted the public was, I believe, this invitation to collective self-confidence, this appeal to their sense of responsibility, to their inventiveness:

> The greatest resource of the Dahomean people is their imagination. The intelligence of three million people could, if properly harnessed, reinvent the world. They should be allowed anew to express themselves. We are today at one of those turning points

where history falters. From it may arise the best or the worst.
The result depends on us all and on no one else. (1973a)

Without any prior consultation with me, Radio-Cotonou,
renamed "The Voice of the Revolution," took the liberty to
broadcast the entire article during its peak hours. Its impact as
a result was greater. An impassioned discussion with students
gave me the opportunity to clear up some misunderstandings
and clarify certain notions. I was thus able to caution them
against the fascination with the Zairian model on the one hand
and the Guinean on the other, against the illusions of voluntarism, the enormous risks of "fascization" and other forms of
rot attendant on a revolution that depended solely on the
army. Perhaps with excessive candor, I called for the creation
of a "great revolutionary organization" that would give urban
and rural workers the means to establish, after free debate, the
appropriate political organization and control over the management of the country, the actions and the deeds of the government. Nkrumah's failure and that of his Convention's
People's Party (CPP) was an example which, to me, merited
reflection. To this end, it was necessary to read and re-read the
fine analyses of it done by Samuel Ikoku and translated by
Yves Benot (Ikoku 1971). I invited my audience to learn and
digest the "elementary virtues of capitalism" in order to use
them for development within the framework of a new vision of
society, and not to "throw away the baby with the bath water"
in a gesture of demagoguery. All the while maintaining that a
necessary path led from anti-capitalism to socialism, I warned
against the temptation of confusing state capitalism with socialism. Finally, a question on proletarian internationalism
provided me with the opportunity to clarify, by relying on
Nkrumah among others, the idea of a class struggle on a world
scale. I then cautioned—using the examples of the anti-
Dahomean and anti-Togolese pogroms of 1958 in Abidjan, the
more recent tribulations of West Africans in Zaire and of

Asians of British nationality in Uganda—against the racializa-
tion and ethnicization of problems based on an incorrect identification of the real enemy.

I decided to include in the collection a transcription of this
discussion under the title "A Reply to Nine Questions." By also
including "A Note on the 'Ghanaian' Philosopher Amo" previously published in *Daho-Express*, in response to a radio broadcast by Ibrahima Baba Kake, and an article "Science and
Revolution," also published in *Daho-Express*, in which I tried
to understand—taking myself as an example—why, in a
crowded lecture hall, nobody had understood the scholarly ex-
planations of the brilliant biochemist Jacques Sètondji during
his doctoral defense, I insisted on the "unity of the cultural and
the political in a struggle whose stakes must be to liberate
popular initiative *on all fronts* including the scientific."

Guy-Landry Hazoumé wrote the preface. The work was
very successful.[3]

c) Real History and Philosophy

Time did not come to a standstill. Already from one article
of *Libertés* to the other, between November 21, when "What is
a Revolution?" appeared, and December 25 when I completed
the epilogue, the situation had significantly evolved and, with
it, necessarily, the tone of the analyses. The growing emphasis
on "the internal threat of fascism" was not accidental: it expressed
a widely shared anxiety in the face of the ever-increasing
authoritarianism of the military regime.

The rest is well known. Marxism-Leninism was proclaimed
the official ideology of the State on November 30, 1974, in a
national policy speech made by the President of the Republic
on the new national day which was the anniversary of the
"policy speech" of November 30, 1972. A year later, on November 30, 1975, officially came into existence through another speech—the same that had re-christened Dahomey

"The People's Republic of Benin"—something resembling, it is difficult to tell them apart, the "great revolutionary organization" that we all had called for. But instead of a grassroots initiative, it was a creation of the government itself. It had worked out its functions and appointed its leaders. Instead of a coalition of men and women of different ideological persuasions united by a common vision of society and of its collective management, one had a collection of proselytizers confident of having resolved all problems by their profession of faith in Marxism-Leninism and their zeal to spread the good word. Instead of a democratic structure of collaboration and decision making, one had a Stalinist-type single party, where "democratic centralism"—excessively centralized and totally anti-democratic—left the rank and file activist with no other choice but to noisily conform by communing through slogans and revolutionary songs with the jubilant crowds, even if this also meant fighting hard to be noticed, and later co-opted in the holy of holies—the Central Committee and its Politburo—where criticism was not possible either, except within the limits of a code of good conduct and a verbal ritual that was tacitly observed by everyone. The violation of human rights, the economic crimes, the crimes *tout court* that were carried out during these fifteen long years under a regime of terror draped in pseudo-revolutionary verbiage are well known.

At the end of 1976, by the time *African Philosophy* was published, the regime had already been in power for four years. New developments could clearly be seen. The critique of ethnophilosophy could not but take them into account. The political stakes had become higher and more complex than when I first gave the lecture in Copenhagen and wrote the article in *Diogène*. It was no longer merely a question of liquidating the subtle complexes that held us prisoner to Europe in an endless drama of recognition, nor was it a question of reclaiming a freedom of speech stifled by dictatorial régimes brandishing a nationalist and anti-imperialist discourse. It was necessary to understand the transition from this "rabid particularism"—proclaiming loud and clear its distrust of foreign ideologies—to "an abstract universalism" which, on the contrary, but no less rabidly, imposed Marxism-Leninism on entire populations on the pretext that it is "scientific." The unity of these two apparently contradictory attitudes had to be thought through. I needed to show how one presupposed the other like the two complementary sides of "the same conformist attitude, the same refusal to think, the same inability to carry out . . . 'a concrete analysis of concrete situations.'"

The revisions of the selected articles clearly reflect these concerns. They examine the functioning of state ideologies in general, exposing them as alibis and masks of reality, as forms and instruments of political mystification. They question and expose the ridiculousness of a discourse that thinks it can confer nobility on the most vulgar police dictatorship by pompously christening it a "dictatorship of the proletariat" and "describing as Marxist-Leninist, a neo-fascism of pseudo-revolutionary phraseology," thus reducing "the enormous theoretical and political subversive power of Marxism to the dimension of a truncheon" (Hountondji 1996, 69). It called for a Marxist reading of the real functioning of regimes that call themselves Marxist—or any other revolutionary ideology— for a severe critique of the practices that lay hidden behind official discourses.

I had read Jacques Rancière's small book on *La leçon d'Althusser* with interest. A rather fierce critique by a repentant Althusserian—one brought about by the events of May '68— he recalled, among other useful reminders, that beyond the acceptance of Marxism, the most important thing was the mode of historical appropriation of Marxism and its real functioning in the arena of social struggles. Without saying it, Rancière's critique, in its own way, tied in with what at the time was called in Eastern Europe the critique of "real socialism" (Rancière 1974; Bahro 1979).

The lesson was astonishingly applicable to the Benin situation. The critique of ethnophilosophy led, by the same token, into a critique of what I was later to call "ideologism," which is the use of ideology for purposes of political mystification and subjugation.

In the background to this criticism was constant reference to two types of regimes, two opposing models that I both dismissed without calling them by name: the Zairian model, which to me was an example of nationalism in its most dangerous form, and the Guinean paradigm, which represented the extreme case of revolutionary rhetoric in the service of autocratic rule and of which the new regime in Benin—and its ruler, an ardent admirer of Sekou Touré—was only a copy, fourteen years later.

Secondary school education quickly became an important battleground for the new regime's official ideologues. At first, they had to substitute the teaching of philosophy—conceived as an attempt at promoting balanced and non-partisan thinking—with a more committed teaching approach. Like in Guinea, the new discipline would be called "philosophy-ideology." Then they needed to impose a Marxist content on the teaching. Finally, the notion of a specific competence of specialists in philosophy had to be destroyed, the monopoly of teachers trained in the discipline in the traditional university broken, and the idea instilled that "philosophy-ideology" could be taught by any activist-intellectual, possibly a specialist in some other subject— for example, history, German, economics, or sociology—as long as he stuck to the doctrine of the People's Revolutionary Party (Hountondji 1984a, 1984b, 1995a).

This background must be kept in mind to understand the sometimes important revisions made to certain papers collected in *African Philosophy*. Besides the short additions to the articles that became chapters 2 and 3 in the book, the article "Philosophy and Its Revolutions," which became chapter 4, was entirely revised and rewritten and considerably expanded to take into account the new questions that then preoccupied me (compare Hountondji 1973b with 1996, 71–107). Chapters 6 and 7 on Nkrumah, written in 1973; the special attempts to compare the two successive versions of *Consciencism* and to place them in the context of the Ghana of the period; finally the warning against the temptation of dividing the world in two according to the Stalinist model of a "bourgeois science/ and a proletarian science;" the appeal for a sense of nuance; the constant need to return to reality—all of this could not be understood either without this political context.

2. Theoretical Stakes

Beyond the political anchoring or the concrete history that could not be discussed in the book—because this was not the latter's aim—but which I have just described in bold strokes, the discussion conducted in *African Philosophy* involves specific academic and theoretical issues. These have already been partially outlined in the previous chapter. Through a transverse reading of the book, they can now be presented in a more synthesized way, their internal structure, as well as their specificity, brought out in relation to the political stakes just described.

a) Reading Ethnophilosophy

It was necessary to learn how to read the abundant literature devoted to the definition of a Bantu, African, or more generally, "primitive" philosophy. Its status as literature had to be acknowledged. Beyond its claims to total transparency, to a purely transitive role as a transparent medium whose only task would be to facilitate vision, it was, on the contrary, necessary to take note of its overwhelming reality as a specific genre, and to outline its history. The strategy of self-concealment and self-erasure—through which ethnophilosophy claimed to be nothing, or skillfully hid behind a system of thought (real or imaginary) that it tried to reconstitute—had to be unmasked.

Ethnophilosophy exists. Acknowledging this may appear banal. Yet it is quite strange for a reader who would let himself be taken in by the ethnologist's game and who, entering into his logic, would try with him—at the same time as him—to find this philosophy that is a presumed given. In order to *see* ethnophilosophy, a measure of detachment must be maintained, the immediate complicity with this encompassing discourse broken, and a certain distance from it kept.

Once its existence is acknowledged, the discourse had to be related to its historical origins. The precedence of Western ethnophilosophy had in particular to be recognized, and the fact understood that before the clamor for it by Africans anxious to establish their difference, "African philosophy" was first and foremost a European invention, the product of an intellectual history at the intersection of the most diverse disciplines, notably anthropology, the psychology of peoples, missiological theory, and a good many other concerns. To recognize this could help clear up the atmosphere of a debate that is already in large part polluted, and to restore a freedom of analysis that is threatened by all types of misunderstandings and prejudices.

To read ethnophilosophy was also to acknowledge the pluralistic nature of this literature, to note that "from Tempels to Kagame" there is "continuity and rupture"; that behind the apparent monotony of the numerous monographs devoted to "African philosophy," important nuances, notorious differences of approach and perspective sometimes appear. It was also to acknowledge, conversely, that whiffs of ethnophilosophy can often be detected in works that appear to be far removed from ethnography. In other words, although such works are ostensibly critical of ethnophilosophical unanimism, they nonetheless display, on closer inspection, traces of the worst features of this philosophical practice, hence the need for critical vigilance when reading them.

It was necessary both to recognize these nuances and make these comparisons; to pin down the conflicts behind the surface agreements and conversely the points of agreement and theoretical links behind the apparent disagreements. In its own way, *African Philosophy* practiced just such a reading. More work on many an issue remained to be done, but the path had been cleared. It will be shown later how, in later publications and research, I modified and qualified in one sense, and sharpened in another, and in all cases enriched and developed, my initial analyses.

b) Unshackling the Future

The great issue at stake in the critique of ethnophilosophy, the principal objective, is the liberation of the future. For the African intellectual, the burden of having to conform, on pain of repudiating his identity, to a system of thought that had been worked out in advance, had to be lifted. It had to be demonstrated that no doctrine, no form of thought was forbidden to him, that at a conceptual level, the freedom of the individual could not, in Africa any more than elsewhere, be restricted in advance. The horizon of possibilities had to be reopened. *African Philosophy* rejected any premature foreclosure of the intellectual history of black peoples. It was a matter of principle from which everything else flowed.

The book is quite unambiguous on this point. By substituting a "new concept of African philosophy" to the "vulgar concept" inherited from ethnology, it sought to locate the Africanness of a philosophy "no longer in an alleged specificity of content, but simply in the geographical origin of its authors." The effect of this was to broaden the narrow horizon that had hitherto been imposed on African philosophy, and to give to this philosophy—henceforth understood as methodical inquiry—"the same universal aims as those of any other philosophy in the world" (Hountondji 1996, 66).

The search for intellectual freedom presupposes a "demythologizing" of the idea of Africa. The "dominant, mythological conception of Africanness" had to be demolished, and reestablished the "simple, obvious truth that Africa is above all a continent, and the concept of Africa an empirical and geographical concept and not a metaphysical one (Hountondji 1996, 66).

I later returned at length to this theme in "Que peut la philosophie?" I had been accused of resorting to a mere "geographical criterion" to identify works of African philosophy:

> The avoidance of the debate on the content of African philosophy is proof of the philosophical and political poverty of the discourse of our abstract philosopher. What is the value of a philosophy that avoids the substance of philosophies and seeks refuge conveniently in geography? . . . It is clear: the geographical criterion leads to deception. (Yaï 1978, 71)

I responded quite simply that Africa is a continent, and not a philosophy or a system of values; that this word refers to a section of the world and no more; that the concept is geographical, empirical, and contingent, not determinable *a priori:*

> It was thus necessary to start by demystifying Africanness by reducing it to a fact—the simple and, in itself, perfectly neutral fact of belonging to Africa; by dissipating the mystical halo of values arbitrarily grafted to this fact by ideologues of African identity. To think through the complexity of our history, it was necessary to bring back the theater of this history to its original simplicity; to realize the richness of African traditions, one needed first to impoverish resolutely the notion of Africa, to rid it of all the ethi-

cal, religious, philosophical, political and other accretions that a long anthropological tradition had foisted on it, and whose most visible effect was to limit the horizon, to foreclose history prematurely. (Hountondji 1981b, 52)

In short, the overdetermination of the concept of Africa is an obstacle to the freedom of Africans. Freeing up the future first of all meant reducing this semantic overload, giving back to words their original, simple, and obvious meaning. The reader can easily see, by going through some of Mudimbe's and Appiah's most recent works, the extent to which this refusal of geographical confinement is still widely shared today (Mudimbe 1988; Appiah 1992).

For the same reason, the notion of philosophy had to be reexamined. It had to be shown to describe a history and not a system; a discipline in which results matter less than reasoning, less than the conceptual steps that have led to them, and one whose goal is precisely to go beyond the results in a search for better ones. The long discussion in chapter 4 of this subject; the critique of a dogmatic conception of philosophy that tends to reduce the latter to a set of definitive truths; the examination of the structure of philosophical revolutions in their relationship with scientific revolutions; the reflections on history in general or, from an Althusserian point of view, on the differential histories of levels or instances of modes of production and their articulation within a complex whole whose functioning still has to be studied, all these painstaking, tentative analyses have no other aim but to contribute to liberating the future. The conclusion of the chapter recalls it clearly: "We must be ambitious for Africa and for ourselves; we must be careful not to nip in the bud the unparalleled promise of our history or to prune it prematurely. We must on the contrary open it up, liberate it . . . . Beyond all facile solutions, beyond all myths, we must have the courage to make a fresh start" (Hountondji 1996, 107).

c) A Responsible Subject

Liberating the future also meant giving back the individual his rights and responsibilities, enabling him to learn to think anew for himself instead of lazily seeking refuge, as ethnophilosophy invites him to do, behind the thought of the ancestors. It was thus necessary to put an end to the exclusive valorization of collective thought, and to acknowledge the need, on all important questions, for individual thought; for a personal stance that commits the responsibility of each person, and fosters authentic debates based on a free confrontation of ideas and a search for truth, instead of these semblance of debates where intimidation takes the place of argument, and where a passionate support for a collective catechism is expected of each one (Hountondji 1996, 69).

Yves Bénot was not mistaken in the title of his review in *La Revue du tiers-monde:* "Philosophy in Africa or the Emergence of the Individual" (Bénot 1974).[4] To liberate the future, pluralism had to be established, and such an enterprise presupposes the emergence of free, intellectually responsible men and women who had disentangled themselves from this collective "us," this impersonal "one" behind which it is so convenient to hide, as long as one dares not think for oneself.

My critique of ethnophilosophy and my rejection of collective thought were, to be sure, a bit excessive (Hountondji 1970c, 196–7). This made the task of criticizing me easier for some of my bitterest opponents who had a field day seeing my central argument as a reflection of the bourgeois ideology of private property. Such a good, they contended, is never anything but the result of the private appropriation of a collective good, therefore of an act of usurpation (Niamkey 1977, 1980; Niamkey and Touré 1980; Yaï 1978). I had to show that fundamentally, the problem raised, the real issue at stake in the critique of ethnophilosophy was not so much the *ownership* of philosophical ideas as it was the *responsibility* of the subject defending them (Hountondji 1977, 1981a, 1982a). However, I later acknowledged this criticism by allowing for the idea of collective representation without, in the process, conceding that the study of these representations (which belongs to the province of sociology, anthropology, and linguistics) could be taken for philosophy. The analysis of the collective "unthought" must, on the contrary, enable focused attention on that *against which* a true philosophy must develop, on the set of conceptual constraints inherent in a culture or a language that must be overcome by a responsible thought or, at least, kept at a distance. *African Philosophy* sought to establish the need for such distancing (Hountondji 1982b, 1990b).

The liberation of the subject thus understood involves a psychological or, more specifically, as was mentioned in the previous chapter, a psychoanalytical dimension. The African had to be exorcised of the obsession of the Other, an obsession that leads to a constant effort to tend to appearances, to tend to one's *look*, in the idiom of our children.

I had read William Abraham's *The Mind of Africa* with considerable interest and noted one of his final remarks, which roughly went like this: we have repeatedly been told that the entire world had its eyes turned on us: this is not true. Africa has to be guided by its own motivations (Abraham 1962). I observed for my part, with perhaps excessive harshness compared to the measured tones of the Ghanaian philosopher's warning that "culturally, Europe has never expected us to do anything other than hold up our civilization as spectacle and alienate ourselves in a fictitious dialogue with her over the heads of our people." I deplored the fact that by accepting to be party to this game, we ended up by "looking at ourselves with the eyes of the Other," thus suddenly developing the most extravagant forms of "folklorism" and "collective exhibitionism (Hountondji 1996, 44, 67). Imprisoning oneself in an identitarian discourse seemed to me the result of this mental extraversion, and one of the most dangerous forms of alienation.

Since "Charabia et mauvaise conscience," I was inclined to follow Frantz Fanon in his psychiatric, or at least psycho-pathological approach to cultural alienation. The situation described in *Black Skin, White Masks*—that of the mimeticism of the Black who could not wait to entirely assimilate the behavior, reflexes, and ways of thinking of the white model—was the most perfect instance of cultural alienation. But it also derived, at the same time, from a sort of neurosis whose most acute expression Fanon later described in the last chapter of *The Wretched of the Earth* titled "Colonial Wars and Mental Disorders" (Fanon 1961, 1990; Hountondji 1967).

I had read with particular interest, from among Valentin Mudimbe's already abundant publications, *L'autre face du royaume: Une introduction à la critique des langages en folie.* The brilliant Zairian writer, as much a philosopher as a linguist and, in another context also a novelist and poet, had not yet published the book that was to make him famous in North America: *The Invention of Africa.* But in his 1973 book, one could already sense his distrust of a certain Africanist, and more generally, anthropological discourse. To me, ethnophilosophy seemed to constitute the most dangerous form of this "language gone bezerk," a language that had to be restrained, fixed, stabilized, and mastered by subjecting it to critical and responsible examination, a task that could only be carried out by a subject, a task somewhat reminiscent of those correct opinions, which, in the *Meno,* Plato compared to the statues of Dedalus that could only be held in place by causal reasoning (Plato 1937, 377; Mudimbe 1970, 1980; Hountondji 1979, 64, 73).

This return to the subject, this construction of a rational *cogito* necessarily carried political overtones in the context of the period. The call for freedom of expression and for a responsible criticism also meant the rehabilitation of the free citizen; the refusal to see him crushed.

d) Constructing Pluralism

Liberating the future also meant getting rid of the founding, unanimist prejudices of ethnology and, more generally, of a certain kind of ethnology that tended to spread the view that in sub-Saharan Africa like in all so-called primitive or semi-primitive societies, everyone is in agreement with everyone else.

This set of prejudices function here in two complementary directions. First, in the interpretation of the past and of a given cultural heritage, they tended to erase differences, to minimize change, and to lend support to the idea that the entire society subscribes to one and the same system of beliefs. This is a reductive reading of cultural heritage that denies the possibility of any ideological pluralism in precolonial African societies—like in all so-called primitive, archaic, traditional societies. This interpretation is based on a rejection of history. The societies in question are perceived as societies without a history or, to borrow Lévi-Strauss's correction, cold societies with a non-cumulative history, in contrast to western societies that are constantly in a hot cumulative history (Charbonnier 1969, 32–42). In these conditions, it becomes difficult to see how such societies could contain these differences of opinion, contradictions, and debates that, to a certain extent, make history.

But that is not all. Beyond this reductive reading of the past, unanimist thought valorizes the absence of differences for the present and the future, and holds it up as a model. Thus unanimity is considered—often for political purposes—as a value to be promoted. And to accomplish it, methods designed to nip all contradiction in the bud are actively promoted, sometimes by the most brutal of means.

I borrowed the word "unanimism" from Jules Romains but used it in a different context to signify something different: to stigmatize both the illusion of unanimity in the reading of the intellectual history of a given culture, and the ideological exploitation of this illusion for the present and the future. The French writer had used the term, on the contrary, in a laudatory way (Romains 1904, 1908, 1910, 1911, 1932–46).[5]

To liberate the future, the past had first to be liberated by restoring movement, contradiction, and dynamism to it. The complexity of history which is as old in Africa as anywhere else in the world had to be acknowledged, and the illusion of stasis—as much in the assessment of material history as of the history of ideas and beliefs—renounced once and for all. It was also necessary to assert, against the ideological will-to-level displayed by the authorities, the virtues of a free and plural discussion in which each partner would intervene on his own. Catechisms of all stripes—just so many attempts at uniformizing thought had to be relativized, and the right of each person to verify and examine freely, recognized.

From this point of view, Nkrumah's *Consciencism* seemed, in its recognition of three currents of thought in contemporary African society—the traditional, the Euro-Christian, and the Arabo-Islamic—to constitute an improvement on the ethno-philosophical approach that tended to reduce present-day Africa only to its traditional component. However, by keeping quiet over the complexity, the internal pluralism of each of the three components, by stylizing them as much as possible, by reducing them to their lowest common denominator, and finally, and above all, by asserting the possibility and necessity of a synthesis that would make it possible to reconcile all three currents by proposing the elements of a complete philosophical doctrine "profoundly rooted in materialism" but not necessarily atheistic—a doctrine where he believed he could articulate a metaphysics, a complete ethics, and a political

ideology—Nkrumah restated, at a higher level, the same unanimist presuppositions of classical ethnophilosophy. By situat-
ing the book in the context of Nkrumah's *oeuvre*, by shedding
light on it through a study of the development of his work, and
by comparing the two successive versions of *Consciencism* (the
one before and the one after the Osagyefo's overthrow in the
coup d'état of February 24, 1966), I was able to show that the
ideological voluntarism of the 1964 version was inseparable
from a thesis that was dear to Nkrumah: that of social homo-
geneity, of the absence, that is, of conflicting classes in past or
present-day African societies; the belief, consequently, in the
possibility of a peaceful transition (with no pain or divisive-
ness) from traditional "communalism" to the most modern
socialism.

The discarding of this argument as early as 1965, the increasingly finer analyses of neocolonialism and its social foundations in the dominated countries, the acknowledgment of
the reality of class struggle—all this should have logically led
to the abandonment of this ideological voluntarism. The revisions to the original text made in the 1970 version did not,
however, question this voluntarism. They left untouched the
belief in the possibility of a common philosophy to which all
Africans subscribed. It is really a relic of the earlier period, one
that was incompatible with the new vision of society developed
in such books as *Neo-Colonialism, The Last Stage of Imperialism,
Class Struggle in Africa,* and other works of his later period.
Logically, Nkrumah should not have been satisfied with merely
revising *Consciencism.* He should have rewritten it completely or,
better still, proposed, from a rigorous position of self-criticism, a
new vision of the functions of philosophy in contemporary Africa
(Nkrumah 1964, 1965, 1968, 1970, 1972).

Using this example, *African Philosophy* demonstrated the
firm grip of the unanimist temptation, the difficulty of acknowledging the reality of pluralism—be it in the form of social,

economic, and political cleavages, or of the diversity of theoretical and ideological positions. It demonstrated the still greater difficulty of valorizing the pluralism that is thus acknowledged, and of developing a method from it (Hountondji 1996, 131–55).

The book's last chapter revisits this lesson, drawing general conclusions from it. Real pluralism does not only consist in affirming, against the West's cultural hegemony, the plurality of cultures (an affirmation that could lead, if one is not careful, to freezing these cultures on the pretext of preserving their authenticity). It consists in recognizing the complexity, diversity, tensions, contradictions, internal dynamics of each culture, and in seeing in that a source of richness and creativity, rather than of evil (Hountondji 1996, 156–69).

e) *The Right to the Universal*

Unshackling the future by practicing the *cogito*, and constructing on this basis a responsible pluralism also necessarily meant expanding the basket of questions and topics considered legitimate. The African philosopher was no longer to be forced to reflect on Africa alone, to make it the exclusive subject of his theoretical inquiry. The horizon had to be opened up. The false modesty, the guilty conscience that prevented us up until then from moving out and extending our curiosity to other cultures, indeed simply to other general questions of interest to all cultures with no special relationship to any of them, had to be demolished. For example, I thought it useful to point out that rather than wall himself up in African history, the African historian would stand to gain by also showing interest in the history of Japanese industrialization at the end of the nineteenth and the beginning of the twentieth century. Similarly, the African philosopher need not hide to read Plato or Marx, or to study mathematical logic, neither should he or she feel that his Africanness is being repudiated in so doing.

African Philosophy thus set out to explode all theoretical ghettoes. Similarly, it refused all conceptual manipulation, and the semantic shifts that consisted in subtly changing the usual meanings of words, narrowing their scope or softening their contours as soon as they were applied to Africa. My Kenyan colleague Henry Odera Oruka once mentioned, rather humorously, expressions such as "African religion," "African philosophy," "African democracy," and "African development," in which the usual concepts of religion, philosophy, democracy, and development are manipulated, stretched, and distended to accommodate realities that in other cultures could have simply been designated by openly pejorative and critical terms such as superstition, mythology, dictatorship, or pseudo-development (Odera 1972, 1974; Hountondji 1996, 60).

Here the critique of ethnophilosophy addresses a major issue: that of attributing the same meaning to the same words, the same connotation to the same concepts, whatever their field of application, of avoiding the ambiguities, equivocations, and confusions that have, at all times, been the hallmark of sophistry and lies.

On the rule of univocity, Aristotle seemed to have given the clearest formulation possible in Book 4 of the *Metaphysics*, in his forceful plea for the principle of contradiction:

> Not to signify one thing is to signify nothing (Aristotle 1993, 9).

In this sense, philosophy could not mean one thing in Africa and something else outside. Its content will necessarily be different, naturally, its problems and specific themes necessarily original in relation to those developed in other cultural, social, and historical contexts; but its nature as a discipline, its implications, methodological, and theoretical demands will all be the same, on pain of no longer being philosophy.

I also secretly thought of a remark made by Husserl, in his passionate struggle with psychologism, in which he ends up grounding the principles of contradiction and excluded middle solely on the meaning of the words "true" and "false." This he does, however, without excluding the possibility of a "dispute over words" that would result from a totally different understanding of those terms, and would, at a stroke, make any discussion impossible. To the relativist, who imagined that other free beings could conceivably not be subject to the same logical laws, Husserl replied by simply referring to ordinary human language.

> Either such beings understand the words "true" and "false" in our sense, in which case it is irrational to speak of logical principles not holding, since they pertain to the mere sense of these words as understood by us . . . . Alternatively, such beings use the words "true" and "false" in some different sense, and the whole dispute is then one of words. If, e.g., they call those things "trees" which we call "propositions," then the statements in which the logical laws are expressed of course do not hold; but they will also have lost the sense in which we asserted them. (Husserl 1970, 1:141)

For Husserl, as for Aristotle, the absolute prerequisite to any dialogue, to any sensible discussion, is a univocal language. But no one had demonstrated the limits of this postulate better than Husserl; and I knew it. The ideality of meaning is precarious, constantly threatened in ordinary language by a mass of fluctuating expressions that crowd discourse. I, however, admitted that the word philosophy could not be among those with such fluctuating meaning. And with regard to "philosophy," I asserted, like Husserl, "the absence of limits to objective reason."[6]

In truth, I had to fight on two fronts, to assert the possibility of an authentic African philosophy both against the champions of ethnophilosophy, and the ideologues of European superiority, some of whom—respected and acclaimed philosophers, by the way—curiously saw in philosophy an exclusively Western mode of thinking. Husserl, unfortunately, was among these, and more clearly still Heidegger, who detected a tautology in the "clichéd expression 'Western European philosophy.'"[7]

In an oral presentation I made at a seminar conducted by Jacques Derrida, I had denounced, using similar texts, the ethnocentrism of a certain number of classical philosophers. This critique is not included in *African Philosophy*. It, however, constitutes the background to my thinking on cultural pluralism and the related effort to deconstruct current notions of "Westernness" and "Europeanness" as well as of "Africanness." It also explains my suspicion of "any notion that attempts to link explicitly or implicitly such and such a system of values to such and such a geographical zone or region of the globe." A critique of eurocentrism thus leads to the same task of "ballast-shedding" effected on the notions of Europe and the West, to the same effort at "demythologization" that has been carried out on Africa. This way it will be clearly shown that Europe too is first of all a continent and no more, that the modern United States a subcontinent and nothing else, and that there is nothing inevitable about the long cultural history that has unfolded in these territories.

In short the critique of ethnocentrism leads, like that of ethnological self-imprisonment, to a de-territorialization of cultural values. It makes them free-floating at most, detaches them from their geographical base, or more precisely, relativizes their relationship to a base by demonstrating how accidental, contingent, and not intrinsically necessary this relationship is.

It also leads to a relativization of the significance of these values by showing that they are often inseparable from a set of counter-values that the apologists and other praise-singers of different cultures generally forget to make their own. Science, a European invention I hear you say? But so is syphilis, introduced among Native Americans by visitors from the Old Continent.

> I start from the assumption that values are no one's property, that
> no intrinsic necessity lies behind their distribution across various
> civilizations or their changing relative importance. . . . Cultural
> values are like venereal diseases; they flourish here and there, de-
> velop in one place rather than in another, according to whether
> the environment is more or less favorable; but this purely histori-
> cal accident cannot justify any claim to ownership or, for that
> matter to immunity. (Hountondji 1996, 177)

Such an approach will make it possible to get definitively rid
of any inferiority—or conversely, superiority—complex; to
show that no historical success is permanently irreversible or
no failure insurmountable; that anything is possible at any moment; and that each culture must, in each period, take its responsibility before history. At a stroke this approach made it
possible to claim for Africa—against all attempts to exclude or
wall her in—a right to the universal, the possibility of raising
independent questions that are not a mere restatement of
those raised (understandably by the way) on Africa by Western curiosity. Rather, these questions would reflect the various
preoccupations rooted in African experience itself. It also
made it possible to claim for Africa the possibility of treating
such questions with enough method and rigor to yield answers
that would be universally valid.

f) Recentering Africa

A critique of unanimism and cultural self-imprisonment, a
return to a responsible *cogito*, a demand for a coherent pluralism, and a claim to the right to the universal, *African Philosophy* is also a critique of scientific exclusion and of its corollary:
theoretical extraversion.

From the outset, as has been observed, the book questions
the practice, among westerners, of writing learned disquisitions
on Bantu philosophy without the participation of the Bantu
themselves, but all the same expecting from them in return a

noisy expression of inflated gratitude. Beyond this extreme case, however, in which the people excluded are precisely the subject of the ongoing debate, the book deplores the exclusion of Africans and Africa in general, from science; the fact that research develops without them, and that they remain on the margins of the process of the global production of knowledge.

As a result of this, the few Africans that are co-opted into the international scientific community have no choice themselves but to theorize on the backs of the great mass of Africans, and to tailor their discourse to a public that is in the main Western. Exclusion therefore generates extraversion in African scientific practice—the participation in an activity located elsewhere; the concentration on an audience that, in its vast majority, lives outside of Africa; the "decentering of knowledge in relation to our geo-political space," to borrow an expression that I used shortly after (Hountondji 1980c, 27).

Ethnophilosophy is the daughter of extraversion. The critique of ethnophilosophy thus necessarily led to a critique of extraversion. By initiating a critique of the latter, *African Philosophy* demonstrated a need to open up in Africa a new space of research and discussion, an autonomous space where the themes explored would no longer be a distant echo of those developed by Western knowledge, but the direct or indirect expression of Africa's own preoccupations. The creation of an autonomous body of thought had to begin with the effort to formulate original sets of questions, not out of a search for novelty for its own sake, but out of a concern for authenticity, of a desire to be oneself by freely asking questions that one spontaneously asks oneself and by trying to raise them to a higher level of formulation, rather than by passively accepting the questions that others ask themselves or ask us from their own preoccupations.

The prerequisite for such a renewal of problematic is a change of audience. It involves a reversal of situations that would lead the African researcher to consider his African public as his prime target. This theme, present in all my writings of the period, is again taken up in the articles contained in *African Philosophy*. I expected a lot from the social recentering of the theoretical discourse: not only a renewal of content, but also an actual qualitative leap, and the most unexpected progress in the different disciplines.

If I was so fascinated with Amo's adventure—this man from Ashantiland who, torn from his people at the age of 3, had succeeded in making a breakthrough in eighteenth-century Germany through a number of brilliant works, and returned, in his old age, to his country of origin—it is precisely because his adventure prefigured to me the destiny of all colonial and postcolonial intellectuals, namely the massive extraversion that leads them to participate, in various disciplines, in the movement of ideas in the West and, more generally, in an intellectual history centered elsewhere in the great industrial and scientific capitals. By clearly indicating to us what we should avoid and, by contrast, the direction we ought to take in the search for ourselves, Amo was the counter-model that revealed us to ourselves.

Constructing a new space of theoretical production, seeing to it that sub-Saharan Africa, today marginal in relation to Europe and the West in the exchange of ideas, becomes fully autonomous, a center in its turn, or its own center, such then was the book's goal.

In this new process, it was impossible to avoid a massive appropriation of writing. The rehabilitation of oral tradition, the discovery of the richness and complexity of what Maurice Houis calls "oral civilization," should not blind us to the indispensable role of writing, not only in the transmission of a certain type of knowledge, but in its very construction. On this score, I remained faithful to Husserl's teaching (Houis 1971, 46–72).

I also remained faithful to it in another area. In my assessment of current tasks, I made no distinction between science and philosophy; rather I considered each as the expression of one and the same demand, of one and the same spirit of responsibility, of one and the same "radicalism." I thus transposed to Africa Husserl's demands for Europe. At the level of vocabulary, I expressed this demand through a particular use of the word "science," employed in its broadest sense beyond the traditional opposition between exact and natural sciences, human and social sciences. I also used the word "theory" in its Althusserian sense, as a generic term to designate the unity of a certain type of philosophy and a certain type of science. In any case, science as a project—as the unending task of tearing culture away from its original confinement for the purposes of introducing a teleological perspective into it, an opening that would otherwise have been impossible—was not only good for Europe. Challenging Husserl's eurocentrism on this point, I sought to demarginalize Africa, and to place it firmly at the center of its own history in a world that is henceforth plural; a world whose unity cannot be the result of annexation, or some kind of hegemonic integration, but of periodic re-negotiation.

g) *Rediscovering History*

It became possible on the field thus cleared, beyond the intellectual insistence on cultural constants, to examine the diachronic succession of doctrines and works, the continent's intellectual evolution. Whereas ethnophilosophy had hitherto led people to believe in the permanence of a single, unchanging vision of the world that traversed the ages intact, a history of African thought now became possible and necessary.

The critique of ethnophilosophy liberated the project of such a history. For the moment it was impossible to express an opinion either on that history's antiquity or its richness: only an empirical inquiry would settle the issue. The difficulties of the enterprise could not be ignored either. Wanting at all cost to do a diachronic reading on intellectual material that was thousands of years old, entire portions of which still belonged to an unwritten tradition, was something of a challenge.

In spite of these difficulties, however, the project retained its full significance. *African Philosophy* demonstrated motion in the act of walking, through two case studies that could serve as example. Thus the analysis of the work of Amo, the precise identification of his writings *(De humane mentis apatheia* and the *Tractatus de arte sobrie et accurate philosophandi,* as well as the thesis of his student Meiner, the *Disputatio philosophica),* the interpretive essay dealing with the first of these writings in light of the historical and theoretical context of the period, the effort to work out the issues involved—were all just a beginning of the implementation of one of the tasks laid out by this project, even if this reading led to a "formidable question": that of the legitimacy of this use of Amo, and more generally of the inscription of an intellectual work in the living history of Africa (Amo 1734, 1738, 1968a, 1968b; Meiner 1734; Hountondji 1970b, 1996, 111–30).

Similarly, the critical reading of *Consciencism* in light of Nkrumah's development and of the social and political struggles in the Ghana of the period did not aim solely at shedding light on the intricacies of the book. It proposed a method that is applicable, should need be, to other texts. The reinsertion of thought in the real movement of history should enhance both a recognition of the specificity of works of speculative thought, and their relationship to the social, economic, and political context of the different periods. It should finally found a pluralist vision of philosophy and African culture by sweeping away, once and for all, the unanimist prejudice and the myth of a society without history.

It could not have been pure coincidence. While I was drawing attention to the existence of texts and denouncing the "myth of spontaneous philosophy," bringing all of African philosophy to such accumulated texts (and while this idea of philosophy as history was taking shape) Fr. Alphonse Smet was delivering the first version of his important "Bibliography of African Thought." A careful, meticulous, and erudite scholar, this Lovanium professor was, since his transfer to Lubumbashi, chair of the department of philosophy at the National University of Zaire. In this capacity, he was in charge of the *Cahiers philosophiques africains* (African philosophical journal), a quarterly and bilingual periodical that the department founded at my suggestion. Its specific goal was to initiate, at the level of the continent, the indispensable exchange of ideas wherein alone could reside, in my view, an African philosophy properly speaking. It is in the second issue of this journal at the end of 1972 that the first version of a bibliography appeared, completed by Smet, and later corrected, revised, and enriched by others (Smet, 1972, 1978a; Nkombe and Smet 1978; Mudimbe 1982; Hountondji 1987a, 1988a; Van Parys 1980).

A parallel development took place in the Lubumbashi Department of Philosophy where, in spite of resistance, a movement emerged to rename some courses on the syllabus in light of the new demands. The courses titled "African Philosophy," whose content was of necessity mostly ethnographic and nothing else, were now named "African Philosophical Texts" or "Elements of a History of African Philosophy." Neutral of necessity in a debate among African colleagues that was sometimes rancorous, Alphonse Smet worked to defuse the situation, but at the same time strengthened the new trend by his own research. Moreover, openly deploring what he saw as a misunderstanding of Tempels, whom he knew better than any one else, he later through his research completely renewed the study of Tempels to the point that even the latter's most determined critics had to take a more balanced view of the man

(Smet 1977a 1977b, 1977c, 1977d, 1978b, 1981; Tempels 1948, 1949, 1962, 1979, 1982; Hountondji 1987b).

Be it as it may nobody today dares talk of African philosophy without referring to the literature that expresses it; no one projects it in the absolute as a thing-in-itself, a closed system that remains for all time identical to itself. No one imagines it outside of history. In this return to the real should be seen one of the most tangible results of the critique of ethnophilosophy, whatever else the new problems associated with this rediscovery of history.

h) Politics in Its Proper Place

There remained one last issue that could not be ignored. Against the pervasive ideological fervor of the moment, the wholesale politicization of human activity, *African Philosophy* sought to put politics in its right place.

In a context where, in Benin, the classics of Marxism had become the measure of all truth, and in philosophy, the indispensable reference and necessary condition for any dialogue, it was almost a provocation to talk of "From Lenin to Descartes," as I attempted to do in a lecture delivered in Abomey in 1975 at a national seminar for philosophy teachers, and in the article—unfortunately still incomplete—in which I returned to the issue (Hountondji 1975).

I wanted to show that the materialist thesis, in the form it took in *Materialism and Empiriocriticism*, where it actually boils down to what in epistemology is usually known as realism, could not stand up to the traditional objections of skepticism. At no time, besides, does Lenin seriously try to refute idealism. On the contrary, he readily acknowledged its internal coherence and, by extension, its irrefutable character. However, because he could not refute it, he attempted to banalize it.

The technique used is of disconcerting simplicity. The idealist is a madman! *Ad hominem* argument takes the place of refutation. Because the doctrine cannot be invalidated, a doubtful ancestry is concocted for it, an arbitrary genealogy that makes it possible to dismiss the annoying product with ease. I sought to prove that Lenin was using against idealism a type of argument that others before him had used against skepticism—for example Aristotle, who, in Book 4 of the *Metaphysics*, attempts to settle scores with the sophists who claimed to deny the principle of contradiction (Aristotle 1993, 1–26; Lenin 1970).

Finally, and above all, against the charge of madness, I appealed to the intellectual daring of Descartes who, in his quest for apodictic certainty, readily accepted the risk of madness and, through the argument of the dream, provisionally rejected all belief in the existence of bodies including his very own.

A famous discussion between Foucault and Derrida on the status of madness in Descartes had finally convinced me that, far from practicing the exclusion against madness and mad people that Michel Foucault saw as the founding gesture of classical rationalism, the *First Meditation*, on the contrary, accounted for them in its reasoning. The apodicticity of the *cogito* is thus not threatened by the eventuality of madness. On the contrary, it presupposes madness, and consequently remains of a different order, beyond the opposition between reason and unreason (Descartes 1953a; Foucault 1965; Derrida 1978, 31–63).

Thus Lenin was placed in his rightful place with respect to the philosophical question that, incidentally, he himself considered, after Engels, to be the only truly great question of philosophy, namely the relationship between being and consciousness. I tried to prove that the uncontested authority of the Russian revolutionary, a midwife of history, and henceforth, indispensable in the area of political theory and practice, did not necessarily give him comparable authority in the quite different field of speculative thought.

African Philosophy returns to this important question by another route: in the discussion of Nkrumah's work. The fundamental question of *Consciencism*, the *raison d'être* of this book, unique in Nkrumah's abundant output, is that in his eyes, all politics presupposes a philosophy. He formulates the relationship clearly: "There is only one real philosophical alternative: idealism and materialism. Idealism favors oligarchy, materialism favors egalitarianism" (Nkrumah 1964, 75).

The claim seemed "infinitely hazardous" to me. I found "this wish to put the various figures of metaphysical discourse into one-to-one correspondence with the figures of political discourse" highly debatable. For me, it was arbitrary to found socialism on materialism. Inversely, oligarchy could not, any more than any other unegalitarian doctrine, be founded on idealism or such other form of spiritualism. "Our political choices stand on their own feet. If they need justification, it must be political justification, belonging to the same level of discourse and not to what is the completely different *(ex hypothesi)* level of metaphysical speculation" (Hountondji 1996, 153–54).

That our choices "stand on their feet" does not mean that they are self-determined, or that they are not determined, in the final analysis, by our class location in the same way that our metaphysical choices are. I clarified this point in a footnote to avoid all ambiguity. However, coming directly or indirectly from the same origin, belonging to the same social class, does not imply, as the case may be, any relationship of logical dependence, of premise to conclusion between two types of discourses that are distinct in their object and method.

The issue at stake in this discussion was simple. It was about making ideological pluralism, different beliefs and world views coexist with the necessary unity of action; of ensuring that practical imperatives never serve as excuses to snuff out free and responsible thought; of guaranteeing the possibility for men and women of different philosophical and religious persuasions to continue to struggle together today, as they did yesterday, for the same cause and the same ideal.

To thus preserve unity in difference, all ideological proselytizing had to be abandoned; political problems had to be couched in political terms; that is, in terms of interests and conflicts of interests, of projects of society and practical organization of communal life. Intimidation and other authoritarian techniques used to forge a unity of thought that could not but be artificial had to be abandoned. The unanimist illusion together with the "systematic cast of mind" that made all political projects dependent on specific metaphysical foundations had to be destroyed. The "ideological thesis that politics has a metaphysical grounding" had to be shaken and the "autonomy of the political as a distinct level of discourse" had to be proclaimed loud and clear, in order to liberate and put in their proper place the political and the philosophical debate.

Returning to this question three years after the first version of the article on *Consciencism*, the postscript of *African Philosophy* restates its main conclusions while at the same time refining the explanatory concepts it previously deployed. Expressions such as "a rightist or leftist reading," "a rightist or leftist critique" that initially seemed so illuminating now appeared disconcertingly simplistic. Undoubtedly these expressions could still be useful, but only within precise limits. They were a warning, especially, against the temptation of dogmatism and, more specifically, against a certain catechetical reading. Such a reading, would result in trivializing the authors and their most revolutionary works by taking their interrogations for peremptory answers, by considering as resolved questions that they themselves never claimed to have resolved, and by reducing the immense anxiety that runs through them to a set of catch-phrases.

Ideological purring is a right-wing practice: such was my hypothesis. In the context of the period, the idea was quite simply subversive. It was an implicit invitation not to be content with party slogans, or with ideological courses hastily concocted by the National Center for Revolutionary Education with the help of popularizing texts from the Soviet Union. It made it incumbent on all those with the requisite intellectual tools to read the great classics themselves, and to form their own general opinion. "But on the whole the record is meager. We have failed to develop this heritage, and now we are powerless to prevent it from being taken over shamelessly by political groups that are completely cynical and reactionary . . . . There is a danger that the time may soon come when, in the name of Marxism, we will be forbidden to read Marx" (Hountondji 1996, 183).

That said, beyond the subversive charge of the metaphors that, perhaps wrongly, I took for concepts, I acknowledged in the postscript that the antithetical couple "rightist or leftist reading" could not be literally interpreted, unless one wished to divide the world into two, along the lines of the old Stalinist antithesis of "a bourgeois and a proletarian science."

I think, although I am not sure, that I read Dominique Lecourt's *Lyssenko* when it rolled off the press in May 1976; a book that was a timely reminder of the disastrous consequences of this brilliant and yet simplistic approach (Lecourt 1977). Without mentioning this celebrated affair in particular, I could not rid myself of the very strong feeling that in the Benin of 1976, history was repeating itself on a smaller scale after an interval of 30 years. In this small corner of the world, people were yielding, as they did in the Russia of the 1940s, to the same temptation: "to batten scientific life mechanically on to political life, so as to make the former an immediate reflection of the latter, thus emptying it of its richness, of its essential open-endedness (Hountondji 1996, 180–81).

Nkrumah's Ghana thus acquired the value of a paradigm. By placing them within the African context, it made it possible to reflect on some of the theoretical and practical excesses that are legion in the present or past history of the most diverse societies. It forced people to question the usual meaning of the classical notions of left and right, by showing the flawed nature of any assessment that sought to characterize, politically, a regime or a person on the sole basis of his or its public discourse, and by demonstrating the need to compare, in each case, discourse and practice. To illustrate my argument, I quoted a harsh critique of Nkrumah's regime that had appeared ten years earlier (Fitch and Oppenheimer 1966).

In sum, keeping politics in its place was a way of giving legitimacy, acknowledging the right status, to a discourse whose object is clearly and unambiguously about the totality of problems connected with the management of human societies and of the destiny of the species. But conversely, it was also a way of containing this discourse within the boundaries of its field of legitimacy; to prevent it from overflowing and becoming invasive to the point of claiming to structure all other fields.

Thus, while acknowledging the rootedness of the critique of ethnophilosophy in politics, the profound links that existed between *African Philosophy*—or indeed all my writings and theoretical reflections—and the concrete and ongoing struggles in Benin and Africa, I tried—both paradoxically and simultaneously—to keep politics at a distance, in order not to get stuck in it. I made it the theme of my work, reflected on it, in order not to submit to it, and, at the same time, to ensure the right to existence of an autonomous theoretical space.

3. Some Readings

The success of the book can be measured by some simple indices. The first is that it generated, and to this day continues to generate, bitter controversies. The very ferociousness of some of the criticism is proof that the positions advanced leave no one indifferent. I took note, as the need arose, of the gratuitous accusations of ulterior motives, and seized the opportunity to clear some misunderstandings (Niamkey 1977, 1980; Niamkey and Touré 1980; Yaï 1978; Hountondji 1977, 1981a, 1982a).

But, of course, I did not have only critics. Many people had read with understanding this or that article and the entire book when it was finally published. Some observations especially were cause for reflection. An example is Marc Augé's remarks in his fine study of the "theory of powers" in the lagoon societies of lower Ivory Coast. In it he concluded on the need to take the "ideo-logical" seriously, that is the logic of collective representations of human communities, and tried, at the same time, to make a careful distinction between this project and the hasty generalizations of ethnophilosophy (Augé 1975, 117–21).

The penetrating comment that was directed at my article in *Diogène* was later developed, after the publication of the collection, in another book by Marc Augé devoted to a critical examination of the "questions of anthropology." The brilliant French anthropologist, more attentive than others to his discipline's reception within the populations studied, was especially struck by my contestation of the status of ethnology in its claims of distinctiveness from sociology (Augé 1982, 78–90).

I was indeed suspicious of the special study of so-called primitive societies. I was not impressed by the subtleties of vocabulary or the lexical arrangements that have characterized this project. These learned corrections were unsuccessful in concealing the inconsistency of what seemed to me to be a science without an object: "Ethnology (or whatever name is given to it: anthropology or whatever) always assumes what it needs to prove: the real distinction between its object and that of sociology in general. The difference in nature between 'primitive' societies ('archaic,' if you will) and other societies. At the same time, however, it claims to bracket the real relationship—which is simply that of imperialism—between these societies and the 'others'" (Hountondji 1996, 16).

Beyond ethnophilosophy, "ethnology's fundamental flaw in general," to my mind, lay in its reduction of so-called primitive man to silence, in its attribution to him of an imaginary silence, in seeing in him "the opposite of an interlocutor: he remains a topic, a voiceless face under private investigation, an object to be defined, and not the subject of a possible discourse" (Hountondji 1996, 34).

Besides the questions raised about anthropology, Marc Augé picked up in the postscript to *African Philosophy* the remarks about these "collective codes of conduct, patterns of thought which viewed as a whole, can constitute what might be called a practical ideology." He also picked up the remarks in which I said that " the residual 'logic'," the "very particular coherence" of this practical ideology suggest the backyard of the do-it-yourself man, and make it impossible for this to be mistaken for philosophy (Hountondji 1996, 178).

He rightly saw in these suggestions and observations the answer to a critical question he had raised in *Théorie des pouvoirs et idéologie* about the real implications of the critique of ethnophilosophy. By rejecting the idea of a collective philosophy, should all forms of collective representation be also suddenly denied? Should the baby, to borrow the English expression, also be thrown away with the bath water?

On this specific issue, his concerns were all the more justified because when the *Diogène* article was published I was still in the mood of defiance expressed two years earlier in my Copenhagen lecture, where I went as far as to say— provocatively, I admit—that, in all rigor, "a collectivity does not think, at least not in the literal sense." The truth that Marc Augé could not have guessed at is that in formulating in the postscript the notion of practical ideology—incidentally similar in more than one sense to that of ideo-logic that he had himself developed—I was, after a nine-year interval, embarking on the early stages of self-criticism. From the beginning to the end of the book, during the seven years separating the *Diogène* article from the postscript, I had reflected more deeply on the issue, and made conceptual adjustments, thanks especially to a greater familiarity with Lévi-Strauss, aspects of whose work I had tried, with more or less success, to understand (Lévi-Strauss 1968a, 1987, 1968b, 1952, 1973).[8]

It will be useful in any case to compare Marc Augé's reading—careful as it is critical—sharing to a point of complicity the concerns of *African Philosophy*, with Claude Rivière's "friendly provocation." Attempting mainly to defend a discipline that in his opinion has been unjustly maligned, he felt duty bound to recall that "modern ethnology, the sister of sociology" very clearly appreciates the "differences, conflicts, and social dysfunctions that [had] frequently been analyzed over the past ten years in the context of relationships of dualism or pluralism." He deplored the fact that "too often, the pure philosopher, late by a decade, is ignorant of this socio-ethnology of change, which has no illusions on the pseudo-unanimity of thoughts and political will." He concluded by adding that African philosophy, contrary to European philosophy, needs to be modest because in Africa, it is the younger sister of the social sciences whereas it is recognized as the elder sister in Europe (Rivière 1979, 93, 105).[9]

What a pity, really, to see otherwise difficult issues of epistemology and theory reduced to a quarrel of preeminence between disciplines.

For more evidence of the impact of the critique of ethnophilosophy, it will suffice to mention the anthologies, collections, and other textbooks used to teach philosophy in Africa or the United States, that have quoted large extracts from it over the last twenty years (Smet 1975, 410–30; Azombo-Menda and Enobo-Kosso 1978, 163–76; Tort and Desalmand 1978, 372–73, 375, 378–81; Azombo-Menda and Meyongo 1981, 5–6; Serequeberhan 1991, 111–131; Mosley 1995, 172–90).

It is even amusing to read in one of those collections that I was born in the Republic of Benin (instead of Abidjan), that in 1995 I was still a minister of education (a post I only held for sixteen months: from March 12, 1990, to July 29, 1991) and—less excusably—that my book was published by Indiana University Press in 1987 instead of 1983. More amusing still is to read the introductory chapter to a school text whose main title—"Does There Exist an African Philosophy?"—is followed by two subtitles inviting two possible answers: "no" for the first and "yes" for the second, and to observe that the first author chosen in support of the first answer is a certain Paulin Hountondji. With no difficulty at all, some of his writings are quoted out of context (Mosley 1995; Azombo-Menda and Meyongo 1981, 5–6).

Popularization has its pitfalls that are not always easy to avoid. It must, nevertheless, be possible, in spite of these difficulties, to do good popularization. Out of respect for the user, a sense of nuance and of the complexity of issues in the texts must not be sacrificed to clarity of presentation.

African Philosophy has been translated, it is well known, in several languages. I am indebted for this to some solid friendships, to the indulgence of certain readers who were also brilliant translators, sometimes doubling as original creators, as in Henri Evans's case, and finally, of course, to the publishers who took the risk.

Each of the translations has its history. By responding in September 1980 to the invitation of the Rockefeller Foundation that was organizing in its center in Bellagio, Italy, a colloquium on "African Cultural and Intellectual Leaders and the Development of New African Nations," I did not expect that from the chance encounters made on the fringes of the conference would come some firm decision to make my book accessible to an English-speaking public. Abiola Irele had been invited to present a paper on the movement of ideas in francophone Africa. I was supposed to reply as a discussant.

Irele had made a reputation for himself in anglophone university circles as one of the foremost specialists of francophone African and Caribbean literature. He was preparing a book that would bring together articles he had written between 1968 and 1976 (Irele 1990). I do not think that my presence at the colloquium had anything to do with it; but it so happened that Irele devoted the entire last portion of his paper to an examination of the critique of ethnophilosophy, a subject he treated both with penetration and critical defiance. Aroused by this other "friendly provocation," I improvised in English a reply of almost an hour, experiencing neither apprehension nor embarrassment for a stammering that would otherwise have been disastrous. A heated debate ensued in the conference room. This happened one evening after dinner. The following day during coffee break, a group of participants discussing animatedly around Michael Crowder decided that the book had to be translated. On his return to Ibadan, Irele spoke about this. Henri Evans reported that he had read the book enthusiastically. His translation was a new creation, with a beauty and fluency given only to a Franco-British by birth, one with a wonderful education and a perfect mastery of two cultures, himself a distinguished creator. Jonathan Rée, a philosopher and an associate of the London publisher Hutchinson, collaborated in this translation. The text was sent to me in Düsseldorf. On reading it, I discovered obscurities in a French text that I had thought was perfectly clear. I corrected the inevitable mistranslations. The result is a book by three, faithful to the original French text and probably better written.

Irele's preface did the rest. It situated *African Philosophy* in the context of the movement of ideas on and in Africa. His account went from Levy-Bruhl to Lévi-Strauss through Griaule, Tempels, and Janheinz Jahn; and from Senghor to Wiredu through Fanon, Marcien Towa, Claude Sumner, Stanislas Adotevi, Pathé Diagne, and many more. Irele saw in the book a kind of manifesto, comparable in its polemical thrust, to Alfred Ayer's *Language, Truth and Logic.* He especially saw clearly—and this was a plus to him—that beyond its apparently theoreticist accents, the real issue at stake in the book was none other, when all is said and done, than the improvement of the quality of life in Africa (Ayer 1970; Irele 1996).

Hutchinson of London thus published the book in 1983. Indiana University Press was responsible for distributing it in North America. In 1984, the book was co-winner of the Herskovits Prize of the African Studies Association.

I am no longer quite clear about how or when or by whom the decision to publish a translation in Serbo-Croatian was taken. I believe I was clearly made to understand, at the annual international "Socialism in the World" conference at Cavtat near Dubrovnik in the former Yugoslavia, that such a possibility existed. But I did not take the information seriously until 1983—the centenary of Marx's death—when at a round table that took place from October 24 to 28, on the theme "Marx, Marxism, and the Contemporary World," I received some author's copies of *O Africkoj filozofiji* or, at the very least, news that the book was going to be published. By way of a preface, the editor had included a 1982 interview between Joseph Ki-Zerbo and Vjekoslav Mikecin, editor of *Socialism in the World* (Ki-Zerbo and Mikecin 1983).[10]

I had already observed the interest of certain East European intellectuals for this critique of ethnophilosophy. Imre Marton had had two chapters of *African Philosophy* translated in Hungarian in a collection of handouts for students of Karl

Marx University in Budapest.[11] Janos Sipos of Laurent Eötvos University had translated and published "What Can Philosophy Do?" in the *Hungarian Journal of Philosophy*.[12] Besides, I had been the guest, in November 1980, of the Africa Institute of the Academy of Sciences of the USSR, and had noticed, following an oral presentation titled the "The Shadow of Levy-Bruhl and the Problem of Philosophy in Africa," how well informed were the Africanists who honored my lecture with their presence (Hountondji 1978b, 1978c, 1980b, 1981b).

The German edition published by Dietz in Berlin in 1993 had been produced from the English text following a series of meetings and discussions. I no longer remember at which colloquium I had met a colleague of Karl Marx University in Leipzig in the German Democratic Republic who gave me off-prints of two articles of his. I saw Gerd-Rüdiger Hoffmann again in Vienna, Austria in October 1989 (when Eastern Europe was in full crisis) at a conference organized by another philosopher with an interest in Africa, Christian Neugebauer.

At the same conference, I met Franz Wimmer of the philosophy department in the University of Vienna who was a comparative philosophy enthusiast and had just published the previous year an exciting, collective volume on the subject. We held many discussions. The three colleagues deplored the fact that *African Philosophy* was not available to a German-speaking public, and they made some plans to correct the situation. Four years later, I realized they were not talking in the air (Hoffmann 1985a, 1985b, 1988; Wimmer 1988, 1991; Neugebauer 1987).

Only recently did I discover the existence of a Spanish translation of chapter 3, done from the English and published in 1986 in *Prometeo*. The review's director, Horatio Cerutti Guldberg of the National University of Mexico, took part with me in a colloquium in the University of Alcala de Henarès near Madrid in May 1994 (Hountondji 1986b).

I took these translations, different interpretations, critiques, and questions as invitations to carry on the work that I had undertaken. I needed to deepen and, if necessary, correct and refine my earlier critique of ethnophilosophy. It had to be developed, placed in its rightful place in a broader field of questions. My future work was to be devoted to this indispensable task.

Part III

POSITIONS

Following the publication of *African Philosophy: Myth and Reality*, my research has attempted, in part, to deepen the critique of ethnophilosophy by taking the numerous objections raised into account and by expanding its problematic. Thus, I am gradually trying to formulate a critique of extraversion in general (and not only in philosophy); an analysis of the scientific and technological relations of production on an international scale; and a critique of the actual functioning of research in the periphery as it relates to the world system of knowledge controlled and managed by the rich countries of the North. At the same time, I am raising new questions about science policy—about the ways and means for a critical re-appropriation of endogenous knowledges, as well as a methodical appropriation of all the useful knowledge available in the world; about possible mechanisms for capitalizing and reinvesting knowledge in Africa and, on another level, about the irrationality of daily life, the conditions of emergence or consolidation of a civil society; and about the conditions for the emergence of ethics in politics and the cultivation of a democratic culture.

I hope one day to be able to present the results of this new research and show how the diversity of themes leads to the unity of the same itinerary I have been pursuing, the same demand. I also hope to draw some lessons from my brief incursion into politics. The transition to action from research is a huge problem in Africa, as it is everywhere else. In the particular environment of a poor country—of a country that is said to be poor and that has ended up believing itself poor—the stakes of power are so complex, the motives of people so disturbing, that one needs infinite love to continue to believe in the future.

The following chapters will take us to the threshold of these new questions. After giving an account of the noisy and somewhat polluted debate provoked by the critique of ethnophilosophy, we will attempt to draw lessons from it while allowing both for the necessary "rootedness" in the collective culture and for the demand for freedom.

5

A Polluted Debate

1. The Elegance of the Elders

a) Cheikh Anta Diop's Lesson

I have always kept in mind Cheikh Anta Diop's beautiful example given in Copenhagen during the discussion that followed his brilliant lecture on "L'éveil de la conscience historique de l' Afrique" (The awakening of the African historical consciousness) (C. A. Diop 1970).[1] The "cultural revolution," it will be remembered, was then raging in Mao's country and its leaders were attempting, among other objectives, to erase the past. Consciously playing the devil's advocate, I asked the "elder brother" in a heckling tone what he thought of this, and how he could justify, in this context, his insistence on the recognition of the Egyptian origins of black civilizations. Deep down, I added, what is the use of history if the only dimension that mattered was the future? His answer was of stark clarity: the Chinese can afford, up to a certain point, to bracket their past; they will in any case always find it at the appropriate time. Who has ever doubted the historical depth and antiquity of their civilization? But we Africans, on the other hand, cannot afford this luxury. After several centuries of slavery and of colonial lies, we need to rehabilitate our past. *History's role*, in these conditions, *is to give to our people consciousness of their continuity in time.*

When it was my turn to speak, and after I had presented my paper—the last on the program, as I said—Cheikh Anta Diop did not ask any questions. He picked up a piece of chalk—or was it a marker-pen?—and went to the chalkboard. One by one, he wrote down the names of some of the gods of Pharaonic Egypt, explaining how these gods gradually gave rise to the four elements of Greek cosmogony and, by extension, to the entire problematic of first causes and first principles central to Western metaphysics. Chapter 17 of *Civilisation or Barbarism,* a book that appeared long after the seminar, later developed this argument in greater detail (C. A. Diop 1990, 310–76).

I could not help—any more than so many intellectuals of my generation—being fascinated by the force, the activist conviction, the infectious enthusiasm of Cheikh Anta Diop's discourse. He opened up unbelievable perspectives that could be extremely fruitful. However, at the time, I still found his proofs about a historical continuity—biological as well as cultural—between ancient Egypt and contemporary black Africa insufficient. His intuition was brilliant, but the proof, on some key points, still seemed a touch impressionistic, especially for a lay person with little familiarity with the dating and other investigative techniques used by specialists. Cheikh Anta Diop left me skeptical. He listened to me patiently and understood, I believe, my scruples as a philosopher. I was in such perfect agreement with so many other vital points of his vision—his uncompromising demand for an Africa that is united and strong, that is capable of taking responsibility for itself on all levels—that our differences on matters of detail must have appeared minor. He was less irritated than others by my incredulity; much less, in any case, than Pathé Diagne, who, occasionally, knew how to fulminate against miscreants like a dreadful terrorist—a reaction that in truth impressed no one, known as he was as a friendly person and a heckler.

I later saw Cheikh Anta Diop on several occasions: in Paris at the "Celtic," a café situated just in front of *Présence Africaine* that served as a meeting point; in Dakar, at his radio carbon laboratory; in Addis Ababa, where he took part in December 1976 in the seminar organized by Claude Sumner on African philosophy; in Cotonou, where he also participated in different international colloquia, and undoubtedly elsewhere. The patriarch never tired of encouraging younger colleagues, convinced that a sovereign Africa would above all be an Africa capable of counting on its own expertise, on its own gray matter, and its ability to master its problems using its own resources.

b) *Kagame's Silence*

I sometimes feel I have been unjust to Kagame. I do not believe I had ever met him before Claude Sumner's seminar in Addis Ababa, where he presented a paper on "Le problème de 'l'homme' en philosophie bantu" (The problem of "Man" in Bantu philosophy) (Kagame 1980). All I knew of him were his monumental thesis published in Brussels in 1956 and the book published by *Présence Africaine* that, twenty years later, continued and developed the same problematic. I had also seen his contribution to volume 4 of *Chroniques de philosophie* by Raymond Klibansky (Kagame 1956, 1971, 1976). This time I met a man of flesh and blood: fatherly, calm, and very dignified. I later saw him in Cotonou where he participated at a conference organized by UNESCO, then in Düsseldorf at the 16th World Congress of Philosophy organized by Alwin Diemer. Confronted with a critique that directly took him to task, Kagame did not defend himself or did very little. But he did not change his opinion; he pursued his path with a kind of quiet conviction.

I had just completed an article where again I grazed him a bit, when I learnt of his death in Nairobi on December 2, 1981. I added a footnote to recall, on the one hand, that Kagame's production was more than his work on Bantu philosophy; that it also included important work on oral tradition and the history of precolonial Rwanda and, on the other, to express "my respect for a man whose erudition was only equaled by his goodness, affability and deep rootedness in his African culture." Posterity would remember him, I added, "as a morally upright man, a scholar of robust will who devoted himself, in his own way and with the greatest sincerity, to the rehabilitation of African culture" (Hountondji 1982a). Wiredu got wind of this note or—I am no longer sure—of one along those lines. He teased me, detecting in my attitude ancestor worship, no more no less.

c) The Tolerance of the Elders

On the whole, our elders and senior colleagues welcomed our critique of ethnophilosophy with great tolerance—indeed, benevolence—even if deep down they remained frankly opposed to it. It is not that they were not irritated. Ibrahima Baba Kaké once told me of one of his conversations with Alexis Kagame, during an interview with him in Kigali or Butare either for his radio program "Mémoire d'un continent" (Memory of a continent) or for some other journal. In reply to a question by Kaké asking him what he thought of Hountondji's critique, the priest was said to have quite simply replied: "Hountondji? But he is . . . white!" Such irritation does not surprise me. What, on the contrary, seemed remarkable to me was that it did not occur more often, and that it was combined with so much courtesy and style, so much good faith in discussions.[2]

I could cite many more examples. Alioune Diop for example who by temperament or choice listened more than he spoke, but who nevertheless had strong opinions on the precise issues concerning us, opinions that he had unambiguously expressed in his glowing preface to *La philosophie bantoue* (Bantu philosophy) (A. Diop 1949). After a perfectly understandable reticence to publish Eboussi-Boulaga's article, with which I planned to launch the "Philosophy Column" of *Présence Africaine*, he readily yielded in the end, simply accepting to add a footnote recalling the circumstances of publication of the book and the psychological climate of the period (Eboussi-Boulaga 1968).

I could give the example of Louis-Vincent Thomas. He did not appreciate my criticism of his work on the Diola, but willingly took part in a frank and direct discussion, even accepting to chair with me a roundtable on philosophy in Africa for a special issue that appeared in 1982 in Denyse de Saivre's review *Recherche, pédagogie et culture*. A pity that his untimely death should have put an end to such a frank and cordial dialogue! (Thomas 1959; de Saivre 1982).

I could also give the example of Alassane N'Daw who was willing to discuss whenever he had the opportunity to do so, unlike others who held on tightly to their positions while pretending to ignore the issues. His paper in Düsseldorf had not persuaded me any more than his 1966 article. His 1983 book, a revised version of his doctoral dissertation, did not convince me of the fruitfulness of his approach either. We have, however, always argued, sometimes deriving pleasure from provoking and taunting each other, so much so that when an unexpected and painful incident prevented me from delivering the speech that I had been invited to give at the closing ceremony of the seventeenth Congress of World Philosophy in Montreal, it was to him that I turned to read it for me. And he did so brilliantly (N'Daw 1966, 1981, 1983; Hountondji 1986a).

2. Muddying the Issues

a) *A Terrorist Discourse*

Others who lacked the same class preferred to have recourse, when they could, to forms of discourse that were closer to denigration or sarcasm than to calm and healthy criticism. Maybe it was only fair: there is always someone more iconoclastic than oneself! However, the motives are sometimes murkier than first thought. Thus little ironic barbs unleashed to all present by Niamkey in 1976, then repeated with the same tone, with the same touch of ambiguity, in an article jointly signed by Niamkey and Touré, became quite clear some years later in an article written by Abdou Touré. Read on.

First blow:
For Towa and Hountondji, reference to African philosophy or to philosophy *tout court* is only legitimate to the extent that the African thinker will sit as an *"agrégé,"* duly co-opted by the philosophical conclave, at the Western table of the Socratic symposium. And he will be co-opted only insofar as he consumes the philosophical knowledge developed by Western society. (Niamkey [1976] 1980, 171)

Second blow:
Hountondji could be asked the question that he has left unanswered: who decrees that such and such is a philosopher or, more specifically, an African philosopher yesterday and today? As for today the question is simple because it is enough to be a duly consecrated *"agrégé,"* co-opted by the sacred college of *"agrégés"* and doctors in philosophy, as an expert in Western philosophy. (Niamkey and Touré [1976] 1980, 197)

Final death blow:
Hountondji's aim in this methodological presentation is to exclude all the philosophers of the oral tradition, the important element being writing. And it is in relation to this criterion that *our philosopher, who is conscious of being an "agrégé"* in philosophy

[emphasis mine, P. H.], is ready to welcome any writer that claims to be a philosopher. (Touré 1980, 17)

It was clear: I had, first of all, to be forgiven for being an *"agrégé."* Replying in kind, I expressed my dismay at my discovery that some Ph.D.s in sociology derived their titles from the "popular masses," or at least had enough contempt for these "masses" to be able to make such a claim (Hountondji 1982a). I was not intimidated either by Koffi Niamkey's call— may he excuse me for writing his first name before his last name[3]—for "the death of mandarins" and all this in connection with my poor self. I answered back in kind saying that he would be well advised to familiarize himself anew with the use of his gun. I was, however, astonished to see the manipulations and the distortions he readily inflicted on the texts that he liked to quote, sometimes making them say the opposite of what they actually meant. Authors such as Marx, Gramsci, Canguilhem, Althusser, Foucault, and Terray were all victims of a massacre by a fervent disciple who could not wait to start, quite simply, by being a *reader*, with all that *reading* implies by way of rigor, patience, and intellectual discipline.

One was clearly faced with a terrorist discourse, a discourse of intimidation whose aim was to frighten; a discourse that brandished the worst threats to achieve its end. It solicited the reader's complicity for a symbolic . . . "murder" (for want of anything better); it fought to discredit because it could not refute. On the rhetorical level, the method *par excellence* of such a discourse consists in muddying the water by sowing confusion and doubt in the use of the most basic notions by using the words of ordinary language in a non-ordinary way, and by breaking up language.

b) *Arguments of a Counter-critique*

However, beyond the bitter and other *ad hominem* attacks, beyond the rhetoric of intimidation, the issues raised sometimes had real merit. This had to be taken into careful consideration, and the opportunity seized to refine some concepts, deepen, and, if necessary, create a more nuanced critique of ethnophilosophy. For Niamkey was, in a way, correct. The distinction between worldview and philosophy, or between a rigorous and a vulgar meaning of the word "philosophy," could conceal, if one is not careful, a "contempt" by professional philosophers for so-called popular thought, a "fascination" for philosophy wrongly considered as the queen of the sciences. In "L'impensé de Towa et de Hountondji" (The unthought in Towa and Hountondji), Niamkey robustly shatters two commonplaces on which this claim rests:

> Commonplace no. 1: philosophy as a scientific discipline;
> Commonplace no. 2: philosophy as private intellectual production.

Concerning the first "commonplace," he tries to show, drawing on Althusser, that philosophy, far from being the foundation of the sciences as it claims, has in reality always developed historically as an ideological commentary on the existing sciences, furthering exploitation and mystification. Moreover, the claim to scientificity is never innocent. It is always, on the contrary, a ruse to conquer power:

> The idea of philosophy as science is fraudulent. . . . The distinction Modernity-Tradition . . . Philosophy-Vision of the world, Science–Non-science . . . both hides and manifests a muffled struggle for power, a struggle for domination of "science" over "pseudo-science," a struggle of philosophy against worldview. This struggle, in the final analysis, is the expression of the will of the bearers of knowledge to overthrow the authority of the alleged bearers of false knowledges and to become the new authority. (Niamkey [1976] 1980, 170–73)

Concerning the second "commonplace," our critic, reducing the call for individual thought to a claim of intellectual property, attempts to prove that "in the philosophy business, there is no private production but private appropriation of knowledge that is collectively produced." Drawing on Jean-François Lyotard, who sees in literary property "an instance of the law of value at work" (Lyotard 1973, 7), he also acknowledges that "the signature is the result of the subjection of the 'author' to the law of capital," and that "the signature of a text or of a piece of thought is the result of a publishing contract that in itself is a specific form of employment contract." In precolonial Africa, he explains, "even official modes of thought are marked with the seal of anonymity." One is dealing with "a mode of production that is rather more collegial [where] knowledge or official thought are the work of a college of masters." Referring to his own *troisième cycle* doctoral dissertation, he warns that a better understanding of our precolonial societies would lead to a relativization of "the imperialism of the current form of writing" and to a recognition of the fact that in phylacteries, shrines, and statues exist in "crystallized forms real literary texts that are a feast of the mind to read" (Niamkey 1974, [1976] 1980, 182).

It is necessary, therefore, to recognize, concludes Niamkey, a class strategy behind the critique of ethnophilosophy; necessary not to be impressed by "science and reason, . . . scarecrows brandished by official philosophy to silence the other forms of thought" necessary to return resolutely to "spontaneous philosophy . . . the repressed requiem of philosophy" (Niamkey [1976] 1980, 186).

c) A Succession of Coups d'Etat

In "Controverses sur l'existence d'une philosophie africaine" (Controversies on the existence of an African philosophy), Niamkey and Touré return to the same arguments in greater detail. From the outset we learn that the history of philosophy is "a history of successive coups d'état. . . . Everything here is about relations of power . . . a test of force." The word itself, at best, should only be used in the plural, because there is no unitary concept, still less a universal mode of philosophy.

Once the concept has thus been shattered, the authors can easily demonstrate the subjugation, behind the critique of ethnophilosophy, to an imaginary concept of philosophy in the singular, or more precisely to a "hagiography of Western-elitist philosophy." From which location are Towa and Hountondji speaking? they wonder. The answer is simple. Judging from their tendency to lend their support to "the hegemony of Western philosophy," it is clear that they are working, consciously or not, "for the interests of cultural neo-assimilationism, a perfect corollary of neo-colonialism" (Niamkey and Touré [1976] 1980, 196).

It is necessary, therefore, they continue, to reaffirm the importance of what is commonly known as African "folklore;" to put an end to this "contemptuous attitude by intellectuals for the intellectual productions of non-intellectuals;" this elitist prejudice that tends to devalue precolonial African thought, saddling it with all sorts of pejorative attributes, including myth, unconsciousness, implicit, collective, a-systematic, and spontaneous mythology. It is especially important to recognize the stakes for power behind these apparently purely theoretical critiques. Drawing here heavily on Gramsci—the victim, be it said in passing, of some distortions—our critics see in the opposition between true and false philosophy the expression of a "struggle between official and subaltern ideas, with the former dominant and the latter dominated," and a way for traditional intellectuals—in this case Towa and Hountondji—to lend their support openly to hegemony and class domination.

Then follow other considerations—equally erudite—on the "politics of reading" by which official philosophies annex the thoughts of others, appropriate them, or set them up as imaginary adversaries, thus developing a "differential re-writing of the history of thought," on "logic . . . the first adventure of discourse" necessarily implying "the logical nature of spontaneous philosophy." The authors reject as purely ideological and unacceptable any distinction between myth and reason. Burnet and Vernant are to them in this respect simply "hagiographs of Greek thought": "The notion of myth is an effect of philosophy, that is a value judgment by which a specific type of explanation that is considered to be below the threshold of scientificity is devalued" (Niamkey and Touré [1976] 1980, 208).

From myth to reason there is no discontinuity, no break: "To opt for ideologies of discontinuity without scholarly justification is called intellectual snobbery" (Niamkey and Touré [1976] 1980, 213). Relying strongly on this argument, our critics examine the mode of production in precolonial Africa, and try to demonstrate how the elders, custodians of the knowledge necessary for production, increase the obstacles on the path to knowledge—obstacles that are none other than what Althusser calls in another context "state ideological apparatuses." They also try to demonstrate how "ideological growths" germinating on the legal, economic, and political soils give rise to

> philosophical apologias . . . that exalt the principle of clan, ethnic and brotherly solidarity, and the principle of the primacy of age as a source of wisdom, . . . and how these apologias present conflicts between relatives as a monstrosity . . . attributable to the evil action of nyctosophy (sorcery) . . . all this within a theoretical space in which the great ideological values of loyalty, filial piety, obedience, and life are celebrated, . . . values that function as aggregative philosophies whose goal is to secure the gerontocratic and political order, the authority of the clan in matters spiritual and matrimonial, . . . as theories and ideologies of power which find expression in the practices of nyctosophy. (213)

Here again, the authors refer us to Niamkey's *troisième cycle* doctoral dissertation, "The Logical Articulation of Akan Thought."

Niamkey had founded *Le Koré: Revue ivoirienne de philosophie et de culture* in the University of Abidjan. Both the articles on which I have commented had been published in 1976 in numbers 1 and numbers 3–4 respectively of this review before being included in the working papers of the seminar held in December in Addis Ababa. They came to my notice only at the seminar. My paper, read on the second day, gave me the opportunity to react. Niamkey requested my permission to publish the paper in his review. I gave it. "Sens du mot 'philosophie' dans l'expression 'philosophie africaine'" (The meaning of the word "philosophy" in the expression "African philosophy") was thus published in 1977 in the quadruple issue (5–8) of *Koré*, before its appearance three years later in the proceedings of the Addis Ababa conference. It was out of the question, however, that I should have the last word. Niamkey published in the same number of the review his answer to my answer: "Les modes d'existence matérielle de la philosophie et la question de la philosophie africaine" (On the material modes of existence of philosophy and the question of African philosophy) (Niamkey 1977).

Meanwhile, the French original of *African Philosophy* had appeared. The work had drawn attention to the material mode of existence of philosophy as tradition, as a fact of culture, and tried to establish the equation: African philosophy *equals* African philosophical literature. My Addis Ababa paper recalled this equation, after having demonstrated the prior need to interrogate the *meaning* of the word "philosophy" before any discussion of the existence of an African philosophy. A piece of naïveté, replied Niamkey! There is no single concept of philosophy but a plurality of irreducible concepts. Acknowledging, however, the need for a material basis to philosophy—in contrast to a method that would simply postulate it like one big hypothesis and painstakingly reconstruct it (the substance of ethnophilosophy's method, to my mind)—he set himself the task of taking up the challenge. This he did through a considerable widening of the notions of writing and text—notions that he applied equally to statues, art objects, and even traces of material culture whose decipherment had to be learned. There again, the reader is referred to this famous unpublished doctoral dissertation on "L'articulation logique de la pensée Akan-Nzima" (The logical articulation of Akan-Nzima thought).

3. The Nationalist Reaction

a) An Irritated Africanist

An enthusiast for the languages and literatures of the world, an excellent linguist, a great connoisseur of Yoruba culture, himself a Yoruba, Olabiyi B. Yaï is currently a professor of African languages and literatures at the University of Florida. In 1978, he was still a professor at the Center for African Studies at the University of Ife in Nigeria, after resigning from the civil service of his country of origin, Dahomey, where he had long been a Spanish teacher. "Jo," as all his Benin friends (from his French first name, Joseph) know him, was my classmate. After kindergarten and early elementary school in the Protestant primary school (at Savé in Middle Dahomey), which we attended for the first three years, we entered the *lycée* at Porto-Novo in November 1953, graduated on the same day in 1960, and left for further studies. He went to the University of Dakar and I to the Lycée Henri IV in Paris. Jo never spoke much. He listened politely, sometimes giving the impression of being in agreement with you. But he only needed to feel secure in a circle that he judged sympathetic to his views for him to suddenly display an unsuspected ferocity.

The dean of the faculty of the humanities at Ife was at the time Olu J. Sodipo, formerly head of the department of philosophy. A very active scholar, he had created a review in his department, *Second Order*, whose first issue had appeared in

1976. He was a friend. We had been in touch, I believe, from 1971 when I was also founding the bilingual journal *Cahiers philosophiques africains* (African philosophical journal) at the National University of Zaire. And then I met him shortly before the founding meeting of the Inter-African Council for Philosophy, which I organized in Cotonou in January 1973. He was elected president of the new association. Sodipo was more of an elder brother to me than a father. In total disagreement, deep down, with my ideas on ethnophilosophy, he still paid a careful, sometimes amused, but always tolerant attention to them, all the while pursuing his research on Yoruba thought (Sodipo 1973; Hallen and Sodipo 1986).

I therefore readily accepted Sodipo's invitation to participate, on May 4, 1978, in a session by a group of multidisciplinary researchers during which Yaï was to read a paper on African philosophy. In the absence of an English version of my book—it appeared only five years later—three of its eight chapters, and a few other articles by me, were available in English. But as they were scattered in different journals, Yaï's paper was, in reality, the first introduction, for most of the participants, to the critique of ethnophilosophy. As regards the introduction, it was more of a devastating critique. The revised and expanded version, published in *Présence Africaine* as "Théorie et pratique en philosophie africaine: Misère de la philosophie spéculative" (Theory and practice in African philosophy: The poverty of speculative philosophy) gives an idea of what the discussions in Ifè were like (Yaï 1978).

b) Critique of Elitism

Yaï has some very harsh words for today's African "lumpen-intelligentsia (which) has made the 'dolce vita' the topmost of its priorities." But neither does he accept the "new form of betrayal by intellectuals, insidious and subtle because it is accompanied by an erudite and/or revolutionary discourse, the betrayal of Africa's intellectual or rather historical continuity." One thing is missing in "our new literati," and that is the indispensable contact with the intelligentsia that existed before the encounter with Europe.

It is only on the basis of such a contact with the so-called traditional intelligentsia that an intellectual revolution is possible. Revolution means a *deliberate break with a tradition.* To revolutionize is to *depart from* (Yaï 1978, 66).

The tone is set. *African Philosophy* can now be examined: "a book . . . that tries to resolve in its way a problem that faces the conscious segment of the African intelligentsia, namely the problem of African philosophy. It is even a brilliant book, one that displays uncommon intellectual agility, a book that one would have liked to see serve an otherwise popular cause."

In what he calls contemporary Africa's "philosophical establishment," Yaï distinguishes two trends: that of the ethnologists and the anthropologists who, beyond the inevitable limitations of their disciplines, have the merit of proposing a detailed analysis of modes of thought in Africa thanks to a solid field experience, and (a more recent trend) that of "pure" philosophers who, to him, are just like the Young Hegelians castigated by Marx in *The German Ideology.*

For these "young Turks" (*pace* Yaï) "the advent of African philosophy is contemporaneous with their own philosophical production. . . . All they find in discourses prior to their own are mythologies, cosmogonies and at best 'ethnophilosophies.'" This "abstract-speculative trend" is a response to a precise political preoccupation. The "aristocratic conception of philosophy" professed by our "new 'philosophical heroes'" aims in reality at "providing legitimacy to the hierarchies in contemporary Africa's neo-colonial societies." At the same time, it enables the philosopher to "produce a left-wing discourse without a corresponding praxis, or at worst with a right-wing praxis."

Repeating readily the arguments by Niamkey and Touré, Yaï objects to the question: "does there exist an African philosophy?" and asks in turn, with the same indignation displayed by his two Ivorian colleagues, "From which location is this question coming? Who, today, is arrogating to themselves the right to pose such a question, which is innocent only in appearance?" The question to him is pointless. A debate on existence? No, he proclaims, it is a nonexistent debate!

He makes the same point insistently about the multiple meanings of the word "philosophy." Any definition of this word, he asserts, is "necessarily cultural." Niamkey invoked Canguilhem in support of his position. Yaï refers to Lévy-Leblond and Jaubert to demonstrate the impossibility of defining a discipline once and for all and how "it is scientific work which, based on the piece of reality studied, constructs its own objects"—although, of course, Yaï conveniently forgets to question the limits of such a construct and the conditions of its coherence and accuracy.

c) The Charge of Fraud

The rejection by Yaï of what he calls the "geographical criterion" in the definition of African philosophy, and his total misunderstanding of the efforts to "demythologize" the concept of Africa, have already been mentioned above.[4] In the same vein, he is also shocked to see "our new philosophers . . . 'recruit' their African philosophers on the cheap" by promoting unhesitatingly any publication by any "bachelor's degree holder in philosophy or theology": "A case both of laxity and intellectual fraud that enables Africa to be used when the need to be a philosopher arises, while in the same breath denying it a philosophy, on the pretext of rigor. . . . More serious criteria are needed" (Yaï 1978).

Yaï does not understand my effort to delimit, to construct a new space for theoretical production. He understands even less the need to take into account within this framework, outside of an apologetic goal, and without necessarily overestimating their value, the simple fact of the existence of African works, African texts. Elitism, if elitism there is, certainly does not reside in my attempt to off-load the concept of Africa. It is rather in the heroic and romantic conception of knowledge that subtends Yaï's critique by which only "great philosophers" and other "great scholars" do philosophy and science.

His biggest reproach, however, concerns the argument in chapter 4 of the book where the written text is given clear preeminence over oral literature, as a condition of development of a critical thought. For Yaï, this "simplistic and manichean hypothesis" both underestimates the danger of the rise of a cult of the book that would promote dogmatism and argument from authority, and the extraordinary richness of oral literature, which is also perfectly capable of taking on board the criticism that takes place from one generation to the other, or indeed within the same generation. François Dossou, another colleague from Benin, gave a name a few years later to this deviation: the fetishism of writing (Dossou 1985, 1994).

His other big reproach, like Niamkey's and Abdou Touré's, is the appeal to personal thought. Like the latter, Yaï quotes Gramsci abundantly and sometimes misinterprets him. What is new, on the other hand, is the massive reference to Dietzgen: this nineteenth-century tanner, author of "L'essence du travail intellectuel" (The essence of intellectual work), who, according to Marx and Engels, is said to have discovered materialist dialectic independently of them and even of Hegel. Modestly, and as a logical result of his theory of the material bases of all intellectual history, Dietzgen said that the content of his book was "not an individual product, but a plant *sprouting from the soil of history*": "As a result—excuse this mystical expression—I only have a sense of my self as an organ of the idea. What belongs to me is the *presentation*" (cited by Yaï 1978, 75).

So, it is never the individual that matters. In the final analysis, the individual is explained by the modes of production, the appearance of ideas at different periods. Moreover, oral traditions also know how to name the "authors" of philosophical discourses. The Fa literary corpus, linked to divinatory practices of the same name in Yorubaland, is abundant proof of it. Yaï quotes in this connection a Nigerian author recognized by all specialists as an authority in the field (Abimbola 1976), and advances the following hypothesis:

> In African societies . . . the modes of production were different from those in the capitalist West. Consequently the individuals who happened to formulate such and such philosophy were not much concerned with a claim of private property, of philosophical 'copyright'. To the extent that these philosophies become 'anonymous,' as they do indeed with time and social practice . . . they can convey the impression to the observer who is uninformed or in bad faith, or to the abstract philosopher . . . that he is dealing with "a collective philosophy." (Yaï 1978, 76)

In these conditions, appealing as I did to the theoretical effort of the individual subject is, in the final analysis, to magnify a huge misappropriation, to perpetrate a monumental fraud: that of a class that appropriates the fruits of the manual and intellectual labor of the immense, anonymous majority (Yaï 1978, 76).

In contraposition to this Yaï advocates what Gramsci calls "the spontaneous philosophy of the masses," the "philosophy of praxis."

That is not all. Yaï strongly denounces in the "abstract, speculative philosophers" what looks to him like a form of scientism, a "will to make an absolute of science" and worse still, "to present their own productions as a new, revealed, science." Better still, he blames "the absence of a socio-historical dimension" in this type of discourse, which explains its "political poverty." Referring to Lukacs and Henri Lefebvre, Yaï expects

African philosophers to study before all else precolonial Africa's modes of production. Every other topic is pure idle chatter. In conclusion our critic reaffirms a hidden complicity between "speculative philosophy" and power. "The choice of the abstract and speculative trend in philosophy is a class strategy. The noisy contempt displayed against 'pre-scientific philosophies' or 'practical ideologies' sounds the death knell of the traditional powers as well as the introduction of the dossier of the self-righteous philosopher for the sharing of the new neo-colonial power."

d) The Charge of Eurocentrism

It is no coincidence if another Yoruba Africanist who, because of the arbitrary division of colonial boundaries, was born on the Nigerian side recently took up the charge of eurocentrism. Yoruba civilization is one of the oldest African civilizations, one of the most robust and the best studied. Furthermore it would not surprise anyone that Yaï gained a following not only in Nigeria where his criticism of the so-called speculative philosophy was translated and widely distributed, but also among the large Nigerian diaspora in the United States. Beyond ethnophilosophy, Owomoyela feels that at issue in *African Philosophy* are African cultures themselves, the traditions and mores, the modes of thought and values of ancient Africa. The author, he believes, encourages a total rejection of this heritage and an embrace of frantic westernization. The book to him, is a "plea against African Studies and Africanists;" it "attacks the study of traditional African thought [and] at the same time insists on the philosopher's right to study non-African ideas;" a philosopher who "brushes aside the idea of cultural pluralism, seeing in it a "pretext for a conservative cultural practice" but supports, on the other hand, the irreversible march toward a "'world civilization,' . . . the dissolution of African particularities (real or imagined) in a rising world civilization—which naturally means a cultural *pax Europeana*" (Owomoyela 1987, 84–85, 92).

What a pity that the author is made to say the exact opposite of what he said! Far from rejecting cultural pluralism, *African Philosophy*, on the contrary, and especially in chapter 8—titled "True and False Pluralism"—makes a case for a pluralism recognized both as fact and value. I have replied elsewhere to my Nigerian critic.[5] In fairness to him let us say that he could only read the book in translation, and that the English version, in spite of its elegance and great qualities, still contains some misinterpretations. For example, at the end of chapter 2, the phrases "Alors que faire? ... Réapprendre à penser" were translated as "So what is to be done? ... We must relearn how to think" (Hountondji 1996, 52–53). Literally this was not wrong, but the text should have read "We must start thinking again": to start thinking again in the strong sense of a responsible thought, one that was necessarily critical and free.[6]

However, beyond these inevitable problems of translation, the infelicities in the French text itself, the abrupt and intentionally provocative formulations, it clearly looked as if seasoned Africanists of sometimes distinguished scholarship needed an imaginary enemy, one whom they then proceeded to give themselves from a simplifying and distorted reading of *African Philosophy*.

4. Marxists and Anti-Marxists

a) *The Dahomey Communist Party (PCD)*

I will only mention in passing the reaction of the Dahomey Communist Party. In its "Introduction aux réalités économiques et sociales au Dahomey" (An introduction to the social and economic realities of Dahomey), a work that, at the time, was circulating under coats (sorry, *agbadas*), the PCD thought it necessary to devote a long commentary to this critique of ethno-philosophy. The PCD was a clandestine party, respected for its courageous resistance to the military dictatorship from 1972 to 1990. Some of its members paid for this courage and determination with their lives. At the same time, however, it practiced what seemed to me an ideological narrow-mindedness unacceptable to any free and demanding mind. I was never tempted to join the party, whatever might have been thought in certain ill-informed circles.

In a brochure that was supposed to be the first in a series of studies on Dahomey,[7] the party's Central Committee, after copious quotations from Marx, Engels, Lenin, Stalin, and from the Albanian Enver Hoxha, finally came to examine the social and political situation in the country. The writings of a number of "careerist intellectuals" against whom the party was determined to "defend the purity of Marxist-Leninist science" were subjected to merciless criticism. In this context, *African Philosophy* receives special mention. Mentioned approvingly at first as a good rebuttal of the work of missionaries and various ideologues who denounce the cruelties of colonialism only to theorize and promote imperialist domination in Africa, the book is subsequently criticized severely for its "eclecticism," its "idealism," its "lack of a proletarian consciousness" and "of party spirit."

Nowhere is Marxist materialism acknowledged in the book for what it is: "a great leap forward in the history of human thought." Moreover, the book does not deal with the economic and social problems of Dahomey and Africa. The author "denigrates the Great Stalin" and in the same breath calls himself Marxist. He is calling for an "anarchistic and petit-bourgeois debate," from which ceaselessly fleeting truths will emerge. P. Hountondji's philosophy, to the extent that it makes no place for proletarian ideology, is in the final analysis nothing less than "the synthesis of the ideology of the radical petite-bourgeoisie that dominated the democratic movement in our country from 1967 to 1976" (PCD 1979, 60–63).

A perfect example of dogmatic and scriptural criticism, these remarks would not have deserved mention had it not been for the fact that they were coming from a *political* organization, and were bringing out in broad daylight—with an exemplary candor and lack of sophistication—an ideological bone of contention that is concealed and draped in more tortuous language in other criticisms. My only surprise was to learn that I was a Marxist. To this day, I do not remember having claimed that label. I have written on the other hand that instead of this Marxism in tablet form that so many of our compatriots swallowed like a panacea, of this closed system that had answers to everything, we must recognize that the debate in Marxism has always been in reality plural and contradictory. And we must promote in our countries, among other theoretical traditions, that of a living, plural, multistranded Marxism. A plea for an unavoidable and basic responsibility, this position was unbearable both to dogmatic Marxists and dogmatic anti-Marxists.

b) Abdou Touré's Reaction

In contrast to the PCD that cautioned party activists against a "Marxologist" that could be mistaken for a Marxist, Abdou Touré, gladly playing the Marxologist, needed to create Marxist-Leninist enemies. Providentially, he found three: Amady Aly Dieng, Paulin Hountondji, and Marcien Towa (Dieng 1978; Towa 1971). With a small exception of the first of the three, he believes that these authors have remained "impervious to the abundant literature that questions state ideology, namely Marxism-Leninism whose goal is to vouch for an ostensibly unegalitarian social order. . . . How can one be Marxist-Leninist today?" (Touré 1980, 8).

Abdou Touré correctly quotes some solid critiques of Soviet

bureaucracy and the beginnings of personal dictatorship in the Soviet Union (Korsh et al. 1973; Linhart 1976; Baynac 1975). He is undoubtedly not wrong to recall, on the basis of these critiques, that the famous "cult of personality" can be traced back, well before Stalin, to Lenin himself. He forces reflection on the nature and conditions of the historical triumph of Bolshevism, the obstacles to liberty, and the important issue of human rights and democracy in the known historical forms of socialism, and of all regimes that claim to be based on the teachings of Marx. I was myself going through this exact experience in Benin and *African Philosophy* bears important traces of this experience. Rather curiously, Touré—who was living under a regime whose openly anti-Marxist ideology was more attuned to these repressive practices (akin to those in Benin), and whose only knowledge of the contradiction between the great hope held out by Marxist discourse and the way this discourse had been "taken over shamelessly by completely cynical and reactionary political groups" came from his readings (Hountondji 1996, 183)—calmly believed he could, against all evidence, invent a "Hountondji who is a 'Marxist-Leninist philosopher'" (Touré 1980, 15), that is dogmatic and scriptural, tailor-made to fit his argument.

5. Initial Responses

a) Begging the Question

In contrast to "the old-fashioned ethnography," which did not bother to defend its own theoretical foundations, Koffi Robert Niamkey's and Abdou Touré's "approach" was, to me, a sign of the times. We were witnessing the birth of a scholarly ethnophilosophy, one that is no longer satisfied with describing worldviews by presenting them "naïvely" as philosophies in their own right, but that attempts to justify this method in a subtle and extremely refined way, using the most modern doctrines. It is a cutting-edge ethnography: aggressive, resolute, possessed of science, philosophy, psychoanalysis, politics. It deploys the most high-powered concepts, is ready not only to justify the immersion of philosophy in ethnography, but also to show, definitively, that this practice of philosophy is the only one valid in Africa today (Hountondji 1982, 58–59).

As a matter of fact, it was as if Niamkey had something to prove at all cost. After having written a dissertation on a subject that one could be tempted to classify under ethnology, he could not wait to show, with irrefutable arguments, that he had produced a work of *philosophy*. Was it then necessary? Was ethnology not also a respectable academic discipline?[8]

Confronted with these violent attacks, I began to ask, with the greatest candor possible, a simple question: What are we talking about? I do not think I had announced the topic of my paper before arriving in Addis Ababa. Claude Sumner had probably suggested one to me that I accepted very conditionally. Be it as it may, the title that I ended up choosing, "The Meaning of the Word *Philosophy* in the Expression 'African Philosophy,'" allowed me to kill two birds with one stone. I could both present the main ideas of *African Philosophy*, a book that was to appear within a few days or weeks, and, at the same time, respond to my critics. But the major problem I had with Niamkey's style was that of knowing what words meant, and whether, in the case at issue, we were actually referring to the same thing. The quotes in the book's title were precisely calling attention to this question of method: the question of meaning preceding the question of existence. Specifically, it was about knowing whether in the expression "African philosophy," the simple addition of the epithet "African" had to modify in return the meaning of the substantive. I saw no reason personally not to keep the usual meaning of the word "philosophy" "for as long as it was, at least, to affirm the univocity of a word, and not the identity of *contents* or of the *concrete histori-cal objects* to which it is applicable." I added: "If, to demonstrate the existence of an African philosophy, one has to start by dis-tending the usual concept of philosophy, if it has to be made virtually synonymous with culture, I have difficulties seeing what is gained by such an elaborate proof that has all the mak-ings of an enormous case of question begging" (Hountondji 1980, 83).

Among other specious justifications for his method, Ni-amkey had claimed that he wanted "to put the concept of phi-losophy at work on pre-colonial African forms of thought." Quoting and invoking the authority of Canguilhem in this regard ("to work a concept is to vary its applicability and un-derstanding, to generalize it through the incorporation of exceptional features, in short it is to give it progressively the function of a form through regulated transformations") he could add confidently: "The expansion of the concept of phi-losophy does not signify a neglect of rigor but a rejection both of the liberal and the academic model, to interrogate, beyond the ideological models provided by traditional philosophers, the reality of philosophical practice itself in the specific mode of production in which it is enclosed" (Niamkey 1980a, 196).

Poor Canguilhem! It is not his fault obviously if his best contributions are distorted and quoted out of context in this way to support the most untenable ambiguities.

b) *Misunderstandings and Accusations of Ulterior Motives*
Once the record had been set straight, I could start to clear some misunderstandings.

First misunderstanding: I have been made to say that African philosophy did not exist. Against this baseless inter-pretation, it was important to recall my observation: an African philosophy (an African philosophical literature) exists and has been obviously developing for *at least* several decades.

"At least" here meant the recognition of a written philosophical literature was only a minimal requirement that did not exclude, but, on the contrary, invited an interrogation on oral literature. At the same time, however, the implicit had to be laid to rest, and emphasis exclusively put on *explicit* discourses. This valorization of the explicit freed the project of *African philosophy*—a project that was not only impossible, but also unthinkable in the context of ethnophilosophy's ideological space.

Second misunderstanding: Some critics assume that I have been denying the existence of an African traditional thought. Against this equally absurd interpretation, it is necessary to recall that not all thought is necessarily philosophical, and that I had questioned neither religious nor moral, social, mythical, or political precolonial African thought. I demonstrated in passing the ambiguities that attach to the adjective "traditional" which, employed as practically synonymous with precolonial, could, by a kind of retrospective illusion, empty of all tension, all internal contradictions, the object to which it applies—in this case African thought. I expressed my preference for a return to the noun "tradition." This substantive should be understood in its original active sense: as a movement of transmission, instead of its passive, secondary sense—as the results of this transmission. To that extent, instead of African traditional thought, I would rather talk of African traditions of thought understood as a complex and contradictory heritage. Finally, against ethnophilosophy's apologetic attitude, always ready to justify any custom or social practice in the name of its supposed metaphysical meaning, I had to recall the need for today's African to entertain a free and critical relation with his heritage.

Besides the usual misinterpretations of my work, Niamkey's criticism could, in many respects, be reduced to a vast search for ulterior motives. The first point (commonplace no. 1, above) concerns the distinction between a broad and narrow sense of the word "philosophy," and the need for a return to the strict meaning. To see in such a distinction—or in the opposition between *doxa* and *epistèmè*—a struggle for power and an elitist and idealist conception of philosophy is proof, undoubtedly, of critical vigilance and a certain familiarity with Marxist analysis. But the application of the Marxist suspicion cannot be pushed that far without falling into dogmatism. The role played in the genesis of Marxism itself by a book like *The German ideology*, in which Marx and Engels unceremoniously dismiss what they contemptuously call "ideology" in opposition to science, cannot be forgotten. Can they, therefore, be described as elitist and idealist? Can it be said that this will-to-break with ideology hides—and demonstrates—a struggle for power on the part of an exploitative elite? Unless one is an ideologue or a rhetorician, one cannot make such a hasty conclusion. It would have been better, in my view, to keep away "from easy solutions, half baked theories, conceptual shifts where demagoguery and theoretical indigence naturally flourish."

The second charge concerns commonplace no. 2: the myth of philosophy as private intellectual production. In truth, Niamkey displaced the problem. The real issue was not so much about the *ownership* of philosophical ideas as about the intellectual *responsibility* of the thinker. Ideas, as a matter of fact, are not just products; they are also, above all, meanings that can be affirmed or denied, proved or disproved. In this act of validation (or confutation) the speaker has a responsibility—a theoretical, intellectual responsibility—that "extends and heightens the practical, moral, political responsibility that is recognized in every human being." This is how I had always interpreted the Cartesian theory of judgment. On this point it seemed unsurpassable to me.

In relation to this intellectual responsibility, it was easy to see "the political danger of ethnophilosophy": "Speaking through it is the ideology of group supremacy," or, more precisely, of "a certain idea of the group imposed by a handful of intellectuals and rhetoricians, the ideology that crushes the individual, and by the same token promotes all forms of fascism and neo-fascism from the most subtle to the most vulgar" (Hountondji 1982, 67).

I thus explained, frankly and squarely, the political stakes involved in the critique of ethnophilosophy and why the positions of Niamkey and Abdou Touré seemed to me at that time, in spite of their noisy demagoguery, to support the most tyrannical and cynical regimes, those that were the most indifferent to the suffering of the "masses."

c) *The Double Illusion*

In these type of controversies the sad thing is that, to clear up an ambiguity or clarify a misinterpretation, it is not enough to set the record straight. You must repeat yourself, restate endlessly what you have already said and what you thought was clear to all. So the paper in Addis Ababa could not be enough. Yaï's criticisms as well as those by various readers that took up in part Niamkey's and Abdou Touré's criticisms forced me to repeat, in greater detail, a certain number of responses. Two articles take stock of this discussion: "Que peut la philosophie?" (What can philosophy do?) and "Occidentalisme, élitisme: Réponse à deux critiques" (Occidentalism, elitism: A reply to two critiques) (Hountondji 1981, 1982). I earlier referred to these two texts. I will now simply outline their significance.

What I refused deep down was "a philosophy in the third person (that) consisted in lazily taking refuge behind group thought, in abstaining from taking a personal position and from giving one's opinion on the problems to which, in its own way, this thought of the ancestors was a response." In place of this "lazy recourse to group thought," I appealed for the intellectual responsibility of the thinker, of *each* thinker. I called for a re-examination of the founding concepts of philosophy, by beginning with the very concept of philosophy itself. "African philosophy," it should never be forgotten, is a Western invention. The ethnological concept of philosophy, the project of systematic identification of "exotic" worldviews is inseparable from the history of Europe's consciousness of itself. Eurocentrism, therefore, does not lie in rejecting this project and the concept that subtends it. It consists, on the contrary, in appropriating it naively, without discernment, to make one's contribution to it; in rushing in all sincerity into the paths laid down by Europe; in accepting uncritically to play the role that the West had carved out for any Third World researcher: that of informant or, in the best of cases, of scholarly informant.

To learn anew to be free intellectually and politically, *that* to me was the current requirement. This liberty presupposes the reassessment of the status that had been worked out, the paradigms that had been established, and the canons of thought that had been developed for us. Shutting ourselves up in our cultural past—a purely apologetic relation to our heritage—would respond exactly to what is expected of us. In this regard, nothing will be more Euro-centered than a febrile nationalism that would be content to hold up the treasures of African culture to the face of the world by congealing them, mummifying them, freezing them in their muggy eternity.

If I have pleaded so much for an off-loading, a shedding of the semantic over-determination of the concept of "Africa," it is because our intellectual liberation also depends on it. "Demystifying Africanness by reducing it to a fact—the simple, and in itself, neutral fact of belonging to Africa; by dissipating the mystical halo of values arbitrarily grafted on this fact" did not necessarily lead to an erasure of the continent's cultural history. On the contrary, it was the necessary condition to be able to think through not only the complexity and relative coherence, but also the contradictions that make up the richness of this history, as well as the alternatives to which this history leads—the possibilities that it leaves intact, and that today invite the exercise of our individual and collective liberty.

That is not all. Yaï's harsh critique of the "poverty of speculative thought," his appeal for a link between theory and practice, his demand for a "philosophy of action" that is organically linked to the "spontaneous philosophy of the masses" raised a problem that merited attention. In its way, "Que peut la philosophie?" proposes an answer. There are two ways of "expecting more from philosophy than it can give, of overestimating its power." The first consists in expecting it to provide answers to metaphysical problems about the existence of God, human nature, the immortality of the soul, and other questions of this nature. I did not hesitate to affirm that Kant had definitively dealt with this kind of illusion. I welcomed in passing the empirio-criticism within Marxism that was—whatever Lenin said about it—a healthy reaction of Kantian inspiration against the speculative trends that drew Marxism towards a dogmatic and scriptural metaphysics.

The other version of the same illusion—the other form of dogmatism—is that which consists in expecting from philosophy answers to political, economic, and social problems: answers that propose recipes for national liberation, the emancipation of exploited classes and nations—in short for the revolution. In my opinion, this illusion had been swept away by Marx himself, especially in *The German Ideology*. In any case, it is not the eleventh thesis on Feuerbach that should be used to prove the opposite. "Philosophers have only interpreted the world in different ways; what matters is to transform it." Nowhere in this thesis does Marx claim that philosophy itself can transform the world; "he calls, on the contrary, for a move away from philosophy to a concentration on the practical tasks of transforming the world" (Hountondji 1981, 59). From this point of view, the fiery rhetoric in a book like *A Contribution to the Critique of Hegel's Philosophy of Right* simply shows the extent to which Marx himself was a victim of the same illusion—the same demand for a directly instrumental philosophy—before becoming the Marx of *The German Ideology* and then of *Capital*.

Once this double illusion had been challenged and philosophy given its place, its more modest significance could be recognized and a number of tasks suggested in the fields of both theory and practice. I readily recognized the fruitfulness of a critique such as that begun in the *Critique of Pure Reason* and *The German Ideology* respectively, each in its area and with its own goals. Far from being purely negative, this deconstruction of the metaphysical illusion, this critique of mystification in all its forms resulted, in my opinion, in clearing the field for new forms of action and thought. I also acknowledged the incomplete nature of the enterprise, that it had to be pursued and repeated in each new period and in each historical context. The theory of science in which I always saw "an essential nucleus of philosophy" was only meaningful when placed in a new context. However, it had to be expanded to take account both of the evolution of critical thought since Kant, and of the demands of contemporary epistemology.

d) The Populist Temptation

Chance, as always, and the good offices of a friend passing through Paris led to a meeting with Denyse de Saivre, Editor-in-Chief and (at the time) Acting Publications Director of *Recherche, pédagogie et culture*. Three of us had dinner in the Latin Quarter. During dessert, I agreed to write an article for a thematic issue of the review on education (Hountondji 1980a). Two years later, Denyse decided to devote a special issue of the review to African philosophy. I could not refuse the invitation to participate in its preparation. My job was to identify some authors, chair a round table, and write an article. I leapt on the opportunity to take stock.

The reproach of Eurocentrism is often associated, we have seen, with accusations of elitism, idealism, scientism, the fetishism of writing, and even of intellectual fraud. The list is much too long for an article. Confining myself to the first two, I sought to show, once again, what was incongruous in them. I also wanted to "track to its last hideouts, and clearly identify what is hidden behind this reproach of elitism . . . namely a patent form of what should indeed be called populism." I was in complete agreement with my critics that we should acknowledge "not only the existence, but the unsuspected value, the varied richness of this pre-colonial African thought that is still so badly known," and "emphasize more broadly the creativity of the 'masses' in all areas including that of knowledge." I, however, added in passing that these topics were already contained in *African Philosophy.* Moreover, I added that one could not claim without demagoguery that the heritage so recognized and valued is self-sufficient; neither "could one pretend to believe that the first duty, indeed the only duty, of the new intelligentsia is to exhume, reconstruct, collect, and defend it comprehensively and without reservation."

The opportunity was right to bring out the tendentious use made of Gramsci by my critics, the distorted reading that tilted the writings of the Italian philosopher towards a populist and droning demagoguery. It was almost "child's play" to demonstrate, by referring to the texts quoted by the parties themselves, how the latter had manipulated or misinterpreted them. Although he made himself the apostle of "common sense," "folklore," and "spontaneous philosophy," Gramsci was no less mindful of the need to subject to critical examination these conceptions that were "to a large extent implicit, . . . non articulated, . . . a-systematic, . . . an indigestible collection of fragments of all the worldviews, and whose mutilated and contaminated traces only exist for the most part in folklore." Our critics, therefore, had to look for other masters or another cover: Gramsci did not fit the bill.

Of course, I was in agreement with them on one point: in the debate on African philosophy, no position is politically neutral. But I had already spelled out—with sufficient clarity— the political stakes that I saw in the critique of ethnophiloso-phy: other "stakes" did not need to be arbitrarily invented on the pretext of secret intentions of which I may have been un-conscious. "The recourse to the unconscious of the other . . . can function, in certain specific conditions, like a purely rhetori-cal strategy aimed at hiding the absence of real arguments." I therefore recalled what to me was the real issue at stake:

> What I denounce in, and through, ethnophilosophy, and that I find strangely behind the revolutionary appearance of the popu-list discourse of our new critics is the ideology of group domi-nation or, more precisely, of a certain idea of the group imposed by a handful of intellectuals and rhetoricians, the ideology that crushes the individual, and by the same token promotes all forms of fascism and neo-fascism from the most subtle to the most vul-gar. What is at stake today in the critique of unanimism is, on the one hand, the possibility for our people to evolve, to transform themselves by overcoming, through an autonomous movement of transcendence, the multiple weaknesses that made their defeat by the West possible at a time in history. At issue on the other hand is the status of the individual in modern African societies, the question of democratic liberties, and in particular of freedom of expression. I cannot prevent anyone from seeing in this double need a "struggle for domination." It has to be added, however, that this struggle, if struggle there is, does not oppose, as it has been believed, "professional philosophers" on the one hand and the "popular masses" on the other, but takes place for now between in-tellectuals each as "acculturated," as "westernized," as petit bour-geois as the other. The political stakes of this "struggle" concern, in the final analysis, the fate of our people. It is, however, not clear

that the best way to ensure this fate is to speak the mystifying language of ethnophilosophy to the people. For precisely as Gramsci said "only truth is revolutionary." (Hountondji 1982, 67)

This, therefore, was how a debate that grew more intense with the publication of the book and the articles that followed developed immediately following the publication of the *Diogène* article. It was the opposite of a healthy debate: it was a polluted, highly ideological debate in which the analysis of personal motives took the place of arguments, and rhetoric that of proof. It is understandable: it was too much to hope that such a long practice, and deeply entrenched reflexes such as those informing the discourse of ethnophilosophy, could be questioned without provoking violent reaction. Some people, we saw earlier, had a thesis to defend, a degree to justify, or a career to tend to. Others had strong convictions and could not understand that these could not, in all sincerity, be shared. I had to operate on this terrain, and, when I could, pay back in kind. However, beyond these angry polemics, beyond this passion that our anglophone cousins sometimes thought very French,[9] the force of the controversy and the persistence of criticisms were also indications of problems and difficulties that I had perhaps underestimated in the beginning. These had to be taken into account, and after having cleared the misunderstandings, their merit also had to be examined and responses given to them.

6

Rootedness and Freedom

1. The Time for Rereadings

I never seriously believed that my father was mortal. So when he died on August 20, 1983, things fell apart around me. It took me two years to come to terms with this fact, during which time I produced nothing. I was content with just publishing, occasionally, earlier studies. It was partly thanks to my close and not-so-close relatives, to this extended family that, with friends, remains one of our rare privileges in Africa, that I was finally able to accept his death. In spite of this I have really never believed that he is dead. Wiredu was, in truth, quite right to have teased me about my relation to Kagame; I now know how gods are born.

In my hotel room in Montreal, G., who for once had accompanied me on my travels, had a nightmare; she woke up weeping. She had recently seen father on his hospital bed. I pick up the phone, call J. and E. at home: we had left young F. with them, and I wanted her to go visit with her grandfather. In Cotonou, it was already dawn. I would call again an hour later,

I said to myself, but on the phone, calling me twenty minutes later, was J. He would rather go there himself. He breaks the news to me; it happened the night before. I give him some instructions and put the phone down.

I will not say what I did next. But on that morning of August 21, the Seventeenth World Congress of Philosophy was going to open at the Montreal Convention Center. The International Federation of Philosophical Societies (FISP), under the aegis of UNESCO, organizes this congress every five years. Thanks to the gracious consideration of some members of the organizing committee, including Alwin Diemer, Director of the Institute of Philosophy at the University of Düsseldorf in Germany, and outgoing President of FISP, I had been invited to give one of the plenary lectures scheduled to be delivered on August 27 at the formal closing session, which was under the chief patronage of the governor-general of Canada. As usual, I had not finished preparing my paper. I was counting on the muses to inspire me, once I started to speak, in what I anticipated was going to be one of the best improvisations in my life, never suspecting for a moment that it could, on the contrary, turn out to be the most catastrophic stammering I would ever have.

I went to the conference center. I saw Venant Cauchy, the dynamic president of the organizing committee, who, at the end of the congress, was elected president of FISP for the next five years. Understanding and sympathetic despite the tensions of last-minute preparations, he listened to me. He got me a room, where I locked myself for two to three hours to finish writing my paper. I gave it to Alassane N'Daw who graciously agreed to deliver it. I took leave of my friends, and G. and I took the first flight to Paris and then to Cotonou.

Written in these circumstances, "Pièges de la différence" (The pitfalls of difference) is probably the most conciliatory text that I have ever produced. I did not simply restate the critique of ethnophilosophy, I also tried to clarify, update, and relativize this critique, in a real effort to understand and be fair, as much as possible, to the ideas of the opposing camp. I noted in passing, following Fr. Smet, that the French title of Tempels's work *La philosophie bantoue*, was a questionable translation. The Dutch title *Bantoe-filosofie* could very well have been understood as: philosophical thoughts on the Bantus, in which case "philosophy" would not have appeared "as a reality given *in* the culture studied, but as a reading grid, an interpretive model freely chosen by the analyst." Moreover, Smet's work had provided for a better understanding of the political context of *Bantoe-filosofie*, as did the Flemish Franciscan friar's polemics on behalf of Africans whose rights were being violated by the Belgian colonial administration. Given these new facts, certain criticisms had to be qualified.

Similarly, the counter-critique of the critique of ethnophilosophy, this "learned ethnophilosophy" about which I was so joyously ironic, appeared to me from then on, "if one set aside the rhetorical flourishes in which it draped itself . . . as the necessary reminder of an ancient truth, namely the impossibility of any absolute novelty in the sphere of thought, the necessity for any human project, even, and especially if it wants to be innovative, to be rooted in the concrete soil of a tradition."

The time for re-readings had therefore arrived. I had to reread Tempels, and with him all the literature on ethnophilosophy, in a quest for something other than what it thought it could offer us: "not some philosophy buried deep down in our collective unconscious, . . . but the elements for an objective assessment of the constants in our cultures, with a view to evaluating this millenary heritage freely and critically." Alexis Kagame, Kwame Nkrumah, and Senghor could all be read with "new eyes and be appreciated";

> our cultures themselves could be studied patiently, methodically, in order to discover, on the one hand, their rich contradictions, the

great alternatives and the historic choices which have made them into what they are today, and on the other, their enduring aspects, their material and spiritual constants, all this un-thought which constitutes our common heritage, and with which we must entertain, here and now, a free and critical relationship.

2. Linguistic Relativity and Philosophy

a) *From Herder to Whorf*

I do not know the circumstances in which the editorial board of *Etudes philosophiques* decided to devote a special number to African philosophy. They wanted an article from me for this number. I used this as an opportunity to focus on a certain number of readings that I had been able to carry out thanks to a fellowship from the Humboldt Foundation in Germany. I had studied German for two months at the Goethe Institute in Mannheim. I knew just about enough to be able to work alone, subject to unremitting work and a tireless curiosity. Unfortunately, I failed to take advantage of this unique opportunity by electing, for the rest of my stay, to communicate in other languages with my German hosts who all understood English, and sometimes even French, by accepting almost all the invitations to various international symposia outside of Germany, and by regularly escaping to Paris every other weekend. I bitterly regret this today. Still, I knew enough German to be able to read in the original, albeit slowly, works by Herder and Wilhelm von Humboldt, and by two or three commentators, supplemented by available French translations, including *Introduction à l'oeuvre sur le kavi*, which had just appeared. It was also during the same period that I discovered or rediscovered in French, or in the English original, the writings of Sapir and Whorf.

I was therefore able to return to Kagame's work with a renewed appreciation for his linguistic relativism.[1] Ntumba

Tshiamalenga had defended this relativism in a number of papers that had attracted a lot of attention in Zaire, linking it to German philosophy of language and, gradually to the Sapir-Whorf hypothesis. I noted, for my part, a real convergence between Herder's and Humboldt's inspiration on the one hand, and that of the Rwandan philosopher on the other, a man who was clearly unaware of the former, never quoted them, and preferred instead to use as his model the Aristotelian doctrine of categories of being. I praised Kagame who, with great perceptiveness, had clearly seen, two years before Emile Benveniste's celebrated article, all that Aristotle's categories owed to the Greek language. I was surprised, however, to see that rather than recognize Aristotle's failure, and by the same token, the futility of any project that seeks to establish an inventory of metaphysical categories from a specific language, the Rwandan philosopher's only reaction was, on the contrary, to carry out the same type of analysis, using his own language, Kinyarwanda, even if it meant later proposing a table of correspondences between his four categories and the standard list of Aristotle's ten categories established by scholasticism. Entrapment in the particular: that is the pitfall. Aristotle fell into this trap unwittingly. Kagame, in his turn, fell into it, knowingly and freely (Tshiamalenga 1973, 1977, 1981; Hountondji 1982).

b) Relativity and Relativism

Rejecting this approach in the name of a demand for universality that seemed, and still seems to me, to be the foundation of all thought, I nonetheless drew a lesson from it. This lesson was clear: the particular exists, and it must be recognized. However, rather than shutting up oneself in it, it should be acknowledged the better to live through, contextualize, relativize, and, if possible, transcend it. From this point of view, Wiredu's approach seemed healthier to me. The Legon philosopher[2] distinguishes between *tongue-relative* (or *tongue-dependent*) and *tongue-neutral statements*,[3] that is, propositions that are only meaningful within the conceptual space of a particular language or family of languages, and those whose meaning exceeds these limits. The habit of African philosophers to think mainly—or exclusively—in European languages inevitably leads them to give credence to notions, problems, and positions that, in some cases, would be untranslatable in their own languages, given that they are intimately linked to the semantic fields of European languages. Translation is therefore a decisive test. It reveals what, strictly speaking, cannot be universal, being unthinkable in the target language. The untranslatable is the false universal, the relative that masks itself as universal under cover of the particularities of a language.

Wiredu also recognized, like Kagame, the fact of linguistic relativity. But instead of an apologetic use of it, he makes a coldly critical and polemical use of it. Instead of erecting the semantic particularities of African languages into a system, he warns against the false universality of western philosophical themes. His appeal for a return to African languages is not an invitation for self-entrapment in those languages, but through work on them, for a true conceptual decolonization. That is the meaning of his slogan-like appeal at the end of his paper: "Fellow African philosophers, let us learn to think in our own languages!" (Wiredu 1984).[4]

In truth, Kagame in his own way launched the same appeal. I agreed with him in this respect. But I considered this a *political* struggle. What was in question here, in fact, were the shortsighted language policies of our neocolonial states. On the other hand, I found it unnecessary, indeed highly illusory, to try to ground this struggle for an alternative cultural policy in metaphysics. I did not think it necessary to project on so solid a position philosophical arguments that were so shaky. There again, I readily defended the autonomy of politics.

c) *Anonymous Thought?*

That is not all. After having resolutely resisted, throughout this article, all the arguments in favor of linguistic relativism, after having emphasized the limitations of this position, and shown that it could only be meaningful, at best, "in the most guarded of formulations," and that it could not, in any case, be used to demonstrate "the existence, in so-called traditional Africa, of a 'philosophy without philosophers,'" I suddenly dropped my guard, and effected a leap in the conclusion. I made a big concession by asserting rather abruptly, without any advance warning in the article's arguments, that: "There is indeed thought: anonymous thought, thought without a subject, as it were, logical and coherent in its own way, implicit and binding, forcing in advance choices and minimal orientations on every individual approach."

It is as if I had suddenly gone to the other extreme, without any warning, as if after having denied for a long time that there could exist thought without a thinking subject, after having defended against each and every one the idea of intellectual responsibility, I did a complete roundabout turn to now acknowledge what I had hitherto rejected: namely that the subject is not first, that it is always constituted from an original passivity; that consciousness is not originary, and that the individual is to a certain extent a product.

I had just discovered the fine pages by Marc Augé on the logic of collective representations, and what he calls "the ideo-logic" of lineage societies, an example of which (from the Ivory Coast) he brilliantly analyzed. I referred to it, and willingly acknowledged that comparative linguistics could contribute to knowledge on the ideo-logic thus understood.

The concession I made, however, was only a move. These representations which exist prior to the *cogito*, this pre-formed thought that structures and informs responsible thought in every way possible, does not only exist in *lineage* societies. It is also found, inevitably, in industrial societies, beyond the turbulent history of doctrines and theories. On the other hand, and above all, these representations cannot, under any pretext, be taken for a philosophy. On the contrary, the ideo-logic is, by way of an hypothesis, "the implicit horizon of all possible forms of discourse—quotidian or learned, mythical or rational, religious or profane, philosophical or non-philosophical, scientific or crazy, etc." By identifying it, one also identifies by the same token "that *against which* a philosophy must, if need be, be fashioned or refashioned."

Not only is the ideo-logic not a philosophy, but a study of it does not derive from philosophy either. Rather, it derives from the sociology of collective representations; a discipline, which, with the help of other disciplines—for example linguistics—would have the job of patiently and methodically reconstituting the invisible context of all present thought.

So I did not give up on the idea of responsibility, any more than I did on that of liberty to which it remains wedded. I, however, took more seriously the context, the intellectual and cultural environment in which this liberty is exercised, the complex heritage that is transmitted through education, and that predisposes us to prefer certain forms of behavior to others, certain objects to others, independently of our choices and will, and to which it behooves us to give new meaning, depending on our expectations and demands.

"In a word, there is thought, certainly; but the real problem is what to do with it, how, starting from it, and if necessary working against it, we are to think lucidly here and now, far from any romantic complacency, in the heart of the immense drama through which our societies are going."

d) *The Other Side of the Mirror*
Once this leap was made, I never looked back. Ethnophilosophy has reasons that are sometimes good reasons. I had to learn

to listen to them, acknowledge their relevance and due legitimacy. The collective culture, like the legitimate pride of belonging to a human community whose values one initially accepts, had to be taken seriously; it had to be admitted that individuality is fashioned from this basic personality, even when the latter is later challenged by the former. In a sense, it is true that these ideas are self-evident. If I was silent about them for so long, it was because to me, deep down, the need for rootedness was so obvious that it was better to emphasize the other need: liberty and responsibility. But this was to misjudge the context. This was to assume as over a mental decolonization that was still unfolding, one that wanted us to insist relentlessly on these elementary truths that are important to life, but which colonial arrogance had tried to ruin. It was to forget that self-confidence, the collective pride of being oneself, was the least shared of things in a postcolonial milieu. I learned, or rather re-learned, that at my expense, so much so that after having replied to the attacks against me point by point, or as a friend said, after having fought them off blow-by-blow (*point/poing*),[5] I had to come back to the question of rootedness in its relation to the critique of ethnophilosophy.

Attempting to define, at the end of "What Can Philosophy Do?," the tasks of the African philosopher, I had already acknowledged that after the first task of critique and ideological clarification, and the second of study and deepened understanding of that which is best in the international philosophical tradition, the third task was "a paradoxical one consisting in moving out of philosophy" in order "to contribute to a resolution of the real problems that are masked by the pseudo-problems of the reigning mystification." In this context, one had to move into the field of the social and human sciences themselves, to undertake in those areas, "positive research into African thought in its social, economic and political contexts, and from the point of view of its different trends, contradictions, evolution and changes." Only such a study could finally persuade the skeptics that have been induced into error by the dominant rhetoric (Hountondji 1981, 68–70).

Four years later I still believed in the necessity of such an inquiry.[6] Better still, such a study should no longer merely seek to combat ethnophilosophy on its own ground by holding up, against its static reading of facts of culture a more historical reading, but it should show why and in what sense the ethnophilosopher is correct. It should pay attention to cultural constants, to those continuities that up to then had monopolized all intellectual curiosity, and which had both to be recognized and put in context.

I have never been able myself to devote the necessary time to this type of fieldwork. I nonetheless kept abreast of current research. I recognized the problem, I acknowledged the legitimacy of an approach that privileges the constants of a culture, without however losing sight of an essential imperative: to emerge from and keep one's head "above water," as it were, and put this intellectual material in perspective rather than being stuck in it. I tried from then on to hold on to both ends of the stick—the empirical and the transcendental—realizing fully well that there is freedom only for he who can accept himself and come to terms with his roots, but that, inversely, roots have never been, have never been meant to become, a prison house—neither in Africa nor elsewhere.

3. The Particular and the Universal

a) *What It Means to Speak*
In the spring of 1987, the French Philosophical Society gave me the redoubtable honor of inviting me to give a lecture. I had just been made a program director at the International College of Philosophy at rue Descartes. I was in Paris to conduct a two-month seminar, I believe. Jacques d'Hondt, the

then-president of the association, heard about my appointment. With his colleagues, he decided to invite a philosopher from Africa for the first time.

On March 23 in the Michelet Amphitheater at the Sorbonne, I could not help thinking of Robert Niamkey, of his sarcastic remarks and his learned variations on the theme of the *agrégation*. Putting aside the *ad hominem* character of his remarks and their malice, I found in his sarcasm an indirect echo of my own preoccupations, and almost a distorted version of my critique of extraversion. I had come back to this critique in my Montréal lecture, where I warned intellectuals—and especially philosophers from Africa—against, among other "pitfalls of being different," the search for "international consecration" at all cost—as if this were an end in itself. I did not think, however, that one had to fall into the opposite extreme of refusing all exchange, or the sharing of experiences. I was all the more convinced about this because to me, the problems were in the final analysis all the same, the stakes identical, or very close, from one culture to another.

The identity of these stakes was the theme of my paper. I had titled it "The Particular and the Universal." From the outset, I showed the extent to which the contemporary intellectual debate in Africa—clearly illustrated in the quarrel about ethnophilosophy—was, when examined closely, a new and original version of the ancient debate between Socrates and his many adversaries described by Plato, such as Protagoras, Georgias, or Callicles. Like sophistry, African relativism is strictly speaking irrefutable. Stating as an ethnophilosopher, "To each people its philosophy" is no different from what Protagoras stated in another historical context: "Man is the measure of all things." And it is well known that neither Plato nor Aristotle was really able to refute Protagoras's position; both were satisfied with merely stating their own intellectual choices and basic, fundamental positions.

These positions—which are expressed, in their way, by logical principles, and in particular the principle of contradiction—are in the final analysis, a wager for communication. Language must be possible. Society would be impossible without this continuous possibility to talk and understand one another, and without the acceptance by everyone of, among other constraints, the obligation to use the same words to designate the same things. Coexistence presupposes interlocution, and the golden rule for any such interlocution is univocity. Aristotle wrote: "Not to signify one thing, is to signify nothing" (Aristotle 1993).

The quarrel of ethnophilosophy was, to me, nothing but the contemporary manifestation of this struggle for meaning. The issue at stake was not just African, any more than the significance of the philosophical reaction to sophistry can be circumscribed to Europe or ancient Greece. We are all concerned by this debate where, in the final analysis, "serious theoretical and methodological questions, ideological and political issues, in the deepest sense of the word politics, meaning the global vision that—beyond immediate concerns—we have of the destiny of our societies, and more generally of humanity," are at stake.

b) Kwame Nkrumah's Draft Thesis

"Ethnophilosophy" was not, as I had believed, a new word. The term suited my needs perfectly. I used it in a polemical sense to show that a certain type of discourse that had generally been seen as philosophical, and which was clearly exemplified in Tempels's work, was derived from ethnology and had to be seen as such. I warned against a certain widespread confusion of genres that had ended up imposing as a norm in Africa what was in fact a deviation in relation to the dominant theoretical practices in Europe, even in the original cultures that promoted this so-called norm (Hountondji 1970).

It so happened that around the same period, a year after the publication of my *Diogène* article, Marcien Towa used the same word with the same derogatory connotation, the same critical aim, and the same call to substitute this dominant form of philosophizing in Africa with intellectual practices that were much more coherent and responsible (Towa 1971). The result is that the word "ethnophilosophy" is, to this day, still wrongly considered, by many people, a neologism made up by Towa and Hountondji.

I realized very early on, when re-reading *The Autobiography of Kwame Nkrumah*, that the word was older. In this book, published in 1957, the first head of state of independent Ghana relates in passing how in February 1943, after receiving his master's degree in philosophy at the University of Pennsylvania, he immediately registered at the same university for a Ph.D. in "ethnophilosophy." The word was used with no further explanation. Thus, "ethnophilosophy" was the name of a subject—an academic discipline—and could, in the eyes of the author, be understood without explanation. The dissertation, however, remained unfinished until 1945, the year Nkrumah left for England.

Referring to this occurrence of the word in my Paris lecture, I hypothesized that it must have been created either by Nkrumah himself, or by people in the intellectual circles to which he belonged, in reference to those disciplines today called the ethno-sciences. Ethnophilosophy could only be "the extension into the field of thought in general of the inventory of the corpus of so-called 'primitive' knowledges, [an inventory] that had been undertaken at the time for plants and animals by two pilot-disciplines: ethnobotany and ethnozoology" (Hountondji 1987).[7]

Not only the word, but even the critique of Tempels's project was not new. I had mentioned in the *Diogène* article Césaire's reaction in *Discourse on Colonialism* that I had described as political, and that of the Belgian logician Franz Crahay, which was more theoretical. I also mentioned this time the commentary of the Ugandan poet Okot p'Bitek, and all the controversies that developed, in Belgium as well as in the former Belgian Congo, around Tempels's book when it was first published. The articles by Fathers Boelart and Sousberghe, in particular, were remarkable to me. These precursors had to be adequately recognized and their contribution sufficiently acknowledged while one attempted to continue their work, enrich it, and bring out all its consequences in a rigorous manner (Césaire 1972; Crahay 1965; Bitek 1964; Smet 1981b; Boelart 1946; de Sousberghe 1951).

I concluded, therefore, that neither the word "ethnophilosophy" nor the critique of the corresponding project was new:

> What is new . . . is neither the word, nor the thing, but the conjunction of the word and the thing, the use of the word "ethnophilosophy" no longer to designate just a project or a science to come, but a discipline already in the process of formation, one whose first attempts quickly aroused doubts as to its viability and its theoretical basis; a use, as a result, that was no longer prospective and optimistic, but retrospective and polemical. (Hountondji 1987b)

c) *Questions on Ethnoscience*

Once the record had been set straight, all that was needed was to analyze the meaning of the word in Nkrumah's writings. I could not do that, because I did not have any text by the author on his draft thesis, let alone on the thesis itself, at my disposal. However, having accepted that the word referred to the generic concept of ethnoscience, I could not avoid questions about the relationship between ethnophilosophy and other specialties in the ethnosciences, and between ethnophilosophy and philosophy: in short, the question of the status of ethnophilosophy and its articulations with other disciplines, its ideological and theoretical justifications, and its scope and limits.

To answer these questions, I had to concentrate first on the notion of ethnoscience. The simple enumeration of the disciplines, which today claim to be specialties in this field, will be enough to bring out an essential ambiguity. If ethnoscience defines itself, in the most traditional of cases, as an inventory of pre-existing knowledges—in the sense that ethnobotany, ethnozoology, ethnobiology, and ethnomineralogy are understood as the inventory of knowledges of such things as plants, animals, living things, or minerals in oral cultures—there is another use of the word to mean, instead, the application of a given science to the study of a particular aspect of so-called primitive culture. So ethnolinguistics is not the study of some primitive linguistic theory, but rather, the application of linguistics, as a modern science of language, to the language practices in oral cultures. Ethnodemography is not the inventory of preexisting demographic forms of knowledge, but the application, to so-called primitive peoples, of the theories and methods of investigation bequeathed by demography. These two uses are irreducible and their ambiguity cannot be eliminated: "In the first case, ethnoscience defines itself as a descriptive science, as knowledge born of pure restoration, as knowledge on knowledge. . . . In the second case, on the contrary, one is dealing with active knowledge, knowledge on a practice that is presumed unreflexive, a construct for which only the ethnologist is accountable" (Hountondji 1987b, 151).

The ambiguity thus recognized forces us to ask a question about the site of knowledge. Where, in reality, is located the knowledge? Where does this theoretical construct, from which a *corpus* is built, take place? In the culture being studied itself? Or in the work of the ethnologist? Allowing for the fact that nothing is ever simple, and that, apart from extreme cases, an ethnoscience is necessarily both the original construct of an

ethnologist and an account of preexisting "indigenous theories," and that "in truth the knowledge is nowhere, or rather it
is everywhere, on both sides," in continuous motion, moving
ceaselessly "from the culture-object of the study to the learned
corpus of the anthropologists, depending in certain cases on
new theoretical work," I nonetheless held on to my question,
clarifying it in the following terms: "How, according to which
modalities, why, to whose benefit is this circulation of knowledge taking place? Where does it all end? Is there total circulation, . . . final return to the point of departure or, on the
contrary, dispossession, drainage with no return?" (Hountondji 1987b, 152).

These questions, which, I assumed, were far from Nkrumah's
concerns, seemed unavoidable to me. To complete the clarification of the critique of ethnophilosophy, it was necessary to
interrogate the status, the scope and the limits of ethnoscience,
its theoretical and practical effects, its real relationship to the
knowledges of which it claims to account, and its place in the
general economy of modern science. One had to examine the
origin, modes of functioning, transmission of "traditional"
knowledges and other so-called "indigenous theories," their
place in the overall scheme of intellectual and technical practices in Africa and elsewhere, their real relationship to official
science in and outside of ethnoscience, the role they can play
today and their future.

I could not, either at the lecture itself, or in the published,[8]
expanded version of it, draw all the consequences of this inquiry on the uses of the word "ethnoscience."[9] My comments,
however, were clear. The semantic imprecision was an indication of an unresolved question, or, more precisely, of a repressed question. By identifying this question as I had done, I
found, in the heart of ethnoscience in general and its specialties, the same ambiguity I found in ethnophilosophy. I showed
that the critique of ethnophilosophy could be extended to

ethnoscience. I suggested, besides, that from one to the other, the logical relation was probably the reverse of the chronological relation, and that ethnophilosophy, which appeared late on the scholarly scene after other ethnosciences, logically came before them. A daughter of ethnoscience, ethnophilosophy, in a sense, would be its mother. It is "the common foundation of the ethnosciences, the system of theoretical and methodological, indeed, of ideological presuppositions that makes them possible, and by extension it is the site where all the difficulties of ethnoscience crystallize and become visible to the naked eye" (Hountondji 1987b, 153).

I did not go much further. I could not do any more glossing on a thesis I had not read. William Abraham, the author of *The Mind of Africa*, and, according to some malicious rumors, the co-author of Nkrumah's *Consciencism*, assured me in 1982 that the thesis did exist.[10] It was only recently, in May 1996, that, during a brief visit to Stanford University, I was shown—in confidence—the copy that Abraham himself obtained from the national archives of Ghana, a copy that carries the following warning on the first page "This copy is supplied on the condition that no reproduction of it by any photographic process may be made without the permission of the chief Archivist."[11]

d) Political Bantuism and Its Limits

Thanks to the work of Fr. Smet, the extent of Tempels's involvement in the political struggles of the Congo, and the resulting troubles he had with the colonial administration for his support of Blacks, are today well known. Also well known is the increasingly exclusive place that his religious preoccupation came to occupy in what he wrote after *Bantu Philosophy*—a preoccupation present in the 1945 book—and his troubles, this time with the Catholic hierarchy, over his concern with adapting the catechism. Finally, we know the founding role that he attributed to his approach to all the social sciences, and the importance of scientific concerns: simply the desire to understand (Smet 1977a, 1977b, 1978a, 1981a; Tempels 1948, 1949, 1962, 1979, 1982).

At this lecture, therefore, I could better appreciate the rationale of ethnophilosophy by using the case of Tempels. After the devastating critique by Césaire and some others, and after what could have appeared to others as an unjust hounding of Tempels on my part, I had to attempt some rehabilitation. I tried to do it as best I could. For want of total rehabilitation, such an examination at least had the advantage of recognizing the demand for rootedness expressed by the good missionary and showing how generous he was, while enabling me to identify, in a clearer manner, the shortcomings of his discourse.

Contemporary with *Bantu Philosophy*, Tempels's *Ecrits polémiques et politiques*, re-edited by Fr. Smet, first appeared— anonymously—in 1944–45 in an Elisabethville daily, *L'essor du Congo* (Tempels 1979). The very title of these articles, five in all, are revealing: "The Philosophy of Rebellion," "Social Justice," "Native Administration, The Solution: An Administrator in Each Territory," "On Native Marriages," "For the Legal Protection of the Marriages of Our Natives."[12] The Franciscan missionary was clearly linked, in the colony, to a group of progressive Belgians, who did not hesitate to denounce the brutality of the methods used by the administration, and who pleaded for a social policy with greater respect for local traditions. This is the group that wrote the collective volume *Dettes de guerre*, to which belonged, among other judges, E. Possoz, the author of *Eléments de droit coutumier nègre*, quoted several times in *Bantu Philosophy* (Possoz 1943).

Thus, it was no longer possible to repeat without nuance Césaire's sarcastic remarks: "Decent salaries! Comfortable lodging! Food! These Bantus are pure minds, I tell you, etc.," For if there were in the Belgian colony any officials of goodwill who supported the social demands of the poor and destitute,

Tempels was certainly one of them. The project that informs *Bantu Philosophy* is simply an extension of this political position. Beyond the material demands, Tempels believed he discerned a more profound demand: that of the Congolese for respect, as African and Black, for their culture. The missionary believed that to satisfy this demand and rehabilitate an undervalued Bantu culture, in order to get everyone to respect the humanity of Blacks, in a context where the dominant ideology locked them up in irreducible difference, he had to start by showing the system of coherent values and norms to which they made constant reference, and which informed the daily conduct of the average Congolese.

However, that is not all. There is clearly a category of Blacks that Tempels could not stand: that of the so-called *évolués* (acculturated). From the beginning to the end of *Bantu Philosophy*, he tries to discredit them, presenting them as deracinated people who had become strangers to their culture, "embittered people," "materialists who had lost their bearings in their ancestral culture, without any foothold in western thought and philosophy," "men of *lupeto*, of money" who were ignorant of all other values, and remained slaves to childish magical practices, "under the thin veneer of the ways of the whiteman."

I could not fail to see the way in which the missionary hounded the *évolués*, precisely that social group from which the initiatives for the popular revolts and uprisings came, and from which the "agitators" of the rebellion and the leaders of the protest movement were recruited. To me, this was no coincidence. There is a type of "progressive position" that starts by isolating and discrediting the natural leaders of a movement, and then erects itself in their place, as the spokesman of the "masses." The group around *L'essor du Congo* practiced this kind of progressive politics: protective of and paternalistic with the oppressed populations, it could not tolerate the emergence of authentic local leaders, or the development of a radical political discourse that could, in the long run, endanger the colonial system. The avant-garde of the rear-garde: this, undoubtedly, must have been the way in which these "Europeans of good will" (considered highly subversive by the colonial administration) appeared to the local leaders of the protest movements.

These limitations are clearly reflected in Tempels's philosophical discourse, in his rather peculiar understanding of the Bantu system of thought. For it is not enough to note, on the mode of a simple report, and with a false air of objectivity, the Black's belief in the superiority of the White, and still less to see in that the logical consequence of a collective ontology. By claiming to give metaphysical consecration to what, after all, is nothing but a prejudice that can be fully explained in historical terms, the missionary unwittingly revealed the political implications of his theoretical positions.

The ambiguities of political "bantuism" appeared quite revealing to me. Beyond the particular circumstances of its development, beyond the Katanga of World War II and the immediate post-war period, beyond the little book by Tempels that, in a certain way, theorized these positions, I saw a discourse that was at once progressive and conservative in ethnophilosophy. From that I drew a number of lessons on the ambiguity of cultural nationalism: it can function, in periods of resistance, as a powerful factor of collective mobilization, but can also constitute, outside of these periods, a major obstacle to consciousness by society of the real contradictions and cleavages within it.

e) A Trapped Alternative

I was also attentive, of course, to Tempels's other motivations, and to what they could teach us about the ethnophilosophical approach in general. The African intelligentsia for a long time only knew *Bantu Philosophy* out of its context. Recent research has highlighted the missionary's later activity, as a charismatic prophet and founder of an original movement, within the Catholic church in Katanga, known as *Jamaa*, a Swahili word for family (Fabian 1966, 1971; De Craemer 1977; Smet 1977). I was able to read short articles such as "Bantu Catechism," "The Christianization of Pagan Philosophies," the two volumes of *Our Encounter*, of which only one had received church approval, and some other texts where Tempels develops a kind of mysticism of communion and brotherhood (Tempels 1948, 1949, 1962). As a result, it became obvious that the study of Luba "philosophy" in the 1945 book was only a step, a detour to better respond to questions that derived from an other discipline: missiology, the meditation on evangelization and missionary activity. Tempels was already quite clear about this. Bantu philosophy could not remain as it was or be sufficient onto itself; it had to be transformed and raised to a higher level.

"Bantu civilization will either be Christian or be nothing at all."

This set of circumstances did not detract from the theoretical scope of the study itself. The hypothesis of a collective philosophy was better, all things considered, than that of the pre-logical mind it tried to refute. Ethnophilosophy as a discipline gets its meaning, and all its scientific interest, from the fact that it advances an alternative to the theory of the pre-logical mind. This alternative, to my mind, was flawed. But then one had to begin by acknowledging its merits.

f) Regaining Creativity

What, then, is the alternative? How can one philosophize in a responsible way avoiding, on the one hand, the danger of naïvely and uncritically accepting the many prejudices often unwittingly promoted by western philosophical discourse, and, on the other, of entrapping oneself in a so-called African collective philosophy that can only further extend one's alienation?

In the conclusion to my presentation at the Michelet Amphitheater, I called for a way out of the false alternative between what could be called Eurocentrism and, following the African American trend, Afrocentrism: "The choice is not between a eurocentric view and another that could be called African, but between two modes of dealing with culture in general, be it European or African culture, two different approaches, one of which, taking the part for the whole, seeks to reduce, simplify, force into a unity, and the other, in contrast, is resolutely pluralist, mindful of internal contradictions and the powerful dialectic that is at work in all cultures" (Hountondji 1987b, 169).

I restated here, but in a more incisive manner, the conclusions of my article "What Can Philosophy Do?" and the one on linguistic relativity (1982b). In conclusion, I returned to the question—on the site of knowledge—I posed earlier in the paper, no doubt in awkward and unclear terms. I discerned in ethnophilosophy a form of "knowledge by construction, which wants to be taken for knowledge by restoration." In truth, the "site" of philosophy is always the singular author, and the culture studied is always the pretext, "the supporting base (more imaginary than real) for this arbitrary construction."

The comparison with the ethnosciences had, therefore, enabled me to open up the debate. Whether it is about philosophy or science, the real issue is not to claim an African heritage by seeking refuge behind this acknowledgment—real or fallacious—of preexisting knowledges. Beyond such an acknowledgement, the essential thing is to put in place a strategy of reappropriation of what is still valid in these knowledges today, with a view to resolving the problems of the day more effectively.

"The facile apologia for our systems of belief and other collective representations cannot but lead to an impasse. What we need to do today is not to make a spectacle of our cultures to others and to ourselves. It is to embark on a renewed creativeness on all fronts, in all fields."

4. The Field of the Thinkable

a) *A Science of Collective Representations*

So one had to exist first, to take root in a tradition, but at the same time, one must be capable of keeping one's distance from—and entertain a critical and free relation with—that cultural tradition. One must invent again and again. I came back to this theme three years after my lecture at the Michelet Amphitheater. The *Genève-Afrique* team, on which I had some friends, wanted to publish a book on Robin Horton. I did not know much about the work of this British anthropologist who had chosen to settle in Nigeria, and had distinguished himself with a resounding article entitled "African Traditional Thought and Western Science." His ideas had provided the substance for a long debate in Sodipo's journal, *Second Order*. I felt sympathy for this man whom I also saw as a victim of all kinds of unfounded assumptions. I had the pleasure of meeting him at the University of Ife in 1978 during the debate with Yaï. He understood French, and so I preferred to stammer in French than in English (Horton 1967, 1970, 1982; Horton and Finnegan 1973; Horton et al. 1990).

Readily agreeing to contribute to this volume, I titled my article "For a Sociology of Collective Representations." This was the period when, alas, I had little time to do intellectual work, when I could only manage short editorials and, occasionally, a few analytical articles for a bimonthly journal that, with some friends, I had started some months earlier, at the height of the struggle against the dictatorship. I was, however, able to state the main point of my comments in a few pages: "A pseudo-science [*une fausse science*] is not always, or necessarily, a bogus science [*une science fausse*]. To say that ethnophilosophy is a 'pseudo-science,' is to express reservations on its status as a science, but not necessarily on its content; it is to highlight the gap between what it is (ethnography) and what it claims to be (philosophy), and to draw attention on the consequences of this gap" (Hountondji 1990b, 187).

The cultural facts described by ethnophilosophy can be, and often are, real. There is therefore no question of denying or refuting them as facts, only of interpreting them differently—in a critical and non-apologetic manner. Summarizing and complementing "Occidentalism, Elitism," I referred to the counter-critique of the critique of ethnophilosophy. I recalled the main arguments of this counter-critique, the misinterpretations and the other question-begging aspects that ground it, and the weaknesses—serious and unacceptable then as they are now—of an approach that seeks to absorb philosophy into ethnology. But I found no difficulty in accepting, in conclusion, the important fact on which the ethnographer has always insisted: that in every society there exists "a minimal consensus, a small common denominator, a spiritual cement that ensures the system's cohesion." The study of these collective representations belongs to sociology or anthropology. Today, such a discipline can be constituted with extant material. Work such as that of Robin Horton, Ruth Finnegan, Jack Goody, and Marc Augé is proof of what can be done in this area (Goody 1977; Augé 1975, 1977, 1982). However, something more needs to be done: to formally institute this new science of collective representations, and once the apologetic temptation has been removed, to define its tasks and general objectives, which are to help the societies concerned to be more fully conscious of their shortcomings and of the means to overcome them, "so as to promote this indispensable quality, and necessary condition for freedom: lucidity."

b) The Study of Oral Texts

Yaï was correct on this point—I had not given oral texts all the attention they deserved. Nonetheless, I had always recognized their rightful place in the grand project of restoring any given intellectual heritage. Work such as that of Wandé Abimbola, to cite one example, is vitally important. I had never ruled out, *a priori*, that philosophical texts could not be found in the oral tradition. I have always stayed quite clear of what one of my compatriots called "the fetishism of writing" (Dossou 1994). The real problem, however, is a problem of method, the same problem we saw earlier: whether it be collective representations or a *corpus* of oral texts, the apologetic approach leads nowhere.

The problem is basically the same when we move to written texts. Yaï, after many others, is not wrong to caution against the cult of the book, and the widespread bias according to which anything written is necessarily true. The knowledge of authors, the familiarization with the written tradition, the endless work of reading that in the main constitutes the job of the philosopher, all this will only be meaningful if the reader succeeds, from the beginning to the end of this adventure, of this immersion into the thought of others, to remain himself.

This relativization of writing does not, however, remove the question of its relation to orality, and of the respective roles of one and the other not only in the transmission, but in the construction of knowledge. In his fine book, published in the United States in 1992, Kwame Appiah, among many other creditable things, restated why this was an important question (Appiah 1992). I remain convinced that the most ardent apologists of orality would not have wasted so much time and energy defending their views in writing, if writing seemed as superfluous as they say. To transcribe the oral *corpus* of texts, record them, give them permanence through the use of all sorts of techniques—and contemporary culture has put a wide array of these techniques at our disposal—is an elementary precautionary measure for anyone who values them sufficiently to want to see them survive, even if it is necessary to warn against the temptation of considering such a transcription as an end in itself.

c) The Duty to Consistency

The field of the "thinkable" is vast. Everything is material for thought. Everything interpellates us. A symbol is food for thought, as Ricoeur pointed out. But we do not only have symbols. It is possible to gain knowledge from any object or field of objects, from any area of experience, from all and everything. But for there to be authentic knowledge, it is still necessary for this development never to be knocked off course, and for the thinkable to be effectively thought, understood, put in perspective in light of clear practical and theoretical projects, of ends that have been set out in a responsible manner.

I came back to this theme more recently in the United States. The Central Division of the American Philosophical Association (APA) invited me to give a "distinguished lecture" at its annual meeting in Chicago in April 1996. The Fulbright Program, which was celebrating its fiftieth anniversary, financed the program. The culprit in all this? My Nigerian colleague, Malam Olufemi Taiwo of Loyola University in Chicago, whose excellent article on the conditions of production of knowledge in Africa I had read, and whom I later finally met in Toronto in 1994 (Taiwo 1993). I was given the option of choosing my topic. I found nothing better to choose than a meditation on the theme "Intellectual Responsibility: Implications for Thought and Action Today."

I do not think I convinced many people, especially among the many supporters of the "anti-foundationalism" that is currently fashionable in the United States. Abiola Irele had alerted me to this possibility the previous year, when I proposed

"The Challenge of Universality" as a topic for a lecture in his department at Ohio State University. Irele found my universalist convictions very French, or at least, quite European, in the sense of continental Europe, and was surprised that I was not particularly worried by the questions raised by Rorty (1979). In any case, I knew what I was stepping into in Chicago when I attempted to demonstrate, once again, the extent to which the demand for proof was, to me, constitutive of philosophical rationality.[13] I indicated the way in which the idea of intellectual responsibility had run across the history of western thought from antiquity, and the extent to which it was at the heart of any philosophy of consciousness. I explained that this same idea could in reality be found in all cultures, and that it provided the basis for the critique of ethnophilosophy. In Africa today, like everywhere else, we need to develop responsible thought in the most literal sense of the word: a thought that can give an account of itself, and can stand up to the test of debate. Above all, we need, beyond the individual co-optation of such and such a scholar in the field of discourse that is entirely controlled by the North, to put in place an ambitious strategy of appropriation of knowledge by our own societies.

Chapter 7

Reappropriation

1. Extraversion in General

By extending its critique to all the ethno-sciences, ethnophilosophy enabled the articulation of a critique of extraversion in general. It is not only Africa's philosophical production, but also all its scholarly and theoretical production is read more outside Africa than in Africa. It is the entire range of African writings in French, English, or Portuguese that function like products for export, like airport art objects: those monsters of ugliness offered to tourists in our transit lounges, and which, for want of anything better, they buy a few minutes before takeoff.

A discourse always adapts a bit to its addressee. Ethnophilosophy has always seemed to be a type of discourse born of a situation where the speaker, Western or African, knows that he is in every case addressing a non-African public, and that he can set himself up, without great risk of being contradicted, as the spokesperson of the people in question. The exclusion of the latter from the potential public has clear and concrete results on the content of the discourse, the choice of themes and methods, the framing of and the ways of dealing with, the problems.

What is true of ethnophilosophy is also true of ethnoscience. An inventory of so-called traditional knowledges, it is, like ethnophilosophy, a discourse in the third person that seeks to give an account, in the absence of the populations concerned, of what they supposedly know. The question of the value of this knowledge or of its degree of coherence and objectivity is eliminated. It matters little whether these modes of thought are correct or wrong; all that matters is that they exist. Gone is all the researcher's anxiety, his uncertain struggle with truth. The ethnologist is a happy man. He leaves things as they are. Before or after his observations, the world is what it is—always opaque and inhuman. And in this world, knowledge remains an immense, collective heritage wholly administered by the North.

I was struck, reading Samir Amin, by his use of the notion of extraversion. In contrast to a self-sustaining economy that is capable of counting on its own resources, of being self-reliant by ensuring its own internal coherence, the underdeveloped economy is entirely turned to the outside, organized and subordinated to the needs of the ruling classes in the industrial capitals. Samir Amin's approach, which he shares with all the so-called neo-Marxist economists, had the merit of putting into historical perspective and, consequently, of making sense of what is commonly called underdevelopment and taken for an inescapable fate. Underdevelopment has not always existed. It has an origin and a history: the history of the gradual integration of subsistence economies into the global capitalist market through, for the most part, the slave trade and colonization. What has always characterized it, and still characterizes it, beyond the succession of acts of formal independence, is precisely the extroverted nature of its economy;

an economy that aims above all to furnish raw materials to and, secondarily, outlets for the manufacturing industries massively located in the center (Amin 1968, 1974, 1973, 1990; Frank 1969; Wallerstein 1989).

I was therefore able to connect this view to the critique of extraversion developed in *African Philosophy* and subsequent articles. Intellectual extraversion henceforth seemed to me a result, indeed a particular feature of economic extraversion. Of course, the former could not be reduced to the latter. More than ever, the temptation of economism had to be resisted, and the specificity of scholarly activity, in relation to the process of production and exchange of material goods, acknowledged. Nonetheless, I found an approach that situated the production of knowledge in the general context of production *tout court* and that examined North/South relations in the field of science and technology on this basis both illuminating and heuristically fruitful.

Albert Tévoèdjrè, then Assistant Director-General of the International Labor Organization, and Director of the International Institute for Social Studies in Geneva, gave me the opportunity to develop such an approach when he asked me to participate in a seminar devoted to a collective reflection on a new ethics between the North and the South. He himself had just published *La pauvreté, richesse des peuples* (Poverty: The wealth of peoples), and his last chapter, titled "Pour un contrat de solidarité" (For a contract of solidarity), set the tone. I found his approach rather optimistic, but I accepted the suggestion. The result was an article entitled "Recherche théorique africaine et contrat de solidarité" (African theoretical research and a contract of solidarity) (Tévoèdjrè 1978; Hountondji 1978a).

Since then, I have returned to the subject several times: in Katmandu (Nepal), where in December 1979 I took part in a "meeting of experts" [*sic*] organized by the Division of

Philosophy of UNESCO on the conditions for an endogenous development of science and technology; in Constance, where I was honored by the Conference of University Rectors of West Germany with an invitation to its annual congress in May 1982, and where a participant found (correctly, I must admit) my paper on "Science and Culture in the Development Process" much too "emotional" for this type of meeting; in Paris, where another UNESCO conference on "The Exchange of Knowledge for Endogenous Development" gave me the opportunity in October 1983 to present a paper on "The Exchange of Knowledge as Unequal Exchange"; in Dakar in December 1986 at a small workshop chaired by Samir Amin in the framework of a program of the "Third World Forum," where I titled my contribution "Scientific Dependence and the Problem of De-linking"; in Cotonou, in the context of a research seminar that I had initiated at the Université Nationale du Bénin in 1987–88 on endogenous knowledges, and that was a prelude to a series of presentations by colleagues from the Faculties of Humanities, Science, and Medicine; in Cérisy-la-Salle, France, at a colloquium on, and around, Georges Balandier in June–July 1988, during which I made a number of remarks titled "The Situation of the African Anthropologist: A Critical Note on a Form of Scientific Extraversion"; in Porto-Novo, Benin, at a colloquium organized in September 1989 by the Council of Europe, in liaison with a nongovernmental organization (NGO) run by Albert Tévoèdjrè, who had by then returned home after his retirement from ILO; in the United States, where in November 1989 I was obliged to say these things in English, but where the public's great interest in the question, especially at the Center for Africana Studies at Cornell University and at Ohio State University, largely compensated for this effort;[1] more recently again in Toronto, where the African Studies Association had invited me in November 1994 to deliver the second M. K. O. Abiola lecture at its annual meeting. Some of these papers have remained unpublished to this day. Some have been published. The seminar on endogenous knowledges, which benefited from the financial help from the Council for the Development of Economic and Social Research in Africa (CODESRIA), led to the publication of a collective work in 1994.

2. A Rampant Pragmatism

Rereading these articles and papers today, I find them strangely repetitive. It all happened as if I was constantly afraid of not being heard. I did not hesitate to repeat entire paragraphs or to use the same expressions from one paper to the other. The audience, it is true, was never the same, and I was always careful to refer to previous papers and articles in which I had expressed myself in the same terms. For the truth is, it is difficult to put these things differently, or to be satisfied with stating them once, in passing, in the occasional, purely academic analysis. It is difficult to stick to merely making the observation about scientific dependence and to believe that with it the matter is settled, and all work is over. The seriousness of the observation necessitated corrective action, and as long as such action was not effective, I had to repeat the observation tirelessly, verify it, and compare it, if need be, with other approaches.

What struck me at first was the similarity between the structure of economic activity and that of intellectual and scientific activity in the colonial context. One thing missing in each case, an essential step in the process, is *transformation;* the transformation of raw materials into finished products in the first case and, in the second, the theoretical treatment of data, the production of general statements and other scientific results from initial information. The only question at this stage was *how* the transformation takes place, what it consists of, what its stages and moments are, and what its results are. These questions did not arise in the case of industrial manufacture, an activity that had the advantage of being a set of visible operations transforming matter into matter. The work of the researcher on the other hand was subtler. What is the raw material made of in this case? What is the nature of the result? Which operations regulate the transition from one to the other, and how do these operations link up?

On these questions I had my hypotheses. They were based on a rejection of empiricism, and on the lessons of contemporary epistemology. Science is not reducible, in my opinion, to a collection of data and to empirical observation, any more than it can be confused with the industrial object that is only its technical by-product. Science is an activity whose goal is to produce true statements. It is such an activity that was seriously lacking on the ground in the dominated territories. Never would this lack have appeared as a lack to an empirical observer who would have misunderstood the originality, the absolute centrality of theory—be it based on experimentation or not—in the total process of knowledge production. "The colony lacked laboratories as it lacked factories": I owe it to my reading of Husserl, and to a certain familiarity with rationalist and constructivist views of science to have been able to make such a simple and really commonplace observation.

Once this theoretical void—the scientific equivalent of the industrial void—is acknowledged, and the fact accepted that colonial research was regulated from the start by the same "colonial pact" that structured the economy, it becomes possible to get a fair picture of the development that has taken place ever since. On that point again, I remained skeptical. Samir Amin had shown convincingly, using the Ivory Coast example, that it was possible to have "growth without development." I wondered whether the recent increase in universities, institutes, centers, and other research infrastructure did not derive from the same phenomenon. In this field too there was growth without development. I started drawing attention to certain indexes or signs of extraversion and scientific dependence. From one article to the next, the number of pointers might change, but the conclusion remained the same: we need to put in place in Africa an autonomous scientific project that is inseparable from a new project of society.

Decolonization did not put an end, as a matter of fact, to this international division of scientific labor that seemed to reserve theory and invention for the metropolis, and to condemn colonies to the status, first, of huge reservoirs of facts and raw data, and second, testing fields for the results of metropolitan inventions. The system had quite simply become more refined. The former colony no longer exports completely raw facts. It can already start to subject them to some theoretical processing that will facilitate the work of the metropolitan laboratory. But the equipment used is still made in the center; the documentation, the basic scholarly literature is still massively concentrated in the center. The research institutions at the periphery are very often only annexes to the mother-institutions situated in the center. Finally, and above all, whatever the performance of the researchers in the periphery and their institutions, their work aims at giving answers to questions that are of prime interest to the mother-institutions or the industries that sponsor them. Yesterday like today, "the theoretical demand comes from elsewhere just like the economic demand. Theoretical demand here means the set of questions that determine and shape the collection of data, the theoretical tradition from which at a certain point in time emerges, as a result of many complex factors, this set of questions" (Hountondji 1978a, 4).

I was particularly emphatic about this type of dependence: the dependence at the level of the problematic. The science practiced in the former colonies "remains dependent—right up to its problematic and the questions that it raises—on the scientific concerns and, by extension, on the technological and economic needs of Europe." Research in agronomy provided a good example of this alienation. In most African countries, this sector of research, one of those that mobilizes the most important financial resources of the state and the private sector, remains massively oriented toward the improvement of cash crops (oil and oil products, coconut palms, cotton, etc.), at the expense of food crops on which the majority of people depend for their nourishment. Research in this area is therefore directly in the service of an export economy. An effort at reconversion has undoubtedly been made since independence. In none of the countries concerned, however, has this effort led, to this day, to a reversal of the trend.

The example seemed revealing to me: theoretical extraversion "finds its ultimate explanation in economic extraversion." Better still, it teaches us something about "the economic origin of the most complex scientific questions, the material genesis of theoretical questions. . . . Even the most 'abstract' disciplines are not exempt from this constraint. Any scientific problematic, any set of theoretical questions, is linked, directly or indirectly, to theoretical and extra-theoretical conditions of possibility, and it always ends up revealing, as soon as it is interrogated, its complex links with politics" (Hountondji 1978a, 7).

I owed this idea that a theory is defined more by its *problematic*, than by the answer that it proposes, to my reading of the work of Bachelard, and to a certain familiarity with Althusser.[2] Yet, what I observed was that in Africa no effort was made to formulate new and original questions. To answer the questions of others, such seemed to be our destiny. We had become, ourselves, the fiercest defenders of this idea. Our governments openly professed, in matters of science policy, a narrow utilitarianism that put African researchers on guard against the attraction of fundamental disciplines, and that guided them on the contrary toward the applied sciences. It was necessary to react, it is true, against the temptation of easiness that regularly pushed a disproportionate number of young school graduates toward the Faculties of Law and Economics and the Humanities. But our educational systems had made a false start in any case. Rather than tackle the evil at its roots by imagining other systems, we accepted the status quo and only tried to reform it. We formulated our criticisms and, where necessary, our reforms in terms that clearly showed that we had ourselves, without knowing it, internalized an international division of labor that quite simply freed us from thinking. The big thing we thought was development; and to achieve it all that was needed was to apply the inventions of others. Where then has this rampant pragmatism, this shortsighted policy, led us after forty years of independence?

The progress accomplished seemed very limited. We witnessed, indeed, an exceptional development of the descriptive sciences that have no other function than to improve data collection, a function to which the continent seems condemned, and which is at the opposite end of theoretical research. At the bottom end can be seen the development of a number of applied sciences. Between these two poles on the other hand theoretical research is either absent or of recent origin and is still, to this day, very young. Put differently, it is this theoretical research that reveals most clearly what our scientific activity is today: a distant appendage of Western science.

In all, I detected four essential weaknesses that prevent African scientific practice from truly serving African peoples: financial dependence vis-à-vis the outside world, institutional dependence vis-à-vis the laboratories and research centers in the North, the primacy of vertical South-North scientific exchanges over South-South horizontal exchanges—and this leads to the extraversion of local scientific publications—and finally, as a result of this extraversion and of institutional dependence, intellectual subordination to the questions and expectations of the learned public in the West.

Concluding this 1978 article, I called for a "scientific revolution." It was essential, beyond the obsessive fixation on applied and descriptive research, to first recognize the unity of science as a collective project, and the necessity for Africa to be engaged in a responsible way in this historic adventure. What we need is a "radical appropriation of theory, . . . a methodical effort to give ourselves the material and human resources for an autonomous research that is master of its problems and themes."

3. Variation on "Distance"

a) *The Ambivalence of a Word*

The company, Air France, at the time offered its in-flight passengers an illustrated magazine called *Distance*. I had just arrived in Europe for a period of research of at least a year. I was thirty-eight and endured the separation from my family with difficulty. Denyse de Saivre, who wanted to publish a thematic issue of *Recherche, pédagogie et culture* with the title "Vers un nouvel ordre éducatif" (Toward a new educational order), asked me to write an article. I found nothing better to write on than to theorize my frustrations of the moment. I entitled my article "Distances" (Hountondji 1980a).

I used this word in a double sense. Distance meant first of all geographical distance, the distance from which our scientific, economic, and political dependence is organized. But it was also in a positive way the fact of taking a distance, the result of a process of distancing, of establishing a theoretical perspective that is necessary to constitute the scientific object as object. Both a counter-value and a value, distance in the first sense is painfully experienced as a constraint; in the second, on the contrary, it is a conquest of the mind.

The two meanings were in my eyes linked by a "subtle logic." The passive acceptance of distance in the first sense, the acceptance of marginalization as a fatality or a quasi-natural fact can only produce in the field of research a vague descriptive and empirical discourse, "that evacuates from theory, the theoretical proper." Inversely, to overcome dependence, it is necessary to start by seeing it, and to see it, it is necessary already at a more modest level to learn to ask the right questions by questioning things that apparently are self-evident, and by refusing any arbitrary limitations on one's horizon.

b) A Distant Science

So, first and foremost, theory is elsewhere, in the sense of being physically distant. The best universities, the best equipped laboratories, the most authoritative scientific journals, the greatest libraries, and the most credible publishing houses are massively located in the industrialized countries. The result is that the African researcher in search of the sacred fire—the material and intellectual tools of knowledge that is— has to move elsewhere. I was particularly emphatic on this physical constraint that seemed as unavoidable to me as the Husserlian *hylè*, the need to go round a tree in order to see all its sides, the necessary spread in time of a sensible perception. So, more than a privilege or a delight, I saw in this form of cultural tourism one of the constraints characteristic of research at the periphery, and unknown to the metropolitan researcher.

There again I showed how a detour into history could shed light on the present situation; how from the outset the "colonial pact" regulated scientific as well as economic life; how it was necessary to consider the plunder of raw materials destined for the factories of the metropolis as a basic fact; how the collection of new facts and new scientific data, carried out on the same model, has contributed to the enrichment of existing sciences, indeed to the creation of new ones such as "tropical" geography, agriculture, medicine, anthropology, and its derivatives. Just as integration into the world capitalist market had resulted in the destruction of the equilibrium mechanisms of subsistence economies, without in return giving rise to self-sustaining industrial development in the periphery, so, I suggested, integration into world scientific research had resulted in arresting the development of preexisting systems of knowledge, all the while pushing the periphery to specialize in subaltern roles in relation to the global process of knowledge production.

I noted, of course, the changes that have taken place since decolonization. They still seemed purely quantitative and ineffective to put an end fundamentally to extraversion.

c) *Erudite Informants*

I remained fascinated by this extraordinary phenomenon: the internalization of dependence, the tendency to accept and adopt, even in Africa, the erroneous reasoning that tends to justify the system or to make it appear inevitable, just like the mechanisms that tend to perpetuate it. One of these mechanisms is the acceptance by the African researcher himself or herself of this division of labor that leads them, unlike researchers in other countries and regions, to specialize exclusively in the study of local realities at the expense of theory. It is undoubtedly legitimate in any discipline to try to know the natural and social environments to better control them. However, excess in this direction, shutting up oneself in the particular, can only result in precluding a real knowledge of the particular as particular. The detour by way of theory is indispensable: "in science as in love, rushing can be fatal; you must know how to wait and to prepare the way."

I observed, incidentally, that this wholesale Africanization of scientific discourse was more pronounced in the social sciences and the humanities than in the natural sciences. I, however, found the reverse attitude of a certain number of mathematicians, physicists, chemists, and other African practitioners of the natural sciences quite naïve in simply believing that their disciplines were universal, and that they did not have to worry about their relationship with the African environment. Abstract universalism is no better than frenzied particularism, for it eliminates an essential question, namely, that of the ways and means of inculturation, of the collective appropriation of the universal both as result and project.

Knowledge of how to sail—to take off from the present—is therefore necessary. But this must be done with a view to returning to it better armed to situate and understand it. The African historian must be able to be interested as much in the conditions of industrialization in nineteenth-century Japan as in the military conquests of Samory Touré, or in the slave trade and colonial invasion. But if one studies Japan it must be to give oneself a possible model among others, and to better know, through contrast, the history of one's own society.

Thus, theory is elsewhere in a second sense: far from this elementary empiricism, this fascination with the immediate, this self-imprisonment that feeds the usual droning. I went further. If the demand for an "African" specialization were uncritically accepted by African researchers, they would be condemned to remain, at worst, the auxiliaries of Western Africanists and other Tropicalists, and, at best, learned informants in the service of an accumulation of knowledge at the center of the system.

As soon as it is produced, our knowledge is extorted, stolen from us, and integrated into the world system of knowledge administered and managed from the great metropolitan capitals of the industrial countries. However far we go along this path, it will never lead us to an autonomous technological and economic independence, whatever the secondary advantages that we may be able to get indirectly from this alienated activity.

The reality is that we are encouraged by everything to pursue this path. I noted in passing the guilty complacency of certain doctoral committees in great metropolitan universities that took pleasure in awarding "summa cum laude" or "cum laude" doctoral degrees for dissertations that are frankly mediocre. They do this convinced that the recipients would not pursue a career in the country itself, and that at best, after their defense, they would go on to "serve in some bush university and work diligently to reproduce the system."

4. The Impossible De-linking

a) *An Unequal Exchange*

Compared to these two articles, neither the May 1982 conference in Mayence before German rectors, nor the article written for UNESCO as a prelude to the world conference of ministers of culture held in Mexico contributed anything really new (Hountondji 1982, 1984). On the other hand, by inviting me to "a meeting of experts" organized at its headquarters in Paris from October 5 to 7, 1983, on "The Exchange of Knowledge for Endogenous Development: A Study of South/South Cooperation," UNESCO gave me the opportunity to outline my thoughts (still unpublished) on "The Exchange of Knowledge as Unequal Exchange." Applying to the field of knowledge concepts elaborated by Arghiri Emmanuel in his analyses of trade relations (Emmanuel 1977), I suggested that the problem of knowledge transfer was badly framed, and that beyond the North/South transfer—in which the international community saw a possible remedy to underdevelopment—the existence of a massive South/North transfer of knowledge first had to be acknowledged. This transfer not only took the form of data and raw facts, but of systems structured at different levels, and of the considerable contribution of contemporary underdeveloped countries to the constitution of Western knowledge (Emmanuel 1977).

b) *Linguistic Dependence*

I returned to this question a year later in a text entitled "Les langues, la science, le développement" (Languages, science, and development), which served as an introduction to a series of studies prepared for UNESCO by a group of African colleagues on the theme *Langues africaines et échange des connaissances* (African languages and the exchange of knowledge). This series of studies has, unfortunately, remained unpublished to this day.[3] I made use of the opportunity to assess the enormous weight of the ethnocentrist heritage behind the West's discourse on languages, starting from Plato's *Cratylus* to the dawn of the twentieth century, through the *Grammaire de Port-Royal*, the discourse on the noble savage and the invention in the eighteenth century of a linguistic evolutionism that preceded the biological evolutionism of Lamarck and Darwin, to the work of Wilhelm von Humboldt in the nineteenth century and other lesser known works like those by August Schleicher, rediscovered and commented by Patrick Tort, and Lévy-Bruhl's idle chatter on the languages and counting systems of "lower societies." I noted, with Louis-Jean Calvet, the will-to-"glottophagia" that has characterized the language policy of colonial powers, especially France. I could therefore appreciate, in contrast, the intellectual courage and the degree of imagination that it took Cheikh Anta Diop to dare affirm in 1954, in such a polluted ideological climate, the possibility and the necessity of developing African languages as vehicles of more elaborate scientific thought.

What interested me most in writing this introduction was to show how the imperialist discourse on language had wound up being internalized by the colonized and how our language practice in Africa was also extraverted and as subjected to external models as our scientific practice. What interested me was to show how this situation called for a double break: an imaginative and courageous policy—indispensable if we are in the end to promote self-sustaining development in the field of science and culture as well as in that of the economy. I strongly shared Maurice Houis's opinion that "the time for an advocacy of African languages had long gone, and it was now time to formulate, right up to the smallest technical details, an entirely new project." I personally did not think that it was necessary either to waste time refuting the mountain of prejudice accumulated in the course of the centuries against African languages or proving the need to valorize these languages. Like Cheikh Anta Diop it was necessary to get to work immediately (Calvet 1974; Diop 1974; Houis 1971; Humboldt 1974; Tort 1980).

c) Underdevelopment and Culture

The fullest text that I wrote on this topic probably remains "Scientific Dependence and the Problem of De-linking." The workshop organized by Samir Amin from December 1 to 4, 1986, in Dakar brought together around him five or six people under the aegis of his association, the Third World Forum, and the United Nations University. The theme was the cultural dimension of development. He himself had just published *De-linking: Towards a Polycentric World* (Amin 1990). I did not want to miss this unique opportunity to discuss my concerns and the way in which I used the conceptual tools that he had developed to express them. I started by frankly stating how from philosophy I had developed a strong interest in economics, how from a critique of cultural extraversion, I had encountered another concept of extraversion worked out in the context of underdevelopment theory.

Also, I quoted at length the testimony of a "survivor"—for this is how this French biologist came across to me—who had received part of his education in the University of Dakar, and who a few years later, lucidly and honestly acknowledged the extent to which " a good education" had been a disaster. This well-conceived education, 60 percent of which was provided by Africans who were "good teachers, good pedagogues," led, in spite of all its good qualities, to a feeling of dependence on the places where science was really practiced. Jacques de Certaines certainly did not expect in writing these lines to see them used, dissected, and exploited by a keen reader in support of his own hypotheses on scientific extraversion.

The study then went over things that I had already said about the "colonial pact" in science, emphasizing in particular the need for detachment and perspective if particularities are to be correctly situated in their context:

> To forget Africa in order to put it in better perspective, to de-link mentally, to be detached for strategic reasons, to step out of the situation, . . . to aim at the universal is a surer way to understand the particularities of the African context than the short term utilitarianism that from the outset imprisons the African researcher in a scientific ghetto on the pretext that only these particularities are of interest to him. In matters of research, the straight line is never the shortest path, and nothing lasting is possible without a detour through theory.

The diagnosis of current scientific activity in Africa also remains fundamentally the same. Seven signs, seven visible indicators of the alienated nature of this activity are clearly listed down, instead of the four in the 1978 article. But the basic shortcoming remains the weak development of theory and, more seriously still, the internalization and the ideological defense, by Africans themselves, of the international division of scientific labor.

d) The Force of Paradigms

By noting this internalization, by observing the ravages of "an abjectly technocratic, utilitarian and pragmatic ideology that thinks it can avoid theory, without negative consequences," by taking note of "the intellectual poverty, the simplistic empiricism imposed by the colonizer," I acknowledged as a result the "fecundity of models." I had reflected, some years earlier, on Thomas Kuhn's *The Structure of Scientific Revolutions* partly to prepare a paper—"Les paradigmes scientifiques: Problèmes d'une formation optimale" (Scientific paradigms: The problems of optimal training)—that my Moroccan colleague, Mohamed Allal Sinaceur, director of the philosophy division at UNESCO, had asked me to give. Presented at a "meeting of experts" in Katmandu, Nepal, from December 10 to 14, 1979, on the theme "A Philosophical Examination of the Conditions for an Endogenous Development of Sciences and Technology," the paper remained unpublished. I could therefore use some of its material for the Dakar presentation (Kuhn 1962).

The fecundity of models, this internalization by the researcher of colonial norms that to this day regulate the international division of scientific labor, creates in Africa what Kuhn would call "normal science"—one founded on the acceptance of paradigms and theoretical and methodological models that carry consensus within the scientific community. The image of science that emerges from Kuhn's account seemed different to me both from the empiricist vision defended by Bacon and the dialectical, and slightly romantic, vision by Bachelard. Bachelard presents the researcher as a perpetual questioner, and modern science as a process of continuous break with and renewal of ancient conceptions. It is animated by a "philosophie du non," and is engaged in an endless process of re-working of concepts, of objectification and of critical incorporation of ancient doctrines into new ones. As a matter of fact, Bachelard's analyses are more appropriate to science in crisis, "extraordinary/abnormal" science, as Kuhn calls it, than to normal research that is much less voluntaristic, much more routine and conservative.

I concluded for my part that the researchers of the Third World could no longer afford to accept paradigms unquestioningly or be satisfied, uncritically, with practicing "normal science," because this normality is their crisis. To put an end to extraversion, to break with a marginalization that constantly siphons the results of their research to the center of the system, thus depriving their societies from benefiting from this work, they had to "get involved" in the extraordinary, to maintain a critical relationship with the paradigms in each discipline and to raise new problems that, directly or indirectly, are linked to the preoccupations of their societies. Deep down, without being any more Bachelardian than I was Kuhnian, I found that the work of the American epistemologist only gave an account of the routine of the daily work of the researcher in the Center, and of the scientific conformity that is indispensable, in the industrialized countries, to any real progress. But I also found out that this same conformity, transposed to the Third World, would be a disaster. The researcher at the periphery had to be more critical, more demanding, and more radical. Rather than these "cleaning-up" operations that characterized " normal science" in the Center, and that aim essentially at fitting facts to paradigms, the researcher in the periphery has to go back to the paradigms themselves, to interrogate them and, if necessary, to challenge them.

e) De-linking from the System?

However, beyond the individual researcher, what I was calling for with all my heart was a scientific revolution that could inaugurate "autonomous theoretical practices in liaison with an overall effort by our societies to master their destiny." Samir Amin had shown that strictly speaking, the only way out for the Third World, and especially for Africa, was to opt out of the global capitalist market, "to de-link." But he had hardly made this statement than he himself indicated the difficulties and limitations involved: it is impossible to opt out of the system.[4] De-linking, if this term is accepted, could not be synonymous with autarchy or with a withdrawal into the self. To interpret it in such a simplistic or literal way can only lead to an escape into fantasy, as can be observed, for example, in Islamic fundamentalism. Unable to opt entirely out of the world market, it, however, remains possible to subordinate its demands to those of the domestic market and to the imperatives of a self-centered economic program that would respond in priority to the consumer needs of the local populations. How can this demand for de-linking, which can only be relative, thus be translated in the area of scientific activity? I had been struck by a strange text by Arghiri Emmanuel, *Appropriate or Underdeveloped Technology?* published a few years earlier together with a debate between Celso Futardo, Hartmut Elsenhans, and the author (Emmanuel 1982). I was in total agreement with Emmanuel's case against an anti-technicist ideology, which, on the pretext of saving the Third World from the ravages of a cutting-edge technology destructive of local values, would want to see this world settle for a technology made to measure. It is a little like saying: Third World, stay in your place; developing countries, stay where you are! I was myself shocked by this indefensible political paternalism. I was no less surprised to see how, from these premises, the author arrived at singing the unqualified praises of multinational companies, seen to him as the vectors of cutting-edge technologies; and how he was silent, in the circumstances, on the role of these multinationals in the development of what he himself called "unequal exchange." To me, Celso Futardo was perfectly justified in his reaction in finding this approach quite naïve, and in showing that the theoretical and political problem of dependence could not be so easily ignored. The real preoccupation of Third World economists, at least the most lucid among them, concerns the "unpacking" of the imported technology and its integration within the host culture. An appropriate technology presupposes a proper understanding of the theoretical and practical knowledge, and the origin, of the imported product, an understanding that alone can give that culture the ability in the long term to invent new techniques itself.

Opting out of the system, therefore, first of all meant developing a science policy. Too often, new African governments are content with merely administering as well as they can the research institutions left in place by the colonizer—institutions that are only the local subsidiaries of metropolitan organizations: Institut français d'Afrique noire (IFAN), Institut de recherche agronomique tropicale (IRAT), Institut de recherche sur les huiles et oléagineux (IRHO), Institut de recherche sur le coton et les textiles exotiques (IRCT), or the Institut français du café, du cacao et d'autre plantes stimulantes (IFCC). Very often they are satisfied with changing the legal status, the administrative machinery, the management system, and of course, the management teams of these subsidiaries without an in-depth change of the content and shape of their research programs, or even of their goals and real role in the global process of knowledge production.

And yet it is precisely this role that must be changed. To me, the most urgent need was to shake up this division of tasks that condemned us in Africa to import indefinitely the results of research done elsewhere. We must ourselves develop basic research, promote invention in all its forms, and put in place "a research system[5] that is comprehensive and independent."

5. The Appropriation of Knowledge

a) *Aiming High and Far*
At this precise point a new theme quite naturally became obvious, that of appropriation: "We must aim high and far, we must try to appropriate, in the long term, all the scientific heritage

available in the world, . . . develop it ourselves in a selective and independent manner, depending on our real needs and our programs." I observed in passing that the scientific and technological treasure today controlled by the North was in fact created over the centuries by the participation of all peoples. On the other hand, "a methodical and critical re-appropriation of, and an effort to update, what is usually called traditional knowledge" must accompany this vast movement of appropriation. There again we could in part learn from the theoretical heritage of the West, which has undertaken for several decades to make an inventory of our *corpus* of precolonial knowledges, through these specializations in ethnology that are the ethno-sciences. That such an inventory is inscribed as a matter of fact in an ideological horizon that is unacceptable to us is obvious. This situation does not, however, free us from undertaking a critical assessment today of the ethnosciences. It frees us even less from interrogating directly, methodically, critically, responsibly—beyond this assessment of the ethnosciences—the *corpus* of knowledge itself; from testing it, verifying it, checking its validity when possible, and integrating it into living research.

I regret—a little—that this study has never been published. However, I was able to return to the subject shortly after in a paper read again in Dakar in January 1988 during a colloquium organized by an old friend and accomplice, the Dean of the Faculty of Humanities. *Genève-Afrique* agreed to publish this text that I had titled "Collective Appropriation: New Tasks for a Science Policy." In this article, I returned to the analysis of scientific dependence distinguishing this time nine indicators of extraversion instead of four or seven, and proposing *a contrario* nine tasks (Hountondji 1988b).

b) *With the Eyes of Others?*

One of the great observations made at the discussions in Cerisy-la-Salle, in the presence of Georges Balandier, touched on the development over the past number of years of an ethnology of the near, as opposed to an ethnology of the distant, and the remarkable tendency of contemporary anthropology to open up new terrains of study in the very heart of industrialized countries. The question at that point was to assess the consequences, the theoretical and methodological implications of this repatriation of anthropological research. I was preoccupied, for my part, with another question, clearly close to the first, but in fundamental ways totally different from it. The question was: What happens when anthropology is taken over by "exotic" societies themselves, when Africans, for example, undertake to study their own societies or cultures by applying the canons and paradigms of anthropology? To answer this question, it was first of all necessary to acknowledge the role of the illiterate or semi-literate informer as the unavoidable assistant of the metropolitan anthropologist in the colonial era; to recall how the shift gradually took place from the uneducated informant to the more and more educated one, to the point where every educated African had become, as a matter of course, a potential informant for the colonial administrator, the missionary, or the anthropologist. I had to recall how certain schoolmasters of the period—asked by the administration to describe "native customs" (indispensable tools for the courts)—ended up being carried away by their subjects, and producing works of great interest that are still read today.[6] The African anthropologist seemed to me, in the best of cases, like the direct descendant of these top functionaries of the period. The anthropologist enjoys the work, and sometimes achieves a level of competence that is equal to the best that is produced by Western peers. But that changes nothing, however, from the fact that the anthropologist still finds the largest and most constant readership outside Africa, and therefore has to write first for that readership and take into account its expectations and demands.

From this *de facto* extraversion, at least four consequences arise. The first is the acceptance by the African anthropologist of this quest for the exotic that is at the basis of Western ethnography, the tendency, as a result, to look at oneself with the eyes of the other, and to valorize above all one's own cultural difference. The second is a massively empirical orientation that is content with producing field reports without the slightest attempt at theorization—a practice by which most African anthropologists unconsciously accept the role that has been created for them by the system, and moreover tend to marginalize those among them who try, in spite of the difficulties, to swim against the current. The third is a swing effect that leads to a shift, with no transition, from "this indigent empiricism" to a "speculative debauchery" that consists in projecting *behind* the facts and in the place of a real theory, an arbitrary speculative system, a discourse with an imaginary coherence that explains nothing at all, but that is hastily attributed to the entire society.[7] The fourth, finally, is the university's tendency, in Africa as well as in the industrial, metropolitan countries, to perpetuate this model of scientific practice, thus creating optimal conditions for the reproduction of mediocrity. In conclusion, I pointed to the urgent need for a sociology of science in the countries of the periphery, as a prerequisite for the definition and establishment of an alternative science policy.

The article ended there, but it could have continued, and shown in contrast to the current situation, what in Africa today a responsible use of anthropological knowledge can mean. I however did not go that far. Once I had brought out the need to formulate alternatives, I expressed the desire to return to this fundamental problem one day "if God so wishes." The "directions" indicated in the *Genève-Afrique* article were indeed just that: directions. More thinking was still needed along those lines.

6. Reappropriation

a) From One Continent to the Other

The sixth general assembly meeting of CODESRIA that took place in Dakar at the end of 1988 gave me the opportunity to return to these questions in a paper titled "Research and Extraversion: Towards a Sociology of Science in Countries of the Periphery." It was published in *Africa Development* and a few years later in English in a collection edited by V. Y. Mudimbe (Hountondji 1990c, 1992).

I took delight, shortly after, in reading the book *L'écrivain public et l'ordinateur* by Jean-Jacques Salomon and André Lebeau, which the former had autographed for me in Paris (Salomon and Lebeau 1988). I was, however, perplexed by the idea that in the field of science policy the cart could be placed before the horse, and basic research avoided. Yet the authors themselves were the first to warn against the "illusion of the shortcut." Maybe it would have been enough to simply distinguish, while acknowledging basic research as the premier condition for any process of self-directed research, several levels or possible approaches to the basic; to admit that the latter can be situated miles away from this "free research" to which so many intellectuals are attached, and that it can already be found, in the case of basic technological research, very close to applied research. This embarrassment gave me the inspiration for another paper. Included in the papers of a conference organized in Porto-Novo, Benin, in September 1989 by the Council of Europe in association with the International Association of Social Prospective, this paper was titled "Research in the Periphery: Between the Useful and the Pleasant." Unfortunately, it is again one of those texts that I regret have not been published.

The following month, I accepted an invitation by Kwame Anthony Appiah at Cornell University. Appiah had followed the entire debate on ethnophilosophy very keenly, and had just handed over the manuscript of his fine book, *In My Father's House* to the publisher (Appiah 1992). My paper on "Scientific Dependence in Africa Today," stuttered at the Center for Africana Studies, simply repeated in English, basically for this new audience, my analyses on extraversion. The only interesting fact is that this time I gave thirteen indicators of dependence and no longer four, seven, or nine.

I had also been invited to the annual meeting of the African Studies Association scheduled for November 1989 in Atlanta. I was to speak at a round table on Mudimbe's *The Invention of Africa*, a book that had just been published and that, moreover, received the Herskovits Prize at that same meeting. This time I decided to speak in French before an audience most of whose members in fact understood French. From the speech that I improvised, several people retained, and still love to remind me about it occasionally, an exclamation that I meant to be laudatory, but that could indeed be ambiguous: "Valentin has read everything! He has read *everything!*" I must have let out unconsciously, a feeling that I believed I had only shared with the author himself: namely my regret that he had opted for a certain type of apolitical position, of disengagement from Africa, and that he had not put his vast erudition in the service of some core ideas (Mudimbe 1988).

After Atlanta or shortly before, I had the pleasure of accepting Abiola Irele's invitation for a brief stay at Ohio State University. I delivered the same lecture there that I gave in Ithaca. The text was published shortly after, on the decision of Irele and his friend Richard Bjornson, then editor of *Research in African Literatures* (Hountondji 1990a).

b) *An Excursion into Politics*

This entire period was marked in Benin by great political turmoil. I had thought I would complete, by the first semester of 1989 at the latest, the manuscript of a collective volume on

Les savoirs endogènes: the result of a seminar in the sociology of science that I had organized in the 1987–88 school year for students in the master's programs in philosophy, sociology, and anthropology. I received generous assistance from a team of intelligent and hard-working students led by Maxime Dahoun. They carefully transcribed the tapes, rewrote the texts when necessary, and politely urged the authors who failed to link up with one another, as promised, to do so. In spite of all that, I still had to correct the text myself and, sometimes, write short introductory pieces or transitional paragraphs. I had to verify that the volume was coherent, and to write an introduction—all before sending off the final product for publication to CODESRIA in Dakar, which had given us its support.

My involvement in other activities, especially in the development of the democratic movement that was then in full swing in Benin, left me with no time for this. Then came the National Conference of 1990; my stint in the government shortly thereafter (as minister of education under the transitional regime, then minister for culture and communication, and finally as special adviser to the president); the painful compromises; the cup emptied to the dregs, all in the mad hope that my presence would end up serving a useful purpose until the day I finally realized what I was being used for: to give a kind of intellectual and moral legitimacy on the cheap. At that point, on October 28, 1994, I tendered my resignation.

I had thought that I would be able to find enough time for intellectual work, although I was in government. It is true that through sheer stubbornness, a determination to forgo sleep, and to turn a deaf ear to the many calls to attend scores of meetings that did not directly concern me, I managed to write, with very few bibliographical references that I had no time to look up, ten short, incisive articles over the five-year period. And that is not counting the twenty-five editorials or commentaries published in the bimonthly, *L'opinion*, that I edited. But I would have liked to do more, and more quickly. I would have especially liked to be able to get down to more long-term work, work that demanded more staying power and thus more free time, than these articles. The publication of *Endogenous Knowledge* was delayed for four years; I was only able to hand in the final manuscript in 1993, and the book appeared in 1994.

c) "Savage Science"

I was already looking forward to this publication when in 1993 I arrived at L'Ecole des Hautes Etudes en Sciences Sociales in Paris where Marc Augé, then director of the school, had invited me. One day, Yves Hersant was in his office reading a small collection of talks on Radio France-Culture chaired by and then intelligently transcribed and rewritten by Ruth Scheps and titled *La science sauvage: Des savoirs populaires aux ethnosciences*, which had just appeared. I took down the references. Unable to find the book in a bookstore before taking the plane on the same day, or the following day, I had to wait for my next trip to acquire it. I could not resist commenting on it, and CODESRIA gave me that opportunity by inviting me to a conference organized in Dakar from November 29 to December 1, 1993, on the occasion of its twentieth anniversary on the theme "The Social Sciences in Post-Independence Africa: Past, Present, and Future." My paper was subsequently published in a local daily, *La nation* on December 4, 1993, and then in the CODESRIA bulletin in Dakar early 1994 with the title "Primitive Science:" Direction for Use. It killed two birds with one stone, commenting on Ruth Scheps's book while at the same time announcing ours.

First, I pointed to an obvious difficulty in the very way the conversations were conducted: that of remaining within the subject and treating only "savage science"—understood as the set of spontaneous forms of knowledge prior to, or undergirding, the theoretical constructions of so-called modern science (in the sense in which Lévi-Strauss talks of "the savage mind")— without spilling over into other aspects of cultural life. I also noted the difficulty of treating the subject in a consistent way by effectively isolating substantial *bodies of knowledge*. To me, this double difficulty, this gap between the book's promise and its actual achievement pointed to a fundamental difficulty inherent in the very functioning of oral civilizations. I acknowledged that in these societies knowledge could not be as autonomous, neither could the knowledge of things be as distinct from mythico-religious "knowledge," as in literate civilizations.

I pointed especially to a fundamental difference of perspective between these conversations and *Endogenous Knowledge:* the difference between a speculative approach, which is that of the ethnosciences, and an approach that, in the final analysis, is practical and activist: ours.

d) Myth and Knowledge

With the title "De-marginalizing," the introduction to the book begins by recalling the above analysis on the "logic of extraversion," the force of this system where the accumulation of knowledge is almost entirely managed and controlled by the North, and where the products of intellectual efforts from the periphery are sucked up as soon as they become known, irresistibly caught up in structures (of processing, packaging, storing, and redistribution) that are beyond the control of our societies. The big question raised by this observation was, therefore, to know how, through which means, this logic of extraversion could be broken, and the current scientific, technological, and intellectual relations of production on the world scale transformed.

But what is the relationship with so-called traditional knowledges? It was quite simple: by their real status in the intellectual landscape of contemporary Africa, these knowledges reveal more clearly still than official science the marginalization with which all the sectors of our economic and cultural life have been struck for centuries. Ancestral knowledges are marginalized, devalued, and relegated to a subaltern place in relation to laboratory research that itself is already peripheral in relation to research at the center of the system. Thus, they find themselves at the periphery of the periphery.

From this point of view, the important question is how to demarginalize "traditional" knowledges, to open them up, integrate them into the movement of living research; by which methodologies they could be tested, verified, and as the case may be, proved, or on the contrary disproved; how to separate wholly or partially "the wheat from the chaff," to distinguish the rational from the mythical. How can the valuable and true in these real or alleged knowledges be reactivated and updated? How can they be reappropriated in a critical way? How can the silent coexistence between an institutional and scientific discourse and a so-called traditional discourse be transcended by organizing between the two a peaceful confrontation, and by trying to recreate beyond the current divide, the unity of knowledge? Obviously my colleagues and I did not claim to provide answers to this string of questions. But then the questions still had to be asked. I was struck by two things: on the one hand, by the strange amnesia that casts into oblivion efficient technologies that have been attested to historically and anthropologically, which have had their moments of glory but are today disappearing from the collective memory; on the other, by the close integration of the mythical and the rational in so-called traditional and practical forms of knowledge.

In his fine contribution on "'Traditional' Iron Metallurgy in West Africa," Alexis Adandé, an archaeologist, recalled a slogan that made the rounds in francophone Africa during the campaign for de Gaulle's 1958 referendum: "We are incapable of producing a needle, and yet we pretend to be moving towards independence!" He shows how this slogan reflects a totally false idea about the technological level attained by sub-Saharan Africans several centuries before the slave trade and colonization. He recalls how from the first millennium before the Christian era, not only a secondary metallurgy, consisting in transforming metal into different utensils, but also a most prosperous primary metallurgy, consisting in extracting metal from mineral, developed and thrived in sites that are today very well known. The Nok culture region and that of Ile-Ife, a holy city for the Yoruba people of Nigeria, the Aïr region in northern Niger, Daboya in northern Ghana, Bassar country in northern Togo, Waama country in northern Benin, and many other sites, some of which remained active up to the colonial period in the twentieth century, witness how this lost technology was marginalized, repressed, and rendered gradually inactive to the advantage of the metal industries in the former colonial nations whose products, then as now, continue to be imported in large quantities. Along the same lines, the historian Goudjinou P. Mètinhoué showed, in his contribution "Methodological Issues in the Study of 'Traditional' Techniques and Know-How," how a piece of food technology like the production of distilled palm wine was actively fought by the colonial administration under wrong excuses. "Traditional" pharmacopoeia seemed to have fared better. Simone de Souza gives an account of her investigation among traditional practitioners and other "healers" in her contribution entitled "Fruits, Seeds and Miscellaneous Ingredients Used in the Pharmaceutical Practice of Benin" (Adandé [1994] 1997; Mètinhoué [1994] 1997; de Souza [1994] 1997).

Knowledges exist. Sometimes they are of conclusive practical efficacy, as we have just seen. In other cases, their efficacy is more dubious, or at least the experiences that can vouch for them are less well known, more rare, and more personal. The psychiatrist Gualbert R. Ahyi, the surgeon Henry-Valère Kiniffo, and the anthropologist Gbènoukpo Dah-Lokonon believe they can witness to such experiences in their contributions respectively titled: "Traditional Models of Mental Health and Illness in Bénin," "Foreign Objects in Human Bodies: A Surgeon's Report," and "Rainmakers: The Ancestors' Legacy." However, the contributions by Abel Afouda on "Rainmakers the Point of View of an Hydrologist," by the neuropsychiatrist Comlan Th. Adjido on the "Psychosomatic Medicine and Sorcery," and the numerous questions from the audience finally proved, if it was still necessary, that what appears to some as conclusive proof may not be convincing to others (Ahyi [1994] 1997; Kiniffo [1994] 1997; Dah-Lokonon [1994] 1997; Afouda [1994] 1997; Adjido [1994] 1997).

This is not all. Besides practical forms of knowledge, my colleagues and I wanted to examine the structures of thought and the forms of transmission of knowledge in precolonial Africa. Toussaint Tchitchi's contribution on "Traditional Number Systems and Modern Arithmetic," Victor Houndonougbo's reflections on "Fa Ritual: A Stochastic Process: Understanding the Geomantic Cults of Coastal Benin," Jean-Dominique Penel's paper "Epistemological Reflections on Hausa Zoological Names," François C. Dossou's case for orality in his paper "Writing and Oral Tradition in the Transmission of Knowledge," and Bienvenu Akoha's study of "Graphic Representational Systems in Pre-colonial Africa" all open up, in this respect, some fundamental directions for research.

e) A Wager for Rationality

Let us return to the problem: what is the relation between the critique of intellectual extraversion and the interest in so-called traditional knowledges? The answer is simple. To put an end to extraversion, one should start by taking full and clear responsibility for oneself. The achievement of scientific autonomy, the creation of a self-directed research system presupposes the intelligent, that is, the critical, methodical reappropriation of one's own knowledges and know-how as much as the appropriation of all the available knowledge in the world. From this point of view, there is something incomplete, indeed mutilating, in the attitude of the doctor who, faced with the failure of his treatment, finds nothing better than to ask his or her patient to "return to the village," that is, to consult the "traditional healer," or of the physicist who, once out of his laboratory, goes to consult the specialist services of the "local weatherman" to ensure that such a feast or ceremony dear to him will not be affected by unexpected rain, without at all seeking to understand the reasons for the regular or occasional success of the traditional practitioner and the rainmaker, the mechanisms and functioning, the significance and limits of their art. My hypothesis was that an end had to be put to "these tight compartmentalizations between thought and action, this sort of rupture, this unconscious schizophrenia, . . . the silent coexistence of discourses must be transcended, and we must be able, from one mode of thought to the other, from one logical universe to the other, to effect not a leap . . . but a transition, a conscious, intelligible path whose stages are clearly identifiable."

I thus made a wager for rationality consciously. Such a wager necessitates the establishment in each discipline or group of disciplines of new methodologies that will make it possible to test knowledges, evaluate them, and if possible, validate and integrate them. Maybe it also means, more generally, the construction of an expanded rationalism that would enable the incorporation of categories of fact that had hitherto been excluded from the spectrum of possible facts by the dominant discourse of science. That was only a suggestion, an extreme hypothesis, but I was ready after all, to go to that extent to think through the unity of human knowledge.

It was to be expected: some people have interpreted these new concerns as a retreat from the universalist positions expressed in the critique of ethnophilosophy. Souleymane Bachir Diagne, in whom I am pleased to have found one of my best interpreters,[8] reacted in an article titled *"Lecture de 'La science sauvage: Mode d'emploi'"* (A reading of "Savage Science: Mode of Use"). Charles Bowao returns to and develops this critique in another number of the *Bulletin de CODESRIA*. Bachir Diagne wonders about the possibility of testing endogenous knowledges by separating, as I suggest, the mythical from the rational, or as it were, the wheat from the chaff, in a context where, as it is well known, "a configuration of knowledge—and not only in so-called traditional societies—always presents itself as an organized set of permissible questions, theses, procedures, techniques, assertions, accepted results . . . in which it would be artificial to isolate the scientific from the religious or the mythical." In short, he wonders whether it is possible to do this in a context where knowledge always points to an entire paradigm from which it is inseparable. The second question is why should this de-marginalization of endogenous knowledges be the necessary condition for a break with the logic of extraversion and for the creation of a true system of research, when it is well known how, in recent history, the "countries that have been able to carve out a significant place for themselves in the production and development of the sciences and technology have proceeded?" (Diagne 1994; Bowao 1995).

I will quite simply say in response to the first question that if it has the merit of drawing attention to a real difficulty, this difficulty does not eliminate the need for consistency, the duty to recreate the unity of our thought, to integrate competing, or worse still, parallel paradigms that so often govern our practices and thought processes.

The second question calls for a more complex answer. True, we would benefit from closely examining the experience of "the newly industrialized countries"; of these Asian "tigers" that are so astonishing. True, we would benefit from knowing how these countries achieved "their integration in the international system of research" and, I would add, in the international system *tout court*. But for this inquiry to be useful, its starting point must be our own concerns and needs. We must ask the right questions of these experiences—all of which indeed seem successful. These questions must address not only the economic and technological destiny of these countries and the "recipes" that produced them, but also their cultural destiny, their collective personality, the level of their autonomy and sovereignty, the social relationships in their communities, and various other parameters that have contributed in determining the *quality* of this success.

So it is not just a question of integrating the world system: we have been in it for centuries and our current marginalization is only an avatar of this long history. It is about something quite different: to recapture the initiative at all levels, to gain and regain, within the realities of the present-day world, the independence lost, to enable these margins to become their own center and to participate, actively and responsibly, in the construction of a common future.

If this ideal is shared, then the need will be acknowledged, in the field of knowledge and know-how, for this double movement—indispensable to the construction of a self-centered and intellectually independent Africa: a movement of critical appropriation of the scientific and technological heritage available internationally, and at the same time, a no less critical effort of reappropriation of endogenous knowledges and know-how. As a matter of fact both movements are similar, because the knowledge that is accumulated in the North, and which we must possess today, has been produced over the centuries with our collaboration and that of all the peoples of the world. To appropriate it for ourselves is therefore to reappropriate a heritage that for a long time has been misunderstood and neglected, in order to contribute, in a conscious and methodical way, to its promotion and development.

Rationality is therefore not given in advance. It is still to be built. It is not behind us, but before us. No culture is predestined to it, and none is barred from it for all eternity either. Hence the immense responsibility of contemporary generations: that of contributing together, in a thoughtful manner, in a spirit of solidarity and sharing, to the building of the common edifice, so that the germs of irrationality and progressively of ignorance and poverty will be eliminated forever from planet earth.

Afterword

Not everything has been recounted, but the rest can wait. I have tried, in the preceding pages, to take stock of my intellectual itinerary. I have described the circumstances of the genesis and development of a problematic whose broad arguments deserve to be made clearer because they have given rise to different interpretations. I have searched my memory, compared it, on occasion, with those of other people who have been associated with this adventure at various times. I have been frank, concealing as little as possible.

The first part established a few signposts. By tracing in bold strokes my school and university career, from the *lycée* in Porto-Novo to rue d'Ulm by way of the Lycée Henri IV in Paris, it leaves out my debt to my childhood masters—those intelligent, demanding, devoted, and loving teachers who, very early on, gave me the taste for hard work and for work well done. Let me briefly mention Edith Foadey, who died at a young age, Flavien Campbell, known as "The Smile," and his wife Jeanne Campbell, whom I saw recently still looking very young. And before all these, I want to mention those who taught me humility and hope, dignity in deprivation: my very first teacher, Paul Hountondji, the Methodist pastor whose only dream was to open schools wherever he was posted, and who sometimes had differences with his British or French missionary bosses;[1] the educator, and my first female teacher,

Marguerite Dovoédo, herself a pastor's daughter whose strictness was equaled only by her great tenderness.

The first part also shows how I was introduced to Husserl and more generally to the "philosophies of consciousness," as opposed to what Cavaillès calls the "philosophies of the concept." It also traces the origins of a certain predilection for these philosophies, and provides reasons for it without ever claiming, however, that these must be binding on all. Nevertheless, if, by introducing readers to Husserl, this narrative gives them a desire to read him in turn, it would be a happy coincidence, and not a consciously sought goal.

I would probably have felt the same disappointment with the theoretical impasse to which ethnophilosophical writings lead even without this familiarity with Husserl. However, the fact is that I was raised on a diet of methodological rigor, with an ideal of scientificity that has nothing to do, as I have shown, with any scientistic ideology; I had been attentive, more than to anything else, to the history of this ideal, its impact and effects on the greatest classics of philosophical thought, even when they held fiercely opposing positions on the implications and the ways of implementing it: all this strongly put me on guard against the large and unverified assertions of the decipherers of the African soul.

The aim of the second section is to show the meaning, reasons, and issues at stake in a critique of ethnophilosophy. Founded on a unanimist prejudice and a reductive reading of African cultures, this type of discourse develops entirely on the backs of the peoples concerned. Their exclusion here is not accidental, but integral to the discourse. When ethnophilosophy is taken over by the African intellectual himself, then the exclusion of the people leads to the extraversion of the individual who is meant to be their spokesperson, obliging him to look elsewhere—in the countries of the North—for his audience or readership. It is clear how this critique is rooted in a political struggle for independence and democratic freedoms, and in a great ambition for Africa. It is also clear what real theoretical issues are at stake beyond the attribution of ulterior motives to which this critique has so often given rise.

The third section undertakes an assessment of this polluted debate. By extending the lessons of the critique of ethnophilosophy to the ethnosciences and, more generally, to the dominant scientific practices in Africa today, it demonstrates the link between cultural and economic extraversion wherein resides the essence of what is inappropriately called "underdevelopment." At the same time, it shows what is fundamentally right in the demand for rootedness, and how it is possible to acknowledge such a demand without falling into the excesses of cultural relativism. On the contrary, it demonstrates how it is possible to take up the demand for universality that is present in all cultures and develop it to its greatest theoretical and practical value. Finally, it draws attention to different modes of coexistence between the universal and the particular. Rejecting the quiet juxtaposition of the old and the new, the pathological conflict between the modern and what is improperly called the traditional, it shows the need to integrate the "traditional" heritage into the current of living research, and to proceed with the critical reappropriation of endogenous forms of knowledge and techniques. At the same time, it emphasizes the urgent need to appropriate critically all the world's scientific and technological heritage—an act that should be seen as a way of reappropriating a treasure that, it is often forgotten, belongs, in the final analysis, to a common human patrimony.

I referred only in an allusive manner to my short foray into the corridors of power. I should one day return to this experience, draw the lessons from this "excursion into politics," as I described it above. As I went along, I recorded some of my observations in a number of articles published during the period.

I did not, therefore, remain silent, not completely anyway. However, with distance, and beyond the self-imposed silence, I must once again raise the huge problem of the shift to action, and the modalities of implementation, in the real world, of the values in which one believes.

I entered politics a little bit by accident. I obviously had convictions and very clear demands, and held positions that were clear-cut. That is not enough to make a politician. I was not content, like many, to contain my anger and revolt: I was no longer abroad! Moreover, I was incapable of saying the opposite of what I thought, as was often the case in those times of tyranny, informants, and roaring opportunism. It is almost a miracle that I was never arrested.

But I nearly was arrested in 1985. Students told me: your name is on a list of fourteen faculty members that had been distributed to all the police stations. For goodness sake, hide all your tracts and any other subversive literature that you may have in your house in case there is a search. As a result, I waited for the next meeting of the general assembly of the National Union of University Professors (SNES)—one of those meetings where you could be sure there were some "informants"—to announce that I had lots of tracts at home, adding that possessing a tract was not in itself a crime, except under abject dictatorial and ignorant regimes. I was left alone after that. We were still lucky in Benin: the government did not really go all the way. The situation was certainly difficult, and many people had paid with their lives in their determination to resist; hundreds of others were arrested, tortured, and manhandled. But it also was the case that the government hesitated to strike, wondering what was more advantageous or economical. In other countries in the sub-region, repression was more stupid.

I will not spend time on the struggles of the trade unions; on the circumstances in which the executive of the university teachers' union was forced by its membership to convene an extraordinary meeting in 1989 at which it was decided, after long debates and in a general climate of fear, to break ties with the sole union federation—a decision that led to a cascade of disaffiliation by other member unions; on the role that each person played; on the way in which some of the most cowardly—refusing for example to sign the April 27, 1989, petition—quickly managed, after the success of the movement, to pass themselves off as its champions; on the influence of a favorable international conjuncture, and in particular the collapse of the Soviet Union (symbolized by the fall of the Berlin Wall in November 1989); on the preparations for the national conference, this great forum of civil society that, against all expectations, enabled in February 1990 the peaceful transition from a military dictatorship—draped in Marxist-Leninist colors—to a pluralist democratic regime; on my participation in the national conference representing the laity of the Protestant churches. I will not spend time on this.

Few people remember, for example, that Mgr. Isidore de Souza, the conference chair, had been unanimously elected to this job with eight abstentions. Few people gave thought to the meaning of these abstentions. I could talk about it because the eight abstentions in this vote came from the four delegates of the Protestant churches and the four delegates from the Muslim community, representing respectively the hierarchy, the laity, the young, and women. I was seated just next to the imam, an intelligent, cultured, and open man. From time to time a quick consultation took place between the two delegations. I thought, for my part, that we would be necessarily confronted on occasion, as result of a certain type of political debate, with morally equivalent alternatives that no religious absolute would allow us to settle. In such conditions, the religious communities had a duty to observe a benevolent neutrality as their real vocation is to remind politicians of the need to respect the great non-negotiable principles of universal morality: thou shall not kill, thou shall not embezzle public funds. Principles, it should be mentioned in passing that, in my eyes, unequivocally condemned a regime that had made these crimes and misdemeanors the cornerstone of its system.

The rest of the conference, however, demonstrated the eminently positive role played by the Archbishop. We owe the unexpected success of the national conference in part to the humility, patience, and capacity for negotiation of this "man of God," as well as the lingering humanity and the religious faith of the Marxist-Leninist dictator, the tolerance and sense of compromise of various people, and not only to the objective constraints of the moment. This happy outcome does not invalidate, *a posteriori*, our positions on the necessary political neutrality of religions. At most, it shows how, in exceptional circumstances, the will-to-neutrality has been able to create something like a fundamental politics—a non-politician's politics—something I call somewhere else great, as opposed to, small politics. It shows how ethics can explode in the field of politics and, at least temporarily, impose itself on partisan positions. These questions require profound reflection if we are to learn from the lessons of a success that, in different degrees, surprised almost everyone.

I did not expect to find myself, after this conference, a member of the transitional government. I expected even less to find myself, following a ministerial reshuffle, head of a department of culture and communication for which I was little prepared, after having conscientiously worked for sixteen months to rebuild the Department of Education. I must one day return to this experience and assess the transition from an "ethic of conviction" to an "ethic of responsibility," to use Max Weber's beautiful expressions (dear to my master, Paul Ricoeur). I will one day have to explain what men (and women!) are like, why introducing morality into public life is so difficult, and how those who sometimes shout the loudest for it are those who wish it the least and are overall champions in all categories in corruption. I'll have to talk about the cynicism, hypocrisy, and everyday lies that are the daily fabric of small-time politics, and rather than be shocked by it by playing the sensitive soul, to acknowledge that these "qualities" are, in the present state of affairs, a necessary condition for political longevity. But at the same time I must seriously consider whether it is possible to reinvent politics, and, if so, how, on what conditions, and within which parameters.

Beyond these issues of elementary morality, I must one day reflect on the destiny, the possibilities of, and the constraints on a small country like Benin; on the meaning of national independence in a geo-political context where everything conspires to throw us lock, stock, and barrel into the arms of big international finance. One needs to ask whether we really have any future, or a future other than this one; whether we have the right to give up, and, if not, how we can resist; which actions—political, economic, or social—can be consistent with our refusal of domination.

How can civil society be strengthened? How can democracy be anchored in everyday life? How can the weight, the slowness, the inefficiency of our bureaucratic structures be overcome? How can the state be reformed? How can the arrogance and insolence of administrations and monopolies be broken? What can be done so that the ordinary man and woman can truly enjoy the liberties that, in theory, are recognized as theirs by the current constitutions, and how can they exercise their right to initiative and control? How can fear be overcome, and how can it be ensured that in this small corner of the globe, in the absence of larger spaces, dictatorship and arbitrary rule become things of the past forever?

What can be done to enable the small-scale peasant producer, the ordinary craftsperson to live decently off the fruits of his or her work, to gradually regain self-confidence, and to calmly face the future not feeling crushed, as he or she is today, by the problems of survival and the anguish of an uncertain future? How can we minimize the role of middlemen, of these businessmen and -women whose profits, reasonable or inflated as the case may be, are always, in the final analysis, more important and better guaranteed than those of the producers themselves? How can an economic system be established that rewards, against current trends, the producer and not the broker and provides the former with all the knowledge and know-how necessary to sell his product himself by bringing him in contact in the closest way possible with the final consumer? What should be done so that our universities cease to be what they are today, namely huge factories to churn out unemployed youth? What should be the new objectives of our educational systems, systems based on new societal projects that are coherent and sustainable?

On a different level, how can an end be put to extraversion? How can a viable, self-sufficient domestic market be created—a self-centered economy that is less dependent on external markets? At what stage are the various regional and sub-regional processes of integration? Why do our intergovernmental institutions function so poorly? Putting aside, for a moment, the display of voluntarism by our governments, what are the processes of integration at the grassroots level, and how can they be developed? How can a coherent public opinion, a regional and sub-regional civil society that is capable of exerting pressure on state apparatuses from one country to the other, be built across frontiers? Is Nkrumah's great dream—the dream of a strong and united Africa—condemned to remain just a dream, or can it still inspire a rigorous, coherent and progressive action plan? For want of being able to "de-link," as Samir Amin wished, is it at least possible to develop other spaces of autonomous and responsible decision making, outside of the current center of the world system? How can a polycentric and multipolar world be created, beyond the current globalization that is only another name for the expansion of the Western world's grand capital?

I have not stopped asking myself these questions. Neither my period in government, nor my more direct collaboration with the head of state as a member of his cabinet have actually helped me answer them. On the other hand they have made me aware of the obstacles that must be overcome if we are to, if not necessarily resolve them, at least raise them and put them on a clear political agenda.

Very early on, I learned a certain number of technical terms and learned abbreviations frequently used by the specialists. I also took pleasure in using them liberally at cabinet meetings—for example TOFS, which means "Table of Financial Operations of the State." In this small world where people only spoke macro-economics, structural adjustment, financial "deficit," and so on, this gave me a little air of seriousness and respectability. These things needed to be known, without one becoming prisoner to them. I worked at it as best as I could. But I think I beat all the records for sleeping during these endless meetings where, no doubt, important decisions were made, but where the stakes remained, in spite of everything, of rather limited value.

I do not forgive myself for having stayed so far away from my mother when, from her sick bed in Porto-Novo, she was asking to see me. I was in San Domingo for a colloquium in November 1992, the 500th centenary . . . of which discovery? Of the strange discovery by the indigenous people of America of a group of adventurers who had come from another continent led by a certain Christopher Columbus. The theme of the colloquium was "The Peoples of America Five Hundred Years Later." It was one of these trips that brought me some respite from the pressures of being a public figure. The trip was funded this time by the Foundation for Human Progress and, as usual, cost the state nothing. I, however, remained in telephone contact with my staff. This was how I learned, in the course of a briefing on current matters, that my mother had been admitted to hospital for high blood pressure, but that she was already better. As usual, I made light of it.

As soon as I returned, however, I went to the hospital in Porto-Novo. Half an hour of intense conversation punctuated by long silences. I was afraid to tire her out. As usual she was full of projects. This cousin was to get married; she had chosen the fabric for the family and could not wait to be able once again to take over the arrangements. She had a second important plan that escapes me. "Mother, I've always told you that you take on too much. See, you're tired. You need to rest. You'll take care of these things later. Forget the affairs of the family for a while." I meet the doctor, I discuss with my sister and her husband. They had been wonderful, and so remained to the end.

I am shocked to hear in the one o'clock afternoon news on the radio an "Appeal to Black Peoples" launched by the head of state for a cause which seemed derisory to me, the financing of "Ouidah 92, The First International Festival of Voodoo Cultures." I immediately demand an audience with the president. I am received the following day. No, I do not offer my resignation; we all thought a cabinet reshuffle was imminent. So I choose to plead with the president: please forget me in this reshuffle! I hand him my San Domingo conference paper and inform him of my intention to publish it. Three days later it appears with the provocative title "The Minister of Culture Declares: No, the Cultures of Benin Are Not Voodoo Cultures!"

My mother leaves hospital. We are convinced she has recovered. She is settled at my sister's. I leave quietly, this time on an official mission to India. From Bangalore I call Porto-Novo, I am told she is getting better. On my return, however,

I spend some time in Cotonou. I prepare to welcome Wole Soyinka. Abiola Irele has given me a good pretext to invite the Nobel laureate in literature by requesting to organize the Noma award ceremony in Cotonou.[2] Wole agrees to be the guest of honor, and the head of state himself agrees to chair the occasion. I had my plan. Alongside the Noma, I meant to promote, with Wole Soyinka, the project against which the inventors of "Ouidah 92" were fighting, namely, "The Slave Route," a project launched by Father Aristide in Haiti shortly before his overthrow in 1991. Benin, which had created a favorable impression in Port-au-Prince, owed it to herself to take over "The Slave Route" from Haiti. Wole Soyinka accepts. I decide to telephone Porto-Novo every evening. The condition of the patient is stable, but I'm given reassurance. It was convenient to believe it. What naïveté!

Finally, one Friday, I announce my visit for the following day. The host had just left; the other guests were to leave on Saturday. I would thus be able to go to Porto-Novo. Bad luck! Unforeseen worries force me to telephone an hour beforehand to cancel the rendezvous. My mother is annoyed. She wants to talk to me on the phone; the cord is not long enough. She wants to come down from her bed to come closer. The female cousins dissuade her from doing that, and in any case her condition will not allow it. Ten minutes later (a small consolation after all), I am seen on television next to a man of refined and austere elegance. The man is speaking. It is Wole. My mother turns round and blesses the prodigal son. Fifteen minutes later, my telephone rings: Mother is in a coma. Suddenly the things I thought important vanished. I go to Porto-Novo that night. I run everywhere. The patient is in the hospital. For the first time in my life I catch my grandmother, Abigail Dovoédo, crying. She has seen pain in the past and knows how to cope with it. I insist, with the agreement of my family, that Mother be transferred to the university medical center (CNHU) in

Cotonou, which is supposed to be better equipped. A few days later, it is done. In all, she spends twelve days in intensive care, an eternity for us.

Mother did not wake up. I will never know what she had wanted to tell me. Or rather, yes I do! I've always known it. But still! What would have been her last instructions, recommendations, her *ultima verba?* I deprived her of a presence that was her right and that she was demanding. I did not tell her that I was writing a poem for her and that I loved her. But she must have known that, obviously: she guessed everything. I did not know you were mortal, Mother. Forgive me.

Notes

Preface

1. Quantitative methods, it is well known, have been developed to evaluate the impact of scholarly works. Chief among these methods is bibliometrics, which measures the impact of an article or a book by counting the number of times it is cited in general or specialized publications (see, especially, Price 1963). The limitations of such an approach, however, are clear: besides the fact that the periodicals considered never represent more than a tiny fraction of all the periodicals in the world, it is not always clear that the most influential works are always the most cited.

Chapter 1. Landmarks

1. *Hypokhâgne* is the French slang for the first of the two years of preparatory classes for entry into the l'Ecole Normale Supérieure (humanities track) and *khâgne* for the second.

2. I am indebted to Mamoussé Diagne, one of Nietzsche's most careful readers in Africa, for having located this quotation in June 1995 in Dakar: "However to you madman, I'll give this advice by way of a goodbye: where one can no longer love, there should one *pass by!* Thus spake Zarathustra and he passed in front of the madman and the big town" (Nietzsche 1966, 178).

3. [Co-author with André Lagarde of the popular and celebrated high school anthology-cum-history of French literature in six volumes titled *Lagarde et Michard*. Paris: Bordas, 1962–73. Trans.]

4. *Cayman* is Ecole Normale Supérieure slang for a tutor with an *agrégation*.

5. [In English in the original. Trans.]

Chapter 2. The Idea of Science

1. If in the general economy of *Logical Investigations*, the radical return to the subject takes place, as I already indicated above, in the *Fifth* and *Sixth Investigations*—after the decisive objectivism of the first half of the book (from the *Prolegomena* through the *Fourth Investigation*)—this general movement of the text is already intimated in a minor key in the transition from the *Prolegomena* to the *First Investigation*.

2. "Other paths are possible for sense investigations with a radical aim; and the present work attempts to open up, at least in main sections, one suggested precisely by the historically given relation of the idea of genuine science to logic its antecedent norm" (Husserl 1969, 7).

3. *Formal and Transcendental Logic* can be considered the most complete model of the first approach, and *Cartesian Meditations*, perhaps even more than *Ideas*, the best example of the second.

4. I am referring to paragraph 6 of the introduction to the second volume of *Logical Investigations* published for the first time in German in 1901 and including *Investigations 1–6*, and re-issued in 1913 (*Investigations 1–5*) and 1921 (*Investigation 6*).

5. It is well known that the second German edition of *Logical Investigations*, volumes 1 and 2 (1913) is contemporaneous with *Ideas 1*. Husserl left the text of the first edition—chapter 1, Investigation 5 (his opposition to the theory of a pure self)—unchanged. However, he removed paragraph 7 from the text and made the necessary clarifications in a series of footnotes and an "Addendum to the Second Edition."

Chapter 3. Anger

1. [English in the original. Trans.]
2. Getting to know, some five or six years later, J. E. Wiredu (alias Kwasi Wiredu), I discovered that Martin Apeagyei Kissi was none other than the younger brother of the brilliant Legon analytical

philosopher (now in the United States). Was the Copenhagen paper then the fruit of a family discussion? By highlighting both the existence of traditional philosophies in African cultures, like in all the cultures of the world, and the inconsistencies to which one was exposed in trying to extract from this "public and collective . . . culture" an academic philosophy, this text, full of nuances, at any rate, already heralded the subtle anlayses of *Philosophy and an African Culture* (Kissi 1970; Wiredu 1980).

3. In reality, as I was to observe later, Lévy-Bruhl is cited not once in *La philosophie bantoue.* However, the work of Raoul Allier, a privileged target of Tempels, rests entirely on the theory of prelogical thought, and has the further advantage of applying it to the same field as Tempels: the Bantu field (Hountondji 1987).

4. Souleymane B. Diagne was later to develop this point in a thesis that has remained unpublished to this day—"Le faux dialogue de l'ethnophilosophie" (Ethnophilosophy as a false dialogue).

5. Paul Ricoeur, the coordinator of section VI on philosophy in the *Tendances principales de la recherche dans les sciences sociales et humaines,* 2è partie (Havet 1978, t. 2: 1125–1622), was kind enough to mention this contribution, pp. 1135 and 1581

6. The expression is Canguilhem's. He probably remembered a critique of eurocentrism outlined in the conclusion to my *agrégation* oral examination presentation. The year after, he encouraged me in these terms: "You will write a good thesis because you are angry." The topic I had selected at random for this presentation (the most important oral test) was "Development as a Sociological Concept." I also remember one day informing the master of Rue du Four of my plan to write a philosophy textbook for Africa for *Présence africaine* in collaboration with two colleagues (Jacques Howlett and Amadou Séydou). After a few seconds of silence, he reacted in these terms: "A philosophy textbook must be *dogmatic.*" Coming from Canguilhem, it is clear that such a sentence could not be an invitation to intolerance or to some catechistic purring, but to a rigorous consistency that conditions the unity of thought, and which is the opposite of eclecticism. The textbook in question, unfortunately, was never written.

7. The expression is Mamoussé Diagne's (Diagne 1976).

8. This debt to Frantz Fanon was acknowledged in "Charabia et mauvaise conscience" (Hountondji 1967, 16).

9. I quoted to illustrate my point European authors: Tempels, Griaule, Germaine Dieterlen, Dominique Zahan, and Louis-Vincent Thomas; African churchmen: Kagame, Makarakiza, Mabona, Rahajarizafy, Lufuluabo, Mulago, Jean-Calvin Bahoken, and John Mbiti; and finally African laymen: Senghor, Adesanya, William Abraham, Nkrumah, Alassane N'Daw, Basile-Juléat Fouda, Prosper Layele, J. O. Awolalu, and Germain de Souza.

10. I quoted, as examples, a string of articles and books written by authors of my generation or close to it such as F. Eboussi-Boulaga, Marcien Towa, Henry Odera Oruka, Stanislas Adotevi, J. E. Wiredu (alias Kwasi Wiredu), Idoniboye, Elungu, Aloyse-Raymond N'Diaye, Tharcisse Tshibangu, and Njoh Mouelle. I also claimed the publications of Amo in the eighteenth century as constituting an integral part of this literature. These examples, of course, were only illustrative, and I never claimed this list to be exhaustive.

11. Virgile Tévoèdjrè, then Dahomey's ambassador to Kinshasa, was not mistaken about it when, after having graced with his presence a public lecture that I delivered on campus one evening in 1970, the following day he drew my attention in a brotherly way to the political implications of my remarks in the context of a one-party state with no freedom of expression. I had declared to the wild cheers of an enthusiastic public: "African philosophy will be plural or will not exist at all." The brilliant diplomat had seen the issue: this declaration could be, quite simply, subversive.

Chapter 4. The Issues at Stake

1. That is the meaning of the famous expression *abacost*, short for "*à bas le costume,*" that is, "down with suits."

2. This structure became unmanageable if only because of the enormous distances involved between the three campuses: Kinshasa was an hour by plane from Kisangani, one hour fifty minutes from Lubumbashi. By the end of the 1970s, the National University of Zaire broke up into three separate universities, with the three vice-rectors each becoming a rector, and the rector, the chancellor of the universities.

3. Among the reactions provoked by this work must be cited that of Emile-Derlin Zinsou, former president of Dahomey (present-day

Benin), who was forced into exile by the so-called Marxist-Leninist military regime and is author of *Pour un socialisme humaniste, suivi de Lettre à un jeune dahoméen marxiste-leniniste.* Its last chapter is titled "Lettre à Paulin Hountondji, jeune dahoméen marxiste-leniniste." I am sure that the author, one of the most cultured, open, courageous, and patriotic heads of state in the history of independent Benin, must have since realized that such labels should be used with the greatest caution (Zinsou 1975).

4. It will be worth reading the same author's *Idéologies des indé-pendences africaines* (1972) and *Indépendances africaines: ideologie et réalités* (1975).

5. "Unanimism" was the term coined by Jules Romains to describe the spirit of solidarity with humankind celebrated early this century by a number of artists including Georges Duhamel and, according to Lagarde and Michard, rather similar to the social lyricism of the American poet Walt Whitman (1819–92). The "life of unanimity," the collective and unconscious soul is, for Jules Romains, a hidden god that the writer must reveal. It fosters communion between those "archipelagoes of solitude" that are human groups, and thus makes "unanimists" of them. Thus understood, "unanimism" is a value to be promoted, a solidarity that breaks barriers between human beings, and in the process of breaking their loneliness and insularity, endows them with a collective personality. In my view, however, such soli-darity is nothing more than an affective phenomenon. If it remains indispensable to collective action and to infusing life into a collectiv-ity, it cannot claim to suppress in each member of the group this inner loneliness, this minimum space of autonomy and personal thought without which the individual would lose all existence as a responsible subject, and be unable to take part effectively in the life of the collectivity (Romains 1908; Whitman 1968; Lagarde and Michard 1968, 35).

6. See chapter 2, paragraph 5, above.

7. Husserl for example writes: "Reason is a broad title. According to an old familiar definition, man is the rational animal, and in this broad sense, even the Papuan is a man and not a beast. . . . But just as man and even the Papuan represent a new stage of animal nature, i.e., as opposed to the beast, so philosophical reason represents a new stage of human nature and its reason" (1970, 290). Heidegger for his part observed: "The often heard expression 'Western-European

philosophy' is, in truth, a tautology. Why? Because 'philosophy' is Greek in its nature; Greek, in this instance, means that in origin the nature of philosophy is of such a kind that it first appropriated the Greek world, and only it, in order to unfold" (1958, 29–30).

Without mentioning the obvious evolutionist accents in these texts, such deductions are examples of well-known forms of paralogism, like the sophism of the accident that consists in arbitrarily projecting on an accidental fact a perfectly illusory air of necessity. The best minds, unfortunately, do not always avoid this temptation. An African reading of Western philosophy must, for this reason among others, always be vigilant, and try to bring out the tactics and subtleties of an ever-present ethnocentrism.

8. I cannot say for certain that I ever properly "understood" or, if you wish, "took on board" the first two chapters of *The Savage Mind* on the "Science of the Concrete" and the "Logic of Totemic Classifications." By imagining, on the model of this science of the concrete, "the disorderliness of these pieces juxtaposed one against the other like leftovers" in what I called practical ideology, and "the very special coherence of this 'residual' logic," I was aware of raising an issue rather than peremptorily asserting a thesis. I had opened up a whole new set of questions in relation to which the work of Marc Augé was indispensable.

9. It was only much later, in a conversation with a Senegalese colleague at the Centre d'études littéraires et historiques par tradition orale (CELTO) in Niamey that I discovered Marc Augé's penetrating remarks on the critique of ethnophilosophy. I met the man much later still, although we had common friends going back a long time. On the other hand, I had the good fortune of meeting Claude Rivière, then Chair of the Department of Philosophy and Applied Social Sciences at the University of Benin in Lomé, several months before the annual seminar organized in Cotonou by the Inter-African Council on Philosophy on "Philosophy and the Development of Science in Africa." The article cited above refers specifically to a paper read by Rivière at this seminar.

10. Joseph Ki-Zerbo had been since 1979 a member of the editorial board (as distinct from the editorial committee) of *Socialism in the World*. I was also invited to join the same board from 1984. The annual round table meetings in Çavat provided the opportunity for rich, open, and free discussions. I must have attended two or, I be-

lieve, three such meetings, during which I was privileged to listen, sometimes more than once, to such committed and creative authors as André Gunder Frank, Henri Lefèbvre, Georges Labica, Anouar Abdel-Malek, and Samir Amin. The places where these memorable meetings took place are today, alas, probably no more than ruins.

11. The collection also contained texts by André Gunder Frank, Régis Debray, Che Guevara, Jean-Paul Sartre, Senghor, Hassan al-Banna, Abdallah Laroui, Ahmed Sékou Touré, Nguyen Khac Vien, and Amilcar Cabral (Marton 1978).

12. The practice in Hungary is to write the author's last name before their given name, which therefore can no longer be called "first name." So "Karl Marx University" becomes "Marx Károly Egyetem," "Laurent Eötvos University" becomes "Eötvos Lórand Egyetem." My correspondents wrote their names as Marton Imre and Sipos Janos. This convention, respected by all, creates accepted practices and makes for understanding. This is unfortunately not the case in so-called francophone Africa, where the practice of writing the last name first, widespread in the administration and the army and perfectly justifiable for purposes of classification in alphabetical order, insinuated itself into everyday language and even literary writing, thus blurring matters and creating total confusion. Senghor already referred to the problem in connection with the common name "Camara Laye" (*sic*) which, as the reader of *Dark Child* quickly realizes, should be "Laye Camara." The same can be said about the name "Sembène Ousmane" (*sic*) inflicted on an author whose given name (call it first name or whatever) is clearly Ousmane. This is one of those elementary issues on which a minimum, indispensable consensus must be reached in order to settle problems of reading and understanding (Senghor 1954).

Chapter 5. A Polluted Debate

1. The English title "The Awakening of the African Historical Consciousness," probably suggested by the Scandinavian organizers, is clearer than its French translation in the same book: "Une prise de conscience historique africaine."

2. His irritation may have had a solid basis of which I could not have been aware at the time. As I was told later, I had allowed myself

to be "used" unwittingly and unknowingly by some of Kagame's staunchest enemies at the National University of Rwanda. His reaction needs to be understood in this context.

3. The person concerned has always insisted, as a matter of fact, that the reverse be done in his case. However, as I explained above, the elementary need to facilitate reading and understanding imposes an obligation on us to observe collective practices. These can differ depending on the language or society under consideration, as with Hungarian (see above, chapter 4, note 12) or Chinese, where the name "Mao" is both a given name and a surname. Clearly, a more systematic study than has been done thus far of precolonial naming practices in Africa, and the disruptions wrought on them by the colonial administration, is called for. Meanwhile, what is wrong, really, with following the examples of such Africans as Senghor, Kenyatta, Mandela or, to take examples from the Akan, Nkrumah, and Houphouet-Boigny, who have never had problems writing their first names (Léopold, Jomo, Nelson, Kwame, Félix) before their last names?

4. See above, chapter 4.

5. In the preface to the second English edition of *African Philosophy: Myth and Reality*, which was published by Indiana University Press in 1996.

6. One of my great regrets is that these little errors were not corrected in the second edition.

7. The Communist Party of Dahomey (PCD) for a long time rejected, and not without reason, the name "Benin" with which Dahomey was christened on November 30, 1975, by a decision of General Kérékou. It only recently became, in 1994, when it emerged from underground, (and as a result of the process of democratization), "The Communist Party of Benin."

8. I recognized it above: I did myself go too far in the other direction, with not just being satisfied with rejecting the blurring of boundaries between two distinct disciplines, namely ethnology and philosophy, but with encompassing in this critique ethnology as a whole. In my eyes, it was as if the latter was marked by an original sin: that of assuming a difference in nature between its object (so-called primitive societies) and that of sociology (human societies in general), all the while claiming to be unconcerned with imperialist domination. Historically, ethnology developed in the context of this relation of power, and because of this it is based on the exclusion of

the peoples *about whom* it speaks, but whom it assumes forever incapable of becoming viable interlocutors themselves, participants in an international scientific debate. The reader will see a little later how this position needs to be qualified. Be it as it may, such qualification cannot serve as an excuse for the learned rhetoric of our new terrorists, who are prepared to use any means possible to erase all boundaries between disciplines, and impose an artificial expansion of founding concepts.

9. "The English-speaking reader of these essays may well sense more than a hint of the polemical in their author's conduct of his argument, which is not habitual in a debate of this kind within his own intellectual milieu. Their general tone certainly contrasts with the manner in which professional philosophers in English-speaking Africa . . . have gone about canvassing a point of view similar in many ways to that of Hountondji on the same questions" (Irele, introduction to Hountondji 1996, 28–29).

Chapter 6. Rootedness and Freedom

1. My article is titled "Langues africaines et philosophie: l'hypothèse relativiste" (African languages and philosophy: The relativist hypothesis). The subtitle should be corrected as "The relativist thesis."

2. Legon is a town on the outskirts of Accra, capital of Ghana. It is where the University of Ghana, a prestigious institution in colonial times, is located.

3. [In English in the original. Trans.]

4. Wiredu's slogan: "Fellow philosophers, let us learn to think in our own languages!" was launched at a conference organized by UNESCO in Nairobi in June 1980. The proceedings of this conference, however, only appeared in 1984.

5. [The play on the French words *point/poing*—which depends on homophony to convey the idea of both an intellectual and physical effort—is untranslatable. Trans.]

6. The "first version" of "Que peut la philosophie" goes back to 1978, as is indicated in the summary of the article that appeared in 1981.

7. I had not at the time attempted a systematic study of the concept of ethnoscience. Work had been done on it, but I was unaware of

it. I was, however, pleased to read, in a volume of conversations published some years later by Ruth Scheps, the details given by Jacques Barrau on the origins of the word. Botany seems to be the earliest naturalist discipline to have been given the prefix *ethno*—as far back as 1895—by the American agronomist and botanist J. S. Harshberger. "Ethnozoology," a more recent word, goes back to 1914. As for the generic word "ethnoscience," it seems to have been first used in the 1950s at Yale University by a team of young ethnologists claiming to practice a "new ethnography," and attempting under this banner to develop a methodical study of "popular" knowledges and know-how that they called "folk-science." I am to an extent indebted to Mudimbe for making it possible for me to return to this question in a more systematic manner. From Duke University, where he was then teaching, he sent me a list of ten terms on which he asked me to write for his project on an encyclopedia of African religions and philosophy. Who would want to refuse Mudimbe anything? It was, unfortunately, one of those promises that I have been unable to keep, except for one of the ten articles, the one on the "ethnosciences." Thus, I was able to discover, and sometimes to rediscover, some important research *on* ethnoscience in writings such: as articles by W. Sturtevant and M. Fournier, books published under the editorship of Dell Hymes in the United States, and Geneviève Calame-Griaule in France; by Nicole Revel's work on the history and theory of the discipline in her learned thesis on the natural history of Palawan; or Peter Murdock's reference work where, in 1950, the word "ethnoscience" is used for the first time. What appears in these studies is how specific ethnosciences developed long before the word "ethnophilosophy" and the generic term "ethnoscience" were coined. Moreover, if the word "ethnoscience" only appeared in 1950, it sounds paradoxical to derive "ethnophilosophy," a word already in use in the 1940s from "ethnoscience. However, the development of such specific disciplines as ethnobotany, ethnozoology, and ethnobiology is proof that the generic concept of ethnoscience did exist, at least virtually, long before the word was formally coined. It can be admitted, therefore, that Nkrumah, while attempting in the early 1940s to promote a new discipline called ethnophilosophy, had these older disciplines in mind. (Scheps 1993; Barrau 1993; Sturtevant 1964; Fournier 1971; Hymes 1964; Calame-Griaule 1977; Revel 1990; Murdock 1950).

8. The full version, which the *Bulletin de la Société française de*

philosophie could not accept in its entirety, has remained unpublished to this day.

9. The above details concerning the late appearance of the *word* "ethnoscience," of course, do not change anything in the general thrust of the analyses. In the absence of the word, the idea of an ethnoscience clearly existed in specific disciplines which, like ethnobotany and ethnozoology, are abundant proof of it.

10. William Abraham, a Ghanaian, as is well known, and former Chair of the Department of Philosophy at Legon, Accra, was then at the University of California at Santa Cruz in the United States. He remained there until his recent retirement. I had the pleasure, towards the end of my stay in Germany as a Humboldt Foundation Fellow, of having him invited to Düsseldorf by my host Alwin Diemer for a seminar on "Africa and the Problem of Its Identity." This seminar's proceedings were published three years later (Diemer and Hountondji 1985).

11. The word appears right in the title *Mind and Thought in Primitive Society: A Study in Ethnophilosophy with Special Reference to the Akan Peoples of the Gold Coast, West Africa* (Nkrumah 1945). The document comes to a total of 226 pages, typed for the most part, of which seven pages are in Roman numerals, 212 (numbered 1–212) in arabic numerals, plus an appendix reproducing handwritten notes concerning the tribal state, the army, and the tribal organization of the Akan, and, finally, four pages of summary and acknowledgments.

12. The first three articles were partially reworked—this time with a signature to them—for a collective volume that appeared in Elisabethville (present-day Lubumbashi) in 1945 with the title *Dettes de guerre* (War debts), while the other two were published in their entirety in 1944–45 in the Antwerp periodical *Kongo-Overzee*.

13. I was the host of the Central Division of this association, which has three divisions in all, the other two being the East and Pacific Divisions.

Chapter 7. Reappropriation

1. Americans have created a neologism, "Africana Studies," to describe studies concerning both Africa and peoples of African ancestry.

Along these lines, Lucius Outlaw, Chair of the Department of Philosophy at Haverford College, Pennsylvania, organized an international conference in July 1982 on the theme "Africana Philosophy: Philosophy in Africa and People of African Descent."

2. I had read, in my last year of high school in Porto-Novo, *The Philosophy of No* and *The New Scientific Spirit*. One of these books belonged to the school library, the other was probably loaned to me by my teacher Hélène Marmotin. I do not recall which editions I had read. All I can now find among my books is the fourth (French) edition of *The Philosophy of No*, published in 1966. As for *The New Scientific Spirit*, it was already in its fourteenth (French) edition in 1978 (Bachelard 1984, 1968).

3. These studies included, besides my introduction, a text by Wiredu called "Articulating Modern Thought in African Languages: Some Theoretical Considerations," another by Bachir Diagne titled "Note sur la question: Faire des mathématiques en Wolof" (Doing mathematics in Wolof: A note), a contribution by the Benin linguist Marc-Laurent Hazoumè on "Numération en gun, en gen, et en baatonu" (Number systems in Gun, Gen, and Baatonu), one from the Benin mathematician Cyprien Gnanvo titled "Plaidoyer pour la décimalisation" (A plea for decimalization), one by the Kenyan logician Victor Ocaya on logic in Acholi, and an account by G. Mmari, then vice-rector of a university in Tanzania, on the lessons to be learnt from the Tanzanian experiment of using kiswahili in the teaching of science and math.

4. Which led me to make the rather tasteless quip that "rather than the act of de-linking ('déconnecter'), de-linking ('la déconnexion') would quite simply be the act . . . of talking crap—from the verb 'déconner'"!

5. The expression is Jean-Jacques Salomon's, whose book, *Science et politique*, is still worth reading today, among other works by him (Salomon 1970).

6. I cited as examples two authors from Benin, Paul Hazoumè and Louis Hunkarin, but, of course, there are many others (Hazoumè 1956; Hunkarin 1975).

7. Instead of "speculative debauchery," the editor of the article preferred "speculative outline." As a matter of fact, my critique, as later became clear, took aim at the spectacular development of ethnophilosophy, in which I saw both the extreme form of the cult of difference and an imaginary antidote to theoretical poverty.

8. I arrived late, as it sometimes happens, at the CODESRIA conference in Dakar—a few hours after the session in which I was to speak. S. B. Diagne kindly presented my text.

Afterword

1. His *Autobiography*, published posthumously by his family with the support of the Methodist Church of Benin, repays reading (Hountondji 1983).

2. A Japanese prize awarded each year to a book published in Africa.

Bibliography

Abimbola, Wande. 1975. *Sixteen Great Poems of Ifa*. Niger: Niamey, UNESCO/CELHTO.

———. 1976. *Ifa: An Exposition of Ifa Literary Corpus*. Ibadan: Oxford University Press.

Abraham, William. 1962. *The Mind of Africa*. Chicago: University of Chicago Press.

Adandé, Alexis B. [1994] 1997. "'Traditional' Iron Metallurgy in West Africa." In *Endogenous Knowledge: Research Trails*, edited by Paulin J. Hountondji, 63–81. Dakar: CODESRIA.

Adjido, Comlan T. [1994] 1997. "Links between Psychosomatic Medicine and Sorcery." In *Endogenous Knowledge: Research Trails*, edited by Paulin J. Hountondji, 265–78. Dakar: CODESRIA.

Afouda, Abel. [1994] 1997. "'Rainmakers': A Hydrologist's Viewpoint." In *Endogenous Knowledge: Research Trails*, edited by Paulin J. Hountondji, 104–12. Dakar: CODESRIA.

Ahyi, Gualbert R. [1994] 1997. "Traditional Models of Mental Health and Illness in Benin." In *Endogenous Knowledge: Research Trails*, edited by Paulin J. Hountondji, 217–46. Dakar: CODESRIA.

Akoha, Albert B. [1994] 1997. "Graphic Representational Systems in Pre-colonial Africa." In *Endogenous Knowledge: Research Trails*, edited by Paulin J. Hountondji, 309–39. Dakar: CODESRIA.

Althusser, Louis. [1974] 1976a. *Essays in Self-criticism*. Translated by Grahame Lock. London: New Left Books.

———. 1976b. *Positions*. Paris: Editions Sociales.

———. [1968] 1977. *Lenin and Philosophy and Other Essays*. Translated by Ben Brewster. London: New Left Books.

———. [1965] 1990a. *For Marx*. Translated by Ben Brewster. New York: Verso.

———. [1967, 1974] 1990b. *Philosophy and the Spontaneous Philosophy of the Scientists and Other Essays*. Translated by Ben Brewster et al. New York: Verso.

Althusser, Louis, Etienne Balibar, Roger Establet, Jacques Rancière, and Pierre Macherey. [1966] 1990. *Reading* Capital. Translated by Ben Brewster. New York: Verso.

Amin, Samir. 1968. *Le développement du capitalisme en Côte d'Ivoire*. Paris: Minuit.

———. [1971] 1973. *Neo-colonialism in West Africa*. Translated by Francis McDonagh. New York: Monthly Review Press.

———. [1970] 1974. *Accumulation on a World Scale*. Translated by Brian Pearce. New York: Monthly Review Press.

———. [1986] 1990. *Delinking: Towards a Polycentric World*. Translated by Michael Wolfers. London: Zed Books.

Amo, Afer. 1968a. *Anton. Guil., aus Axim in Ghana. Dokumente/Autographe/Belege*. Halle-Wittenberg, Germany: Martin-Luther-Universität.

———. 1968b. *Translation of His Works*. Translated by Leonard Jones with the assistance of Hans Kirsten and Reinhard Koch. Halle-Wittenberg, Germany: Martin-Luther-Universität.

Amo, Antonius Guilelmus. 1734. "Dissertatio inauguralis de humanae mentis apaqeia seu sensionis ac facultatis sentiendi in mente humana absentia et earum in corpore nostro organico ac vivo praesentia." Ph.D. diss. Martin-Luther-Universität, Halle-Wittenberg, Germany.

———. 1738. *Tractatus de arte sobrie et accurate philosophandi*. Halle-Magdeburg, Germany.

Appiah, Kwame Anthony. 1992. *In My Father's House: Africa in the Philosophy of Culture*. Oxford: Oxford University Press.

Aristotle. 1993. *The Metaphysics*. Translated by Christopher Kirwan. Oxford: Clarendon Press.

Augé, Marc. 1975. *Théories des pouvoirs et idéologies: Etude de cas en Côte d'Ivoire*. Paris: Hermann.

———. 1977. *Pouvoirs de vie, pouvoir de mort*. Paris: Flammarion.

———. [1979] 1982. *The Anthropological Circle: Symbol, Function,*

History. Translated by Martin Thom. Cambridge: Cambridge University Press.

Ayer, A. J., 1970. *Language, Truth and Logic.* London: Victor Gollancz.

Azombo-Menda, S., and M. Enobo Kosso. 1978. *Les philosophes africains par les textes.* Paris: Nathan.

Azombo-Menda, S., and P. Meyongo. 1981. *Précis de philosophie pour l'Afrique.* Paris: Nathan.

Bachelard, Gaston. [1940] 1968. *The Philosophy of No: A Philosophy of the New Scientific Spirit.* Translated by G. C. Waterson. New York: Orion Press.

———. [1934] 1984. *The New Scientific Spirit.* Translated by Arthur Goldhammer. Boston: Beacon Press.

Bachelard, Suzanne. [1929.] 1989. *A Study of Husserl's Formal and Transcendental Logic.* Translated by Lester E. Embree. Evanston, Ill.: Northwestern University Press.

Bahro, Rudolph. 1979. *L'alternative.* Paris: Stock.

Balandier, Georges. [1957] 1966. *Ambiguous Africa: Cultures in Collision.* Translated by Helen Weaver. New York: World.

Baldwin, James. 1961. *Nobody Knows My Name: More Notes of a Native Son.* New York: Dell.

Barrau, Jacques. 1993. "Savoirs naturalistes et naissance de l'ethnoscience." In *La science sauvage,* edited by Ruth Scheps, 15–27. Paris: Seuil.

Baynac, Jacques. 1975. *La terreur sous Lénine.* Paris: Sagittaire.

Beladi, Laszlo, Imre Marton, Ferenc Miszlivetz, and Tamas Szentes. 1978. *Fejlödés-Tanulmányok.* Budapest: Université Karl Marx.

Benot, Yves. 1972. *Idéologies des indépendances africaines.* Paris: Maspero.

———. 1975. *Indépendances africaines: Idéologies et réalités.* 2 vols. Paris: Maspéro.

———. 1979. "La philosophie en Afrique, ou l'émergence de l'individu." *Revue Tiers-Monde* 20 (77): 187–98.

Bitek, Okot p'. 1964. "Bantu Philosophy." *Transition* 13: 15–17

Boelart, Edmond-Eloi. 1972. "La philosophie bantoue selon le R. P. Placide Tempels." In *Philosophie africaine: Textes choisis,* edited by J. Smet, 81–90. Kinshasa: Presses Universitaires du Zaire.

Bowao, Charles. 1995. "Désethnologiser: Rouverture du débat Hountondji-Diagne." *Bulletin du CODESRIA* 1: 15–19

Calame-Griaule, Geneviève, ed. 1977. *Langages et cultures africaines: Essais d'ethnolinguistique.* Paris: Maspero.

Calvet, Jean-Louis. 1974. *Linguistique et colonialisme: Petit traité de glottophagie.* Paris: Payot.

Cavaillès, Jean. 1938. *Méthode axiomatique et formalisme.* Paris: Hermann.

———. 1960. *Sur la logique et la théorie de la science.* Paris: Presses Universitaires de France.

Césaire, Aimé. 1956. *Lettre à Maurice Thorez.* Paris: Présence Africaine.

———. 1972. *Discourse on Colonialism.* Translated by Joan Pinkham. New York: Monthly Review Press.

Charbonnier, Georges. [1961] 1969. *Conversations with Claude Levi-Strauss.* Translated by John and Doreen Weightman. London: Cape.

Cohn-Bendit, Daniel. [1968] 1969. *Obsolete Communism: The Left-Wing Alternative.* Translated by Arnold Pomerans. Harmondsworth: Penguin Books.

Communist Party of Dahomey (PCD). 1979. *Introduction aux réalités économiques et sociales au Dahomey.* Paris: Nouveau Bureau d'Edition.

Comte, Auguste. [1830–42] 1966. *System of Positive Polity.* 4 vols. New York: Burt Franklin.

———. [1885] 1974. *The Positive Philosophy.* 2 vols. Translated by Harriet Martineau. New York: AMS Press.

———. [1822] 1978. "Plan des travaux scientifiques nécessaires pour réorganizer le monde." In *Du pouvoir spirituel* by Auguste Comte. Paris: Livre de Poche.

De Craemer, Willy. 1977. *The Jamaa and the Church: A Bantu Catholic Movement in Zaire.* Oxford: Clarendon Press.

Crahay, Franz. 1965. "Le décollage conceptual: Conditions d'une philosophie bantoue." *Diogène* 52: 61–84.

Dah-Lokonon, Gbènoukpo Bodéhou. (1994) 1997. "Rainmakers: Myth and Knowledge in Traditional Atmospheric Management Techniques." In *Endogenous Knowledge: Research Trails*, edited by Paulin J. Hountondji, 83–103. Dakar: CODESRIA.

Damas, Léon-Gontras. 1966. *Névralgies.* Paris: Présence Africaine.

Derrida, Jacques. 1967. *La voix et le phénomène.* Paris: PUF.

————. [1967] 1978. *Writing and Difference*. Translated by Alan Bass. Chicago: University of Chicago Press.

————. 1989. Introduction to Edmund Husserl's *Origin of Geometry*. Translated by John Leavey. Lincoln: University of Nebraska Press.

————. 1994. *Le problème de la genèse dans la philosophie de Husserl*. Paris: PUF.

Desanti, Jean T. 1963. *Phénoménologie et praxis*. Paris: Editions Sociales.

————. 1975. *La philosophie silencieuse: Ou, critique des philosophies des sciences*. Paris: Seuil.

Descartes, René. [1647] 1960. *Meditations on First Philosophy*. Translated by Laurence J. Lafleur. Indianapolis: Bobbs-Merrill.

————. [1644] 1984. *Principles of Philosophy*. Translated by Valentine R. Miller and Reese P. Miller. Dordrecht, The Netherlands: D. Reidel.

————. 1953a. *Méditations, objections et réponses*. In *Descartes 1596–1650. Oeuvres et lettres*, edited by André Bridoux, 253–547. Paris: Gallimard.

Diagne, Mamoussé. 1976. "Paulin Hountondji, ou la 'psychanalyse' de la conscience ethnophilosophique." *Psychopathologie africaine* 12 (3): 443–49

Diagne, Pathé. 1981. *L'europhilosophie face à la pensée de négro-africaine; suivi de Problématique néo-pharaonique et épistémologie du réel*. Dakar: Sankoré.

Diagne, Souleymane Bachir. 1978. "Le faux dialogue de l'ethnophilosophie." Master's thesis, University of Paris.

————. 1989. *Boole, l'oiseau de nuit en plein jour*. Paris: Belin.

————. 1994. "Lecture de science sauvage: Mode d'emploi." *Bulletin du CODESRIA* 1: 10–11.

Dieng, Amady Aly. 1978. *Hegel, Marx, Engels et les problèmes de l'Afrique noire*. Dakar: Sankoré.

————. 1983. *Contribution à l'étude des problèmes philosophiques en Afrique noire*. Paris: Nubia.

Diop, Alioune. [1949] 1969. "Niam M'Paya, ou de la fin que dévorent les moyens." Preface to *Bantu Philosophy* by Placide Tempels. Translated by Colin King. Paris: Présence Africaine.

Diop, Chiekh Anta. 1970. "Awakening of African Historical Consciousness." In *African Humanism–Scandinavian Culture: A Dialogue*, edited by Torben Lundbaek, 140–44. Copenhagen: DANIDA.

———. [1954] 1974. *The African Origin of Civilization: Myth or Reality.* Translated by Mercer Cook. New York: Lawrence Hill Books.

———. 1980. "Existe-t-il une philosophie africaine?" In *African philosophy/La philosophie africaine*, edited by C. Sumner, 24–37. Addis Ababa: Chamber Printing House.

———. [1981] 1990. *Civilization or Barbarism: An Authentic Anthropology.* Translated by Yaa-Lengi Meema Ngemi. New York: Lawrence Hill Books.

Dossou, François. 1985. "Littérature et philosophie dans les programmes de l'enseignement secondaire." Unpublished essay.

———. (1994) 1997. "Writing and Oral Tradition in the Transmission of Knowledge." In *Endogenous Knowledge: Research Trails*, edited by Paulin J. Hountondji, 281–307. Dakar: CODESRIA.

Eboussi-Boulaga, Fabien. 1968. "La bantou problématique." *Présence Africaine* 6: 4–40

Emmanuel, Arghiri. [1979] 1977. *Unequal Exchange: A Study of the Imperialism of Trade.* Translated by Brian Pearce. London: New Left Books.

———. 1982. *Appropriate or Underdeveloped Technology.* Translated by Timothy E. A. Benjamin. New York: John Wiley & Sons.

Fabian, Johannes. 1966. "Dream and Charisma: Theories of Dream in the Jamaa Movement (Congo)." *Anthropos* 61: 544–60.

———. 1971. *Jamaa: A Charismatic Movement in Katanga.* Evanston, Ill.: Northwestern University Press.

Fanon, Frantz. [1952] 1961. *Black Skin, White Masks.* Translated by Charles L. Markmann. New York: Grove Press.

———. [1961] 1968. *The Wretched of the Earth.* Translated by Constance Farrington. New York: Grove Press.

Fitch, Bod, and Mary Oppenheimer. 1966. *Ghana: End of an Illusion.* New York: Monthly Review Press.

Foucault, Michel. [1961] 1965. *Madness and Civilization: A History of Insanity in the Age of Reason.* Translated by Richard Howard. New York: Random House.

Fournier, M. 1971. "Reflexions théoriques et méthodologiques à propos de l'ethnoscience." *Revue française de sociologie* 12: 459–82.

Frank, André Gunder. 1969. *Latin America: Underdevelopment or Revolution: Essays on the Development of Underdevelopment and the Immediate Enemy.* New York: Monthly Review Press.

Goody, Jacques. 1977. *The Domestication of the Savage Mind.* Cambridge: Cambridge University Press.

Griaule, Marcel. [1948] 1965. *Conversations with Ogotemmêli: An Introduction to Dogon Religious Ideas.* Oxford: Oxford University Press.

Hallen, Barry, and J. O. Sodipo. 1986. *Knowledge, Belief and Witchcraft. Analytic Experiments in African Philosophy.* London: Ethnographica.

Havet, Jacques, ed. 1978. *Tendances principales de la recherche dans les sciences sociales et humaines.* Section 2: *Sciences anthropologiques et historiques, esthétiques et sciences de l'art, science juridique, philosophie.* 2 vols. Paris: UNESCO

Hazoumè, Paul. 1956. *Le pacte de sang.* Paris: Institut d'Ethnologie.

Heidegger, Martin. [1957] 1958. *What Is Philosophy?* Translated by William Kluback and Jean T. Wilde. New York: Twayne Press.

Hoffmann, Gerd-Rüdiger. 1985a. "Humanismus und Tradition-Themen der gegenwärtigen bürgerlichen Philosophie im subsaharischen Afrika." *Deutsche Zeitschrift für Philosophie* 33 (2): 97–104.

———. 1985b. "Philosophie im subsaharischen Afrika." *Jahrbuch Asien, Afrika, Lateinamerika: Bilan und Chronik des Jahres 1984.*

———. 1988. "Wie und warum im subsaharischen Afrika Philosophie entstand." In *Wie und warum entstand Philosophie in verschiedenen Regionen der Erde?* edited by Moritz Rüstau and Gerd-Rüdiger Hoffmann, 194–226. Berlin: Dietz.

Horton, Robin. 1982. "Tradition and Modernity Revisited." In *Rationality and Relativism,* edited by Martin Hollis and Steven Lukes, 201–60. Cambridge, Mass: MIT Press.

Horton, Robin, and Ruth Finnegan, eds. 1973. *Modes of Thought.* London: Faber.

Horton, Robin, et al., eds. 1990. *La pensée métisse: Croyances africaines et rationalité occidentale en question.* Paris: PUF/Cahiers de l'IUED.

Houis, Maurice. 1971. *Anthropologie linguistique de l'Afrique noire.* Paris: PUF.

Houndonougbo, Voctor. (1994) 1997. "A Stochastic Process: Understanding the Geomantic Cults of Coastal Benin." In *Endogenous Knowledge: Research Trails,* edited by Paulin J. Hountondji, 147–67. Dakar: CODESRIA.

Hountondji, Paul. 1983. *Autobiographie.* Cotonou, Benin: Renaissance.

Hountondji, Paulin J. 1965. "La notion de úÅ ± λη (hylè) dans la philosophie de Husserl." Mémoire de DES, University of Paris, Sorbonne.

———. 1967. "Charabia et mauvaise conscience: Psychologie du langage chez les intellectuels colonisés." *Présence Africaine* 61: 11–31.

———. 1970a. "L'idée de science dans les 'Prolégomènes' et la première 'Recherche logique' de Husserl." Ph.D. diss., University of Paris X, Nanterre.

———. 1970b. "Un philosophe africain dans l'Allemagne du XVIIIe siècle: Antoine Guillaume Amo." *Les études philosophiques* 1: 25–46.

———. 1970c. "Sagesse africaine et philosophie moderne." In *African Humanism–Scandinavian Culture: A Dialogue.* Edited by Torben Lundbaek, 187–97. Copenhagen: DANIDA

———. 1970d. "Remarques sur la philosophie africaine contemporaine." *Diogène* 71: 120–40.

———. 1971. "Le problème actuel de la philosophie africaine." In *Contemporary Philosophy: A Survey–La philosophie contemporaine: Chroniques.* Vol. VI, edited by Raymond Klibansky, 613–21. Florence: La Nuova Italia.

———. 1972. "Le mythe de la philosophie spontanée." *Cahiers philosophiques africains* 1: 107–42.

———. 1973a. *Libertés.* Cotonou, Benin: Renaissance.

———.1973b. "La philosophie et ses révolutions." *Cahiers philosophiques africains* 3–4: 27–40

———. 1974a. "African Philosophy: Myth and Reality." *Thought and Practice* 1 (2): 1–16

———. 1974b. "Histoire d'un mythe." *Présence Africaine* 91: 3–13.

————. 1975. "De Lénine à Descartes: Le personage du fou et l'argument du rêve." *Annales du DELLSH* 1: 142–53.

————. [1977] 1980. "Sens du mot 'philosophie' dans l'expression 'philosophie africaine.'" *Le Korè: Revue ivoirienne de philosophie et de culture* (5–8). In *African Philosophy–La philosophie africaine*, edited by Claude Sumner, 81–92. Addis Ababa: Chamber Printing House.

————. 1978a. "Recherche théorique africaine et contrat de solidarité." *Travail et Société* 3 (3–4): 353–64.

————. 1978b. "Egy mítosz története" (History of a myth). In *Fejlödés-Tanulmányok 3. Elméleti harcok és harci elméletek*, edited by Imre Marton, 341–52. Budapest: Karl Marx University.

————. 1978c. "A nkrumahizmus végé és Nkrumah (újjá) 'születése'" (The end of Nkrumahism and the rebirth of Nkrumah). In *Fejlödés-Tanulmányok 3. Elméleti harcok és harci elméletek*, edited by Imre Marton, 341–52. Budapest: Karl Marx University.

————. 1980a. "Distances." *Recherche, pédagogie et culture* 49: 27–33.

————. 1980b. "L'ombre de Lévy-Bruhl et le problème de la philosophie en Afrique." Paper presented at the meeting of the Africa Institute of the USSR Academy of Sciences, November.

————. 1981a. "Que peut la philosophie?" *Présence Africaine* 119: 47–71.

————. 1981b. "Mire képes a filozophia?" Translated by Sipos Janos. *Magyar filozofiai szemle* 25: 111–30.

————. 1982a. "Occidentalisme, élitisme: réponse à deux critiques." *Recherche, pédagogie et culture* 56: 58–67.

————. 1982b. "Langues africaines et philosophie: L'hypothèse relativiste." *Les études philosophiques* 4: 393–406.

————. 1983b. *O 'africkoi filozofije': Kritika etnofilozofije.* Translated by Daniel Bucan. Zagreb: Skolska Knjiga.

————. 1984a. "Aspects and Problems of Philosophy in Africa." In *Teaching and Research in Philosophy: Africa*, 11–29. Paris: UNESCO.

————. 1984b. "Convergences." In *Teaching and Research in Philosophy: Africa*, 271–84. Paris: UNESCO.

————. 1984c. "La culture scientifique dans les pays de la périphérie." *Culture pour tous et pour tous les temps*, 65–78. Paris: UNESCO.

———. 1985. "Pièges de la différence." *Diogène* 131: 51–61.

———. 1986a. "Pièges de la différence." In *Philosophie et culture: Actes du XVIIe congrès mondial de philosophie* (Philosophy and culture: Proceedings of the XVIIth world congress of philosophy), edited by Venant Cauchy, 389–96. Montréal: Editions du Beffroi.

———. 1986b. "On 'African Philosophy.'" Translated by Fernando Léal. *Prometeo: Revista latinoamericana de filosofia* 2 (5): 18–33.

———, ed. 1987a. *Bilan de la recherche philosophique africaine: Repertoire bibliographique* (Philosophical research in Africa: A bibliographic survey) *Première partie:* 1900–85. Vol. 1, no. 31. Cotonou, Benin: Conseil Interafricain de philosophie.

———. 1987b. "Le particulier et l'universel." *Bulletin de la société française de philosophie* 81 (4): 145–89.

———. 1987c. "On the 'Universality' of Science and Technology." *Technik und sozialer Wandel: Verhandlungen des 23. Deutschen Soziologentages in Hamburg 1986*, edited by Burkart Lutz, 382–89. New York: Campus.

———, ed. 1988a. *Bilan de la recherche philosophique africaine: Repertoire bibliographique* (Philosophical research in Africa: A bibliographic survey). *Première partie:* 1900–85. Vol. 2, no. 31. Cotonou, Benin: Conseil Interafricain de philosophie.

———. 1988b. "L'appropriation collective du savoir: Tâches nouvelles pour une politique scientifique." *Genève-Afrique* 26 (1): 49–61.

———. 1988c. "La vie quotidienne en Afrique noire: Eléments pour une critique." In *Albert Tévoèdjre, compagnon d'aventure*, edited by Albert Ekué and Edmonde Jouve, 301–18. Paris: Berger-Levrault.

———. 1988d. "Situation de l'anthropologue africain: Note critique sur une forme d'extraversion critique." In *Les nouveaux enjeux de l'anthropologie: Autour de Georges Balandier*, edited by Gabriel Gossin, 99–108. *Revue de l'Institut de sociologie* 3–4: 99–108.

———. 1989a. "L'effet Tempels." In *Encyclopédie philosophique universelle-L'univers philosophique*, vol. 1, edited by André Jacob, 1472–80. Paris: PUF.

———. 1989b. "L'espérance têtue: La vie quotidienne dans un pays de la périphérie." *L'événement européen* 8: 119–38.

————. 1990a. "Scientific dependency in Africa today." *Research in African Literatures* 21(3): 5–15.

————. 1990b. "Pour une sociologie des représentations collectives." In *La pensée métisse: Croyance africaine et rationalité occidentale en question*, edited by Robin Horton et al., 187–92. Paris: PUF.

————. 1990c. "Recherche et extraversion: Eléments pour une sociologie de la science dans les pays de la péripherie." *Afrique et développement–Africa development* 15 (3–4): 149–58.

————. 1992. "Recapturing." In *The Surreptitious Speech: Présence Africaine and the Politics of Otherness*, edited by V. Y. Mudimbe, 238–48. Chicago: University of Chicago Press.

————. 1993. *Afrikanische philosophie, mythos und realität*. Translated by Gerd-Rüdiger Hoffman, Christian Neugebauer, and Franz Wimmer. Berlin: Dietz.

————. 1994b. "Primitive Science: Direction for Use." *Bulletin du CODESRIA* 1: 8–10.

————. 1994c. "La science dans les pays pauvres." *La nation*, December 24, 1993.

————. 1995a. "Philosophie et démocratie en Afrique: Défis et interrogations." Unpublished essay.

————. 1995b. "Producing Knowledge in Africa Today." *African Studies Review* 38 (3): 1–10.

————. 1996. *African Philosophy: Myth and Reality*. Second edition. Translated by Henri Evans. Bloomington: Indiana University Press.

————, ed. [1994] 1997a. *Endogenous Knowledge: Research Trails*. Translated by Ayi Kwesi Armah. Dakar: CODESRIA.

————. [1994] 1997b. "Introduction: Recentring Africa." In *Endogenous Knowledge: Research Trails*, edited by Paulin J. Hountondji, 1–39. Translated by Ayi Kwesi Armah. Dakar: CODESRIA.

Howlett, Jacques. 1974. "La philosophie africaine en question." *Présence Africaine* 91: 14–25.

Humboldt, Wilhelm von. 1974. *Introduction à l'oeuvre sur le kavi et autres essais*. Paris: Seuil.

Hume, David. [1888] 1978. *A Treatise of Human Nature*. Edited by L. A. Selby-Bigge. Oxford: Clarendon Press.

———. [1889] 2000. *An Enquiry Concerning Human Understanding.* Edited by Tom Beauchamp. Oxford: Clarendon Press.

Hunkarin, Louis. 1977. "L'esclavage en Mauritanie" and "Le Zangbéto." In *La vie et l'oeuvre de Louis Hunkarin suivi de Deux écrits de Louis Hunkarin,* edited by Guy-Landry Hazoumé, A. I. Asiwaju, and Jean Suret-Canale, pp. 207–30; 233–49. Cotonou, Benin: Librairie Renaissance.

Husserl, Edmund. 1939. "Die Frage nach den Ursprung der Geometrie als international historisches Problem." *Revue Internationale de Philosophie* 2: 203–23.

———. [1954] 1965a. "Philosophy as a Strict Science." In *Phenomenology and the Crisis of Philosophy.* Translated by Quentin Lauer. New York: Harper & Row.

———. [1935] 1965b. "Philosophy and the Crisis of European Humanity." In *Phenomenology and the Crisis of Philosophy.* Translated by Quentin Lauer. New York: Harper & Row.

———. [1928] 1966. *Phenomenology of Internal-Time Consciousness.* Translated by James S. Churchill. Bloomington: Indiana University Press.

———. [1913] 1970a. *Logical Investigations.* 2 vols. Translated by J. N. Findlay. London: Routledge and Kegan Paul.

———. [1954] 1970b. "The Crisis of European Sciences." In *Transcendental Phenomenology: An Introduction to Phenomenological Philosophy.* Translated by David Carr. Evanston, Ill.: Northwestern University Press.

———. [1939] 1970c. *Origin of Geometry.* In *Transcendental Phenomenology: An Introduction to Phenomenological Philosophy.* Translated by David Carr. Evanston, Ill.: Northwestern University Press.

———. [1913] 1975. *Ideas: General Introduction to Pure Phenomenology.* Translated by W. R. Boyce Gibson. New York: Collier Books.

———. [1929] 1969. *Formal and Transcendental Logic.* Translated by Dorion Cairns. The Hague: Martinus Nijoff.

Hymes, Dell, ed. 1964. *Language in Culture and Society: A Reader in Linguistics and Anthropology.* New York: Harper & Row.

Ikoku, Samuel. 1971. *Le Ghana de Nkrumah.* Translated by Yves Bénot. Paris: Maspéro.

Irele, Abiola. 1990. *The African Experience in Literature and Ideology.* Second edition. Bloomington: Indiana University Press.

—. 1996. Introduction to the second edition of *African Philosophy: Myth and Reality* by Paulin J. Hountondji. Bloomington: Indiana University Press.

Kagame, Alexis. 1956. *La philosophie bantu-rwandaise de l'Etre.* Brussels: Académie Royale des Sciences Coloniales.

—. 1971. "L'ethnophilosophie des Bantu." In *La philosophie contemporaine: Chroniques,* t.IV, edited by Raymond Klibansky, 589–612. Florence: La Nuova Italia.

—. 1976. *La philosophie bantu comparée.* Paris: Présence Africaine.

—. 1989. "The Problem of Man in Bantu Philosophy." *African Mind, Journal of Religion and Philosophy in Africa* 1 (1): 35–40.

Kane, Abdoulaye. 1987. *Les systèmes de numération parlée des groupes ouest-atlantique et mandé: Contribution à la recherche sur les fondements et l'histoire de la pensée logique et mathématique en Afrique de l'ouest.* Ph.D. diss., University of Lille.

Kiniffo, Henry-Valère T. [1994] 1997. "Foreign Objects in Human Bodies: A Surgeon's Report." In *Endogenous Knowledge: Research Trails,* edited by Paulin J. Hountondji, 247–63. Dakar: CODESRIA.

Kissi, M. A. 1970. "African Wisdom and Modern Philosophy." In *African Humanism–Scandinavian Culture: A Dialogue,* edited by Torben Lundbaek. Copenhagen: DANIDA.

Ki-Zerbo, Joseph, ed. 1992. *La natte des autres: Pour un développement des autres en Afrique.* Dakar: CODESRIA.

Ki-Zerbo, Joseph, Joseph Mikecin, and Vjekoslav Mikecin. 1983. "O flozofiji I marksizmu u Africi." In *Paulin J. Hountondji O "africkoj filosofiji,"* edited by Joseph Ki-Zerbo, et al. Zagreb: Skolska Knjiga.

Korsch, Karl, Paul Mattick, Anton Pannekoek, Otto Ruhle, and Helmut Wagner. 1973. *La contre-révolution bureaucratique.* Paris: UGE.

Kraniauskas, John. 1987. "Filosofia africana: Mito y realidad de Paulin Hountondji." *Prometeo: Revista latino-americana de filosofia* 3 (10): 117–20.

Kuhn, Thomas. 1970. *The Structure of Scientific Revolutions*. Chicago: University of Chicago Press.

Lagarde, André, and Laurent Michard, ed. 1962. *XXe siècle*. With Raoul Audibert, Henri Lemaitre, and Thérèse Van der Elsts. Paris: Bordas.

Laleye, Issiaka Prosper. 1970. *La conception de la personne dans la pensée traditionnelle Yoruba: Approche phénoménologique*. Berne: Herbert Lang et Cie.

Lecourt, Dominique. 1977. *Proletarian Science? The Case of Lyssenko*. Translated by Ben Brewster. London: New Left Books.

Lenin, Vladimir Ilich. [1927] 1970. *Materialism and Empirio-Criticism: Critical Comments on a Reactionary Philosophy*. New York: International Publishers.

Lévi-Strauss, Claude. 1952. *Race and History*. Paris: UNESCO.

———. 1968a. *Tristes Tropiques*. Translated by John Russell. New York: Atheneum.

———. 1968b. *The Savage Mind*. Chicago: University of Chicago Press.

———. 1973. *Totemism*. Translated by Rodney Needham. Hammondsworth: Penguin Books.

———. 1987. *Structural Anthropology*. Translated by Monique Layton. Hammondsworth: Penguin Books.

Levy-Leblond, Jean-Marc, and Alain Jaubert. 1975. *(Auto) critique de la science*. Paris: Seuil.

Linhart, Robert. 1976. *Lenine, les paysans, Taylor*. Paris: Seuil.

Locke, John. [1690] 1975. *An Essay Concerning Human Understanding*. Edited by Peter Nidditch. Oxford: Clarendon Press.

Lundbaek, Torben, ed. 1970. *African Humanism–Scandinavian Culture: A Dialogue*. Copenhagen: Danida.

Lyotard, Jean-François. 1973. *Dérive à partir de Marx et Freud*. Paris: Union Générale d'Edition.

Marton, Imre, ed. 1978. *Fejlödés-Tanulmányok 3. Eleméleti harcok és harci elméletek*. Budapest: Karl Marx University.

Marx, Karl. 1947. "Thesis on Fuerbach." In *The German Ideology* by Karl Marx and Frederick Engels. Translated by W. Lough and C. P. Magill. New York: International Publishers.

Masolo, D. A. 1994. *African Philosophy in Search of Identity*. Blooming-ton: Indiana University Press.

Meiner, Johannes Theodosius. 1734. *Disputatio philosophica continens ideam distinctam eorum quae competunt vel menti vel corpori nostro vivo et organico*. Ph.D. diss., Martin-Luther-Universität, Halle-Wittenberg, Germany.

Merleau-Ponty, Maurice. 1962. *Phenomenology of Perception*. Trans-lated by Colin Smith. New York: Humanities Press.

Mètinhoué, Goudjinou. [1994] 1997. "Methodological Issues in the Study of 'Traditional' Techniques and Know-How." In *Endoge-nous Knowledge: Research Trails*, edited by Paulin J. Hountondji, 43–62. Dakar: CODESRIA.

Moritz, Ralf, Hiltrud Ruestau, and Berd-Rüdiger Hoffmann, eds. 1988. *Wie und warum enstand Philosophie in verschiedenen Regio-nen der Erde?* Berlin: Dietz.

Mosley, Albert, ed. 1995. *African Philosophy: Selected Readings*. Engle-wood Cliffs, N.J.: Prentice Hall.

Mudimbe, V. Y. 1973. *L'autre face du royaume: Une introduction à la cri-tique des langages en folies*. Lausanne: L'Age d'homme.

———. 1982. "Panorama de la pensée africaine contemporaine de langue française." *Recherche, pédagogie et culture* 56: 15–29.

———. 1988. *The Invention of Africa*. Bloomington: Indiana Univer-sity Press.

Muglioni, Jacques. 1988. "L'actualité d'Auguste Comte." In *Auguste Comte, qui êtes-vous?* 181–210. Lyon: La Manufacture.

———. 1993. *L'école ou le loisir de penser*. Paris: CNDP.

Murdock, Peter. 1950. *Outline of Cultural Materials*. New Haven: Human Relations Area Files.

N'Daw, Alassane. 1966. "Peut-on parler d'une pensée africaine?" *Présence Africaine* 58: 32–46.

———. 1981. "Prolégomènes à une lecture philosophique de la pen-sée négro-africaine." In *Philosophy in the Present Situation in Africa*, edited by Alwin Dietmer, 23–26. Wiesbaden: Franz Steiner.

———. 1983. *La pensée africaine*. Dakar: NEA.

———. 1985. "Identité et pluralisme culturel en Afrique." In *Africa and the Problem of Its Identity—L'Afrique et le problème de son identité*, edited by Alwin Dietmer and Paulin J. Hountondji, 149–53. New York: Peter Lang.

N'Diaye Aloyse-Raymond. 1970. *L'ordre dans la philosophie de Malebranche*. Ph.D. diss., Université de Paris-Sorbonne.

———. 1982. "La nature des idées et la philosophie de l'homme chez Malebranche." *Revue Sénégalaise de philosophie* 1: 11–31.

———. 1983. "La méthode des *Méditations métaphysiques* d'après les réponses de Descartes aux objections." *Revue Sénégalaise de philosophie* 3: 91–107

———. 1983. *Arnauld et la philosophie*. Ph.D. diss., Université de Rennes, France.

———. 1987. "En Afrique noire." In *Doctrines et concepts: Cinquante ans de philosophie de langue française, 1937–1987*, edited by André Robinet, 77–87. Paris: Vrin.

Neugebauer, Christian. 1987. "Die Ethnophilosophie in der philosophiediskussion Afrikas." *Zast* 1: 47–71.

———, ed. 1991a. *Philosophie, ideologie und gesellschaft in Afrika: Wien 1989*. Frankfort am Main: Peter Lang.

———. 1991b. "Aristoteles, Tempels und Hegel im afrikanischen diskurs-ein philosophiehistorischer Bericht zur afrikanischen Philosophie." In *Philosophie, ideologie und gesellschaft in Afrika: Wien 1989*, edited by Christian Neugebauer, 61–94. Frankfurt am Main: Peter Lang.

Niamkey, Koffi. 1974. *Essai sur l'articulation logique de la pensée akan nzima*. Ph.D. diss., Université de Paris.

———. 1977. "Les modes d'existence matérielle de la philosophie et la question de philosophie africaine." *Le Korè: Revue ivoirienne de philosophie et de culture* (5–8): 25–35.

———. [1976] 1980. "L'impensé de Towa et de Hountondji. In *African Philosophy* (La philosophie africaine), edited by Claude Sumner, 165–88. Addis Ababa: Chamber Printing House.

Niamkey, Koffi, and Abdou Touré. [1976] 1980. "Controverses sur l'existence d'une philosophie africaine." In *La philosophie africaine/African Philosophy*, edited by Claude Sumner, 189–214. Addis Ababa: Chamber Printing House.

Nietzsche, Friedrich Wilhelm. 1966. *Thus Spake Zarathustra*. Translated by Walter Kaufmann. New York: Penguin.

Nkombe, Oleko, and A. J. Smet. 1978. "Panorama de la philosophie africaine contemporaine." In *Mélanges de philosophie africaine*, edited by A. J. Smet, 263–287. Kinshasa: Faculté de théologie catholique.

Nkrumah, Kwame. n.d.[circa 1945]. *Mind and Thought in Primitive Society: A Study in Ethno-philosophy with Special Reference to the Akan People of the Gold Coast, West Africa.* Ghana: National Archives. File. P. 129/63–64.

———. 1964. *Consciencism: Philosophy and Ideology for Decolonization and Development with Particular Reference to the African Revolution.* London: Heinemann.

———. 1965. *Neo-colonialism: The Last Stage of Imperialism.* London: Nelson.

———. 1968. *Handbook of Revolutionary Warfare.* London: Panaf Books.

———. 1970. *Class Struggle in Africa.* London: Panaf Books.

Odera, Henry Oruka. 1972. "Mythologies as African Philosophy." *East Africa Journal* 9 (10): 5–11

Owomoyela, Oyekan. 1987. "Africa and the Imperative of Philosophy: A Sceptical Consideration." *African Studies Review.* 30 (1): 79–100

Parti Communiste du Dahomey (PCD). 1979. *Introduction aux réalités économiques et sociales au Dahomey.* Paris: Nouveau bureau d'édition.

Penel, J. D. (1994) 1997. "Epistemological Reflections on Hausa Zoological Names." In *Endogenous Knowledge: Research Trails*, edited by Paulin J. Hountondji, 169–88. Dakar: CODESRIA.

Plato. [1892] 1937. *The Dialogues of Plato*, vol. 1. Translated by Benjamin Jowett. New York: Random House.

Possoz, Emile. 1943. *Eléments du droit coutumier nègre.* Elisabethville (now Lubumbashi), Congo: Lovania.

Price, Derek de Solla. 1963. *Little Science, Big Science.* New York: Columbia University Press.

Rancière, Jacques. 1974. *La leçon d'Althusser.* Paris: Gallimard.

Revel, Nicole. 1990. *Fleurs de paroles: Histoire naturelle Palawan. 1: Les dons de Nägsalad.* Paris: Peeters-SELAF.

Ricoeur, Paul. 1949. "Husserl et le sens de l'histoire." *Revue de métaphysique et de morale* (juillet–octobre): 280–316.

————. 1950. Introduction to *Idées directrices pour une phénoménologie* by Edmund Husserl. Paris: Gallimard.

————. 1951. "Analyse et problèmes dans *Ideen* 11." In *Phénoménologie, existence*. Paris: A. Collin.

————. 1978. "La philosophie." In *Tendances principales de la recherche dans les sciences sociales et humaines*. Vol. 2, edited by Jacques Havet, 1125–622. Paris: La Haye.

Rivière, Claude. 1979. "Les destins associés de la philosophie et des sciences sociales en Afrique." *Ethnophilosophie* 34 (1): 89–105.

Romains, Jules. 1904. *L'âme des hommes*. Paris: Gallimard.

————. 1908. *La vie unanime*. Paris: Gallimard.

————. 1910. *Un être en marche*. Paris: Gallimard.

————. 1911. *Mort de quelqu'un*. Paris: Gallimard.

————. 1932–46. *Les hommes de bonne volonté*. 27 vols. Paris: Flammarion.

Rorty, Richard. 1979. *Philosophy and the Mirror of Nature*. Princeton: Princeton University Press.

SAC. 1969. "Base théorique de travail de la Commission interafricaine de philosophie." *Bulletin de liaison de la Commission interafricaine de philosophie* 3.

Saivre, Denyse, ed. 1982. "Table ronde." *Recherche, pédagogie et culture* 9 (56): 3–14.

Salomon, Jean-Jacques. 1970. *Science et politique*. Paris: Seuil.

Salomon, Jean-Jacques, and André Lebeau. 1988. *L'écrivain public et l'ordinateur*. Paris: Hachette.

Sartre, Jean-Paul. [1936] 1965. *La transcendance de l'Ego: Esquisse d'une description phénoménologique*. Paris: Vrin.

————. 1946. *L'existentialisme est un humanisme*. Paris: Nagel.

Scheps, Ruth, ed. 1993. *La science sauvage: Des savoirs populaires aux ethnosciences*. Paris: Seuil.

Senghor, Léopold Sédar. 1964a. "Laye Camara et Lamine Diakhaté ou l'art n'est pas un parti." In *Liberté 1: Négritude et humanisme* by Léopold Senghor. Paris: Seuil.

————. 1964b. *Liberté 1: Négritude et humanisme*. Paris: Seuil.

Serequeberhan, Tsenay. 1991. *African Philosophy: The Essential Readings*. New York: Paragon House.

Smet, A. J. 1972. "Bibliographie de la pensée africaine" (Bibliography of African thought). *Cahiers philosophiques africains–African Philosophical Journal* 2: 39–96.

———. 1975. *Philosophie africaine: Textes choisis I, II et bibliographie sélective.* 2 vols. Kinshasa: Presses Universitaires du Zaire.

———. 1977a. "Histoire de la philosophie africaine: Problèmes et méthode." In *Philosophie africaine: Textes choisis I, II et bibliographie sélective.* 2 vols., edited by A. J. Smet, 47–68. Kinshasa: Presses Universitaires du Zaire.

———. 1977b. "In mémoriam: Le père Placide Tempels." *Documentation et information africaines.* 17 October: 959–61.

———. 1977c. "Le père Tempels et son oeuvre publiée." *Revue africaine de théologie* 1: 77–128.

———. 1977d. "L'oeuvre inédite du Père Placide Tempels." *Revue africaine de théologie* 1: 219–33.

———. 1978a. "Bibliographie sélective de la philosophie africaine. Répertoire chronologique." In *Mélanges de philosophie africaine,* edited by A. J. Smet. 181–261. Kinshasa: Faculté de théologie catholique.

———. 1978b. "Le concept fondamental de l'ontologie Bantu. Texte inédit du père Placide Tempels." In *Mélanges de philosophie africaine,* edited by A. J. Smet. 149–80. Kinshasa: Faculté de théologie catholique.

———. 1981a. "Langues Bantu et philosophie dans l'oeuvre de Tempels." *Langage et philosophie* 6: 13–19. Kinshasa: Faculté de théologie catholique.

———. 1981b. "Les débuts de la controverse autour de *La philosophie bantoue* du P. Tempels: Quelques lettres inédites." *Revue africaine de théologie* 5 (10): 165–81.

———, trans. 1982. Preface to *Plaidoyer pour la philosophie bantou et quelques autres textes* by Placide Tempels. Kinshasa: Faculté de théologie catholique.

Sodipo, J. O. 1973. "Notes on the Concept of Chance and Order in Yoruba Traditional Thought." *Second Order* 2: 12–20.

de Sousberghe, Léon. 1951. "A propos de *La philosophie bantoue.*" *Zaire* 5: 821–28.

de Souza, Simone. [1994] 1997. "Fruits, Seeds and Miscellaneous

Ingredients Used in the Pharmaceutical Practice of Benin." In *Endogenous Knowledge: Research Trails*, edited by Paulin J. Hountondji, 191–215. Dakar: CODESRIA.

Sturtevant, W. 1964. "Studies in Ethnoscience." *American Anthropologist* 66 (3): 99–131.

Taiwo, Olufemi. 1993. "Colonialism and Its Aftermath: The Crisis of Knowledge Production." *Callalloo* 16 (3): 891–908.

Tchitchi, Toussaint-Yaovi. [1994] 1997. "Traditional Number Systems and Modern Arithmetic." In *Endogenous Knowledge: Research Trails*, edited by Paulin J. Hountondji, 115–46. Dakar: CODESRIA.

Tempels, Placide. 1948. "Catéchèse bantoue." *Bulletin des missions* 22 (6): 258–79.

———. 1949. "La christianisation des philosophies païennes." *Trait d'Union*.

———. 1962. *Notre rencontre*. Léopoldville (now Kinshasa), Congo: Centre d'études pastorales.

———. 1969. *Bantu Philosophy*. Translated by Colin King. Paris: Présence Africaine.

———. 1979. *Ecrits polémiques et politiques*. Edited by A. J. Smet. Kinshasa: Faculté de théologie catholique.

———. 1982. *Plaidoyer pour la philosophie bantou et quelques autres textes*. Kinshasa: Faculté de théologie catholique.

Tévoèdjrè, Albert. 1978. *La pauvreté, richesse des peuples*. Paris: Editions ouvrières.

Thomas, Louis-Vincent. 1959. *Les Diola: Essai d'analyse fonctionnelle sur une population de basse Casamance*. Dakar: IFAN.

Tort, Patrick, and Paul Desalmand. 1978. "Sciences humaines et philosophie en Afrique: La différence culturelle." Unpublished essay.

———. 1980. *Evolutionnisme et linguistique*, suivi de August Schleicher. *La théorie de Darwin et la science du langage: De l'importance du langage pour l'histoire naturelle de l'homme*. Paris: Vrin.

Touré, Abdou. 1978. "Le marxisme-léninisme comme idéologie. Critique des trois théoriciens africains: A. Dieng, P. Hountondji, et M. Towa." Unpublished essay.

Towa, Marcien. 1971a. *Léopold Sédar Senghor: Négritude ou servitude?* Yaoundé, Cameroon: Cle.

———. 1971b. *Essai sur la problématique philosophique dans l'Afrique actuelle.* Yaoundé, Cameroon: Cle.

Trân-Duc-Thao. 1951. *Phénoménologie et matérialisme dialectique.* Paris: Minh-Tân.

UNESCO. 1970. *Tendances principales de la recherche dans les sciences sociales et humaines. Partie I: Sciences sociales.* Paris: UNESCO.

Van Parys, Jean. 1980. "Trente textes de philosophie africaine: Présence africaine, 1955–1975." In *La philosophie africaine* (African Philosophy), edited by Claude Sumner. Addis Ababa: Chamber Printing House.

Wallerstein, Immanuel. 1974–89. *The Modern World System.* 3 vols. New York: Academic Press.

Whitman, Walt. 1968. *Leaves of Grass.* London: Aldine Press.

Wimmer, Franz, ed. 1988. *Vier Fragen zur Philosophie in Afrika, Asien und Lateinamerika.*Vienna: Passagen.

———. 1991. "Was geht uns die Philosophie in Afrika an?" In *Philosophie, Ideologie und Gesellschaft in Afrika: Wien 1989,* edited by Christian Neugebauer, 139–51. Frankfurt am Main: Peter Lang.

Wiredu, Kwasi. 1980. *Philosophy and an African Culture.* Cambridge: Cambridge University Press.

Yaï, Olabiyi Babalola. 1978. "Théorie et pratique en philosophie africaine: Misère da la philosophie spéculative (critique de P. Hountondji, M. Towa, et autres)." *Présence Africaine* 108: 65–89.

Zinsou, Emile-Derlin. 1975. *Pour un socialisme humaniste, suivi de Lettre à un jeune dahoméen marxiste-leniniste.* Yverdon: Kessebring.

Index